THE PRIVATIZATION PROCESS IN CENTRAL EUROPE

● ●

CEU PRIVATIZATION REPORTS | VOLUME 1

THE PRIVATIZATION PROCESS IN CENTRAL EUROPE

- ECONOMIC ENVIRONMENT
- LEGAL AND OWNERSHIP STRUCTURE
- INSTITUTIONS FOR STATE REGULATION
- OVERVIEW OF PRIVATIZATION PROGRAMS
- INITIAL TRANSFORMATION OF ENTERPRISES

ROMAN FRYDMAN
ANDRZEJ RAPACZYNSKI
JOHN S. EARLE
et al

CENTRAL EUROPEAN UNIVERSITY PRESS
BUDAPEST · LONDON · NEW YORK

3-18-94

© Central European University Privatization Project 1993

First published in Great Britain 1993 by
Central European University Press
25 Floral Street, London WC2E 9DS

British Library Cataloguing in Publication Data

A CIP catalogue record for this book is available from the British Library

ISBN 1 85866 002 5 Hardback
ISBN 1 85866 000 9 Paperback

ISSN 0968–5278

Library of Congress Cataloging in Publication Data

A CIP catalog record for this book is available from the Library of Congress

Typeset by Mayhew Typesetting, Rhayader, Powys
Printed and bound by SRP, Exeter

CONTENTS

Detailed Table of Contents to be found on the first page of
each country chapter

CONTRIBUTORS

The following persons contributed to the preparation and writing of the first two volumes of these reports:

Project officers and staff
Joel Turkewitz
Dana Săpătoru, Sina Toussi
Alexander Dreier, Roger East, Georgy Feher

Regional project participants
Bulgaria
Todor Gradev – Project Coordinator
Center for the Study of Democracy, Sofia

Reneta Indjova – Research Fellow
Agency for Economic Coordination and
   Development

Spartak Keremidchiev – Project Coordinator
Center for the Study of Democracy, Sofia

Stephan Kyutchukov – Research Fellow

Vesselin Pasev – Economic Advisor
Council of Ministers

Todor Popov – Senior Expert
Agency for Privatization

Todor Radev – Research Fellow
Institute of Economics, Bulgarian
   Academy of Sciences

Dimiter Stefanov – Deputy Chairman
Agency for Privatization

Czechoslovakia
Alena Buchtíková – Research Fellow
Institute of Economics, Czechoslovak
   State Bank

Richard Bureš – Information Manager
Federal Ministry of Finance

Eva Macourková – Research Fellow
Institute of Economics, Czechoslovak
   Academy of Sciences

Michal Mejstřík – Acting Director
Centre for Economic Research and
   Graduate Education Charles University

Vladimir Rudlovčak – Deputy Minister
Federal Ministry of Finance

Estonia
Ardo Kamratov – Deputy Minister
Ministry of Economy

Alar Kein – Research Fellow
Institute of Economics, Estonian
   Academy of Sciences

Erik Terk – Director
Estonian Institute of Future Studies

Veiko Tali – Research Fellow
Institute of Economics, Estonian
  Academy of Sciences

Liina Tõnisson – Deputy Chairman
Parliamentary Committee of Economy

Hungary
Lajos Csepi – Managing Director
State Property Agency

Mária Móra – Deputy General Manager
Kereskedelmi Bank RT

Erika Katona – Research Fellow
Central Statistical Office

Erzsébet Lukács – Counsellor
State Property Agency

Gabriella Pál – Research Fellow
Rajk Lászlo College

Lászlo Urbán – Director
Center for Parliamentary Management

István Zsoldos – Research Fellow
Rajk Lászlo College

Latvia
Inga Auzina – Chief Specialist
Antimonopolies and Competition Policy,
  Ministry of Economic Reforms

Eduards Dimitrovičs – Consultant
Permanent Commission of the Supreme
  Council

Natalija Gračova – Engineer
Latvian Institute of National Economy

Natalija Jackovicka – Chief Specialist
Ministry of Economics

Normunds Luste – First Deputy Minister
Ministry of Economic Reforms

Ilma Ruduša – Department Head
Antimonopolies and Competition Policy,
  Ministry of Economics

Lithuania
Jonas Čičinskas – Professor
Economics Department, Vilnius University

Giedrius Jankauskas – Specialist
Ministry of Foreign Economics Relations

Atanas-Zenonas Kaminskas – Director
Privatization Department, Ministry of
  Economy

Antanas Merčaitis – Deputy Minister
Ministry of Economics

Nijole Žambaite – Expert, Member of the
  Board
Lithuanian Free Market Institute

Poland
Joanna Debska – Director
Foreign Affairs Bureau, Ministry of
  Privatization

Jaroslaw Gora
Foundation Center for Privatization

Janusz Lewandowski – Minister
Ministry of Ownership Transformation

Wojciech Maciejewski – Dean and Professor
Department of Economics, Warsaw
  University

Piotr Makowski – Research Fellow
Department of Mathematics, Warsaw
  University

Krzysztof Rybinski – Research Fellow
Department of Economics, Warsaw
  University

Wanda Wojciechowska – Director
Department of Programming and
  Statistical Surveys
Central Statistical Office

Romania

Ion Andrei – Vice President
National Agency for Privatization

Luoana Dana Dulgheru – Researcher
National Institute for Economic Research

Elena Gheorghiu – Senior Researcher
National Institute for Economic Research

Costea Munteanu – Director General
Romanian Development Agency

Dan Dimitru Popescu – Deputy Secretary
of State
Ministry of Economy and Finance

Ladislau Randjak – Information Technology
Expert
National Agency for Privatization

Theodor Stolojan – Prime Minister

Russia

Alexander S. Bim – Head of Department
Institute of Market Economy, Russian
Academy of Sciences

Anatoli Chubais – Deputy Prime Minister
and Chairman, State Committee for
the Management of State Property

Gennady R. Margolit – Senior Research
Associate
Institute of Market Economy, Russian
Academy of Sciences

Yelena A. Nickulina – Research Associate
Institute of Economic Forecasting,
Russian Academy of Sciences

Vladimir T. Tolkushkin – Vice Chairman
Statistical Committee of Commonwealth
of Independent States

Dmitry V. Vasilyev – Deputy Chairman
State Committee for the Management of
State Property

Yury A. Yurkov – Deputy Director
Center for Economic Situation &
Forecasting, Ministry of Economy of
Russia

Edward Yu. Zhydkov – Research Associate
Institute of Economic Research, Ministry
of Economy of Russia

Ukraine

Volodymyr Lanovoy – Minister
Ministry of Property, Transformation and
Entrepreneurship

Olena Manninen – Research Fellow
Institute of Economics, Ukrainian
Academy of Sciences

Oleksander Paskhaver – Head Scientific
Fellow
Institute of Economics, Ukrainian
Academy of Sciences

Victor Rodionov – Department Head
Macro-Economics Department, Ministry
of Statistics

Inna Shovkun – Senior Research Associate
Institute of Economics, Ukrainian
Academy of Sciences

Vadim V. Vasilyev – Administrative
Director
State Property Fund of Ukraine

Oleksander Zavada – National Advisor
Cabinet of Ministers of Ukraine

ABOUT THE CEU PRIVATIZATION PROJECT

The reports presented here are the first in a series to be produced by the Privatization Project of the Central European University. The Project is designed to create a regional framework for the promotion and improvement of public policies in the area of privatization in Eastern Europe (including former Soviet republics). In particular, the Project aims at the following four objectives:

- the creation of a forum for the collection and exchange of information concerning privatization in all the countries of the region;
- the training of local government and academic personnel, as well as other forms of contributing to the human capital required for a successful completion of the privatization process;
- the creation of a research and advising facility making the services of experts from both the Western world and other countries of the region available to the regional governments;
- the definition and elaboration of the emerging corporate governance issues in Eastern European economies, including the development of standards for professional and ethical conduct of corporate directors in the private sector.

It is the policy of the Project to involve local personnel in its activities, as much as possible. This policy is based on the belief that local participants have special access to information and unique knowledge of the conditions in the region, which, when conjoined with the Western expertise provided by the Project, will greatly enhance the understanding of East European privatization.

The headquarters of the Project are located in Prague, with offices in New York and all of the countries of the region. The Central European University in Prague provides facilities for some of the educational and training programs of the Project. It also serves as a informational clearing house and as a meeting place for participants.

At this stage, the Project conducts research and other activities in Bulgaria, Czechoslovakia, Estonia, Hungary, Latvia, Lithuania, Poland, Romania, Russia, Ukraine, and has approximately sixty Eastern European participants and collaborators. The participants in each country include high level government officials, two to three part-time senior researchers (often working in ministries, national statistical offices, and specialized institutes), and one or two full-time junior researchers. They collect and process information, conduct Project-related research, and maintain contact with the headquarters in Prague and New York.

The activities of the Project

1. CEU Privatization Reports

The *CEU Privatization Reports* present the results of research and analysis conducted by Project participants. The purpose of the *Reports* is to provide policymakers and analysts in Eastern Europe, as well Western official, academic, and professional circles, with reliable and comprehensive information concerning the state of privatization in the region.

The individual *Reports* are based on research carried out by the Project teams in each country. The information is collected on the basis of a questionnaire containing a large number of standardized categories. The preparation of each report involves several iterations during which issues and answers are further clarified. The final version of the *Reports* is written by the Project Directors, with the help of the staff in Prague and New York.

Following the first two volumes of the *Reports*, providing an overview of the whole privatization process, future issues will cover specific areas, including leasing, management contracts, small, large, and mass privatization, the privatization of banking and agriculture, and the effects of privatization on labor-market dynamics.

2. Educational and training programs

The Project is engaged in several educational programs, both in the public and the private sector, aimed at upgrading the human capital necessary for the successful execution of the ambitious privatization plans in the region. In particular, the Project is now involved in the following initiatives:

- The Privatization Project, together with the Committee for the Management of State Property of the Russian Federation, established the Institute of Privatization and Management in Moscow, which is in the process of providing a massive program of training for the personnel of the Committee, involving approximately 5,000 officials of the territorial and local offices of the Committee.
- The Privatization Project, jointly with the Center for International Private Enterprise of the U.S. Chamber of Commerce, is running the Corporate Governance Training Program, which trains members of the boards of directors of the newly formed East European joint-stock companies in the state and private sectors. The program is also preparing a general model of corporate governance standards for the region. Pilot courses involving present and future company directors from Czechoslovakia, Hungary, Poland, and Romania were conducted during the summer of 1992.
- The Privatization Project is working closely with the Economics Program of the Central European University in Prague on a joint program designed to integrate the general teaching of economics to Eastern European postgraduate students with a practical research- and policy-oriented experience in the field of privatization.

3. Short-Term research and technical assistance projects

The Privatization Project is equipped to provide, upon request from government officials in the participating countries, special targeted short-term research and technical assistance for Eastern European policymakers dealing with particular problems of the moment. The following initiatives have been undertaken by the Project in this connection:

- At the request of governments considering the implementation of

mass and voucher privatization programs, the Project organized a workshop on voucher privatization in Versailles, France, in June 1992. The workshop provided a forum for exchange of ideas between decision makers in the region and top Western experts on voucher privatization.
- At the request of the Polish government, the Project has been involved in the evaluation of the design and the legislative framework of the Polish mass privatization program.

4. Other Project publications

In addition to *CEU Privatization Reports*, the Privatization Project also sponsors the publication of the results of research conducted under its auspices. Among the forthcoming books by Project authors are:

R. Frydman and A. Rapaczynski, *Markets By Design: Privatizing Privatization in Eastern Europe*, Basic Books, 1993
J. S. Earle, R. Frydman, A. Rapaczynski (eds), *Privatization in the Transition to a Market Economy*, Pinter Publishers and St. Martin's Press, 1993

A list of other publications sponsored by the Project is available upon request.

The Privatization Project is a part of the Central European University, which is a private, independent, and non-partisan educational institution. Although some Project participants are government officials, the opinions expressed in the *CEU Privatization Reports* and other Project publications are exclusively those of the authors, and do not reflect the views of the respective governments or other organizations.

ACKNOWLEDGEMENTS

The Privatization Project is grateful to Mr. George Soros for his unfailing and generous support. Mr. Soros's vision of open societies in Eastern Europe has provided a source of encouragement for the Project participants. The Project also gratefully acknowledges support received from the Pew Charitable Trust.

The interest of Prime Minister Theodor Stolojan of Romania in the early activities of the Project was in part responsible for its continuation. The staff of the Soros Foundations in the countries of the region has provided valuable logistical support for the Project.

The authors would also like to thank Dr. Frances Pinter for her extraordinary efforts in coordinating and expediting the publication of this volume.

BULGARIA

CONTENTS

1. INTRODUCTION

Brief history of reforms

Bulgaria's first reform program was launched in February 1991 in an unfavorable economic and political environment. In 1990, an unprecedented 13 per cent fall in production coincided with both an acceleration of inflation and a rapidly increasing dollarization of the economy. A moratorium on repayment of foreign debt, declared in March 1990, deepened Bulgaria's isolation from the world's financial markets, while the collapse of traditional foreign trade relations with the Soviet Union and other Comecon countries forced Bulgaria to pay in hard currency for essential energy inputs and raw materials.

Main points of the reform program

The reform program, launched in February 1991, envisaged the reduction of the budget deficit, the unification of the exchange rate, and the attainment of a current account surplus. The program was underpinned by a strict monitoring of wages and of the growth of the money supply. The lack of foreign currency reserves precluded currency convertibility. The reform program was approved by the International Monetary Fund (IMF), which conditionally provided a stand-by loan for one year. Major decisions concerning the implementation of the program and other economic matters have been made by a tripartite commission representing the interests of government, employers, and trade unions.

2. ECONOMIC ENVIRONMENT

The structure of output

In 1991, the Bulgarian gross national product (GNP), in current prices, was Leva 138.4 bln ($8.4 bln).[1] The share of industry in gross domestic product (GDP) has been around 60 per cent. The share of agriculture,

---

[1] The Leva-dollar exchange rate used here is the average rate for the year as calculated by *PlanEcon Review*. For the period covered by this report, these rates were as follows: 1989, 0.84; 1990, 2.6; 1991, 16.1; 1992, 22.5 (the average rate during the first eight months).

Table 2.1 The structure of GDP (per cent of the total)

	1988	1991
Industry	63	61
Agriculture	10	12
Services and others	27	27

Source: *PlanEcon*

a likely sector of Bulgarian comparative advantage, increased only slightly between 1988 and 1991.

As in the other countries of the region, most of the nation's output is produced by large enterprises. These enterprises also employ a large fraction of the labor force.

Table 2.2 State enterprises in 1990 (by sales revenues; in thousands of Leva)

Revenues	Number of enterprises
up to 99	9
100–199	19
200–499	61
1,000–1,999	159
2,000–2,999	296
3,000–4,999	182
5,000–9,999	317
10,000–99,999	439
100,000–199,000	917

Source: National Statistics Institute

Output

In 1990, GDP declined by 11.3 per cent. Industry, agriculture, and services fell 11.4 per cent, 14.4 per cent, and 9.8 per cent, respectively. In 1991, GDP plummeted an additional 23 per cent. The largest decline, 27 per cent, was registered in industry, followed by an 18 per cent drop in services, and a 7 per cent decline in agriculture. In 1991, many enterprises were forced to cut production below 1990 levels, mainly because of shortages of raw materials, packaging, and spare

Table 2.3 State enterprises in 1990 (by employment)

Number of employees	Number of enterprises
Less than 10	25
11–30	120
30–50	162
51–80	274
81–140	343
141–200	287
201–500	744
501–1,000	388
1,001–2,000	207
2,001–3,000	70
3,001–5,000	27
5,001–10,000	9
Over 10,000	4

Source: National Statistics Institute

parts, as well as a loss of markets. By July 1991, half of the country's enterprises were functioning at less than 60 per cent of capacity.

During the first four months of 1992, industrial output fell by 17 to 20 per cent relative to the same period in 1991, and by about 52 to 55 per cent compared with the first four months of 1990. Sales of goods and services by all enterprises, including non-industrial, decreased by almost 30 per cent.

Table 2.4 Industrial production (seasonally adjusted; January 1990 = 100)

	Jan	Feb	Mar	Apr	May	June	July	Aug	Sept	Oct	Nov	Dec
1991	69.9	56.9	54.5	52.0	52.0	50.4	55.3	54.5	48.0	48.8	48.0	55.3
1992	45.5	60.2	43.9	42.3								

Source: PlanEcon

INVESTMENT
In 1990 and 1991, gross investment in fixed capital fell by 11 per cent and 19 per cent, respectively. The share of net investment in GDP, 23 per cent, remained high in 1991.

Price liberalization

The prices of over 90 per cent of goods and services were liberalized on February 1, 1991. Under pressure from trade unions, the government retained control over the prices of fourteen basic foodstuffs, energy, and domestic public transport. Actual prices of these goods fluctuated within a range of approximately 10 per cent of the centrally set price ceilings. The second wave of price liberalization, mainly covering energy and fuels, was implemented in June and in the third quarter of 1991.

In April 1992, the government announced new price limits for some of the fourteen important food items under its control, and liberalized the prices of the rest. It also set new minimum procurement prices for a number of agricultural products. Price increases of 35 per cent for electric power, and 60 per cent for coal were announced. A package of compensation measures for the population was also approved.

Inflation

In 1990, the GDP deflator rose 23.8 per cent. Price reform carried out in 1991, however, resulted in a dramatic 271.4 per cent increase of the GDP deflator in 1991.

Following the ''big-bang'' price liberalization in February 1991, retail prices rose 123 per cent in the first month, and an additional 50 per cent in March. The increase in retail prices slowed to the average monthly rate of 4.8 per cent between April 1991 and March 1992. However, the monthly inflation rate for foodstuffs remained very high. In August 1991, it was still twice the rate of increase of the overall consumer price index.

Table 2.5 Retail Price Index (month-to-month per cent changes)

	Jan	Feb	Mar	Apr	May	June	July	Aug	Sept	Oct	Nov	Dec
1991	13.6	122.9	50.5	2.5	0.8	5.9	8.4	7.5	3.8	3.3	5.0	4.9
1992	4.8	5.8	3.9	3.2	12.0	3.0						

Source: PlanEcon

In April 1992, the monthly inflation rate of retail prices declined to 3.2 per cent. However, following the upward revision of the price control ceilings, prices began to rise rapidly during the first two weeks of May. Consequently, retail prices rose by 11.9 per cent in May 1992, with prices of foodstuffs up 11.7 per cent, non-food items up 5.4 per cent, and services up 28.5 per cent. Retail price increases slowed in June. After an increase in July of 2.8 per cent, they rose by only 1.2 per cent in August 1992.

Behavior of wages

On July 1, 1991, Bulgaria's minimum monthly wage was fixed at Leva 620 ($38), and the government approved free wage bargaining. Negotiations between the unions and the government were completed by September 15.

Nominal wages increased 24 per cent in 1990 and 162 per cent in 1991. Real wages fell in both years, 2.2 per cent and 53 per cent, respectively. However, the real wage index in industry fell by much less, 14 per cent, in 1991. It subsequently fell 9 per cent in January, and 4 per cent in February, 1992. It increased by 12 per cent in March.

Table 2.6 Real wage in industry (December 1990 = 100)

	Jan	Feb	Mar	Apr	May	June	July	Aug	Sept	Oct	Nov	Dec
1991	74.8	49.4	32.8	38.4	41.9	43.2	43.2	42.2	51.6	53.8	60.4	64.5
1992	58.5	56.4	62.9									

Source: *PlanEcon*

Nominal wages, in current US dollars, dropped sharply from $115 per month in January to $32 in March 1991. They recovered to $97 per month by March 1992.

Table 2.7 Average monthly industrial wage (in current US dollars)

	Jan	Feb	Mar	Apr	May	June	July	Aug	Sept	Oct	Nov	Dec
1991	129.2	39.5	31.6	38.0	39.7	44.7	49.7	47.2	63.0	66.4	81.6	90.9
1992	85.4	85.0	96.8									

Source: *PlanEcon*

Employment and unemployment

Bulgaria has one of the highest unemployment rates in Eastern Europe. Approximately 420,000 Bulgarian workers – about 10.5 per cent of the total labor force – were registered as jobless at the end of 1991. Half of those were young people, including new university graduates.

By August 1992, the number of unemployed workers rose to 506,000, or 14 per cent of the labor force. This represented a 60 per cent increase over the previous twelve-month period. Government estimates that unemployment will reach only 645,000 by the end of 1992 are considered optimistic.

Table 2.8 Unemployment rate (as per cent of labor force)

	Jan	Feb	Mar	Apr	May	June	July	Aug	Sept	Oct	Nov	Dec
1991	1.9	2.6	3.4	4.4	5.1	5.8	7.0	7.9	8.6	9.1	10.0	10.5
1992	10.7	10.9	11.2	11.5								

Source: PlanEcon

By the end of 1991, the government had distributed approximately Leva 700 mln ($43.48 mln) in unemployment benefits. Further increases in benefits were promised. However, maximum payments have amounted to only about half of the minimum wage. In April 1992, a fund for professional training of the unemployed was set up. The fund is supported by employer contributions.

The number of people employed in the state sector fell from almost 3.7 mln at the beginning of 1991 to just under 3 mln in November. While this fall has been partly attributed to the emigration of ethnic Turks, a corresponding growth of the private sector employment may also have been a factor (see Section 3B below).

State budget

A mild deficit of Leva 225 mln, or 0.6 per cent of GDP, in 1989, was followed by a much greater deficit of Leva 3.8 bln, or 8.8 per cent of GDP, in 1990. Although the nominal deficit increased to Leva 5.2 bln in 1991, it fell to 4.2 per cent as a proportion of GDP.

For the first ten months of 1991 the budget was basically balanced.

In November 1991, the budget deficit surged to Leva 1.8 bln ($111.8 mln). Further increases in social expenditures, such as unemployment benefits, and falling tax revenues resulted in an additional deficit of Leva 5 bln ($310.6 mln) in December 1991. The overall annual deficit for 1991 was Leva 5.8 bln ($360.2 mln).

In an effort to reduce expenditures, the government continued to cut subsidies to state enterprises. The goal of spending only 7.2 per cent of the 1991 budget on subsidies to state enterprises was not achieved. The share of subsidies was 11 per cent.

TAXATION
There are two corporate tax rates in Bulgaria, assessed according to the level of foreign ownership and investment in the Bulgarian company. Companies with 49 per cent foreign ownership and $100,000 foreign investment are taxed at a rate of 30 per cent. Companies with lower levels of foreign investment are subject to a 40 per cent tax rate. Corporate tax rates for banks are higher: 50 per cent for commercial banks and 60 per cent for the savings bank. In addition to the state corporate tax, the companies have to pay a 10 per cent local tax and a special 5 per cent budget surcharge tax. Profits from economic activities in "free trade zones" are exempt from tax for five years, after which they are taxed at 20 per cent.

A turnover tax with rates of 10 and 22 per cent is still in force as well as progressive income tax (10 to 70 per cent).

Monetary policy

INTEREST RATES AND CREDIT POLICY
In 1990, the base short-term interest rate was set by the government. Pursuing a policy of "cheap money," the government maintained the base rate at 4.5 per cent for the whole of 1990. On January 15, 1991 the government increased the rate to 15 per cent.

In February 1991 interest rate management was entrusted to the newly independent National Bank of Bulgaria, and interest rate policy became an instrument of inflationary control. On February 4, at the onset of price liberalization, the base rate was raised to 45 per cent. It was adjusted three times during the year reaching a maximum of 57 per cent per year. It was kept around 50 per cent till mid-1992 and then reduced to 48 per cent in July, 44 per cent in August, and 41 per cent in September. Banks extended credit at rates exceeding the basic rate by 6 to 8 per cent.

Despite the low or negative real base rate throughout 1991, the volume of credit fell precipitously in 1991. Although the nominal value of aggregate credit increased by 25 per cent, its real value decreased relative to 1990.

In 1991, 60 per cent of overall credit was used by non-financial institutions, about 30 per cent by the state sector, and 5 per cent by households. Credit for the private sector comprised about 5 per cent of aggregate credit.

Debt

Bulgarian gross hard currency debt nearly tripled between 1985 and 1990. It reached $11.9 bln in 1990, out of which $2 bln was held by official creditors. A moratorium on servicing of commercial and official debt was announced in March 1990. As a result, the country's credit rating plummeted, and Bulgaria could not obtain any additional commercial loans in 1991. The country's gross hard currency debt increased by only about $500 mln in 1991, mostly representing the capitalization of unpaid interest.

In July 1991, the government concluded rescheduling agreements with six of Bulgaria's official creditors, postponing repayment of its loans until 1998. Agreements have not yet been negotiated with the remaining seven of the country's official creditors. Talks with the London Club, representing commercial creditors, are at a standstill. Bulgaria is apparently proposing a substantial reduction of its debt to commercial banks.

Despite the moratorium, the new government, which took office in October 1991, obtained additional sovereign loans. These included: $133 mln from Norway, $100 mln from Japan (co-financing the World Bank's structural adjustment loan), and 40 mln Ecu from the European Bank for Reconstruction and Development.

The Bulgarian currency is internally convertible. There are no restrictions on exchange of Leva for other currencies by enterprises. Some limitations are, however, in force for individuals.

Foreign trade

Foreign trade liberalization has been one of the main elements of the reform package. The former system of trade permits has been largely replaced with a simple procedure requiring only a customs declaration. Any Bulgarian company may obtain a license to engage in export and import operations. Special permits and export certificates are required only for thirty-three products covered by quotas. In June 1991, all export surcharges were discontinued. However, an import duty of 15 per cent was retained. Two hundred and forty products are exempt due to their deficient domestic supply. These products include basic foods, farm produce, raw materials, clothing, textiles, non-ferrous metals, some minerals, machines, and medical equipment.

According to *PlanEcon*, Bulgaria's convertible currency exports, in current US dollars, increased from $2.4 bln in 1990 to $3.3 bln in 1991, while convertible currency imports remained unchanged at approximately $2.7 bln. But overall exports and imports diminished dramatically, and the numbers require some explanation. The key is the change in trade with ex-Comecon countries, which, while now much smaller, is done in convertible currencies.

Converted to the US dollar equivalents, exports to the former Comecon countries totaled $4.4 bln in 1990, but only a very small fraction of this total was in convertible currencies. Following the breakdown of Comecon trading arrangements, Bulgaria's exports to these countries plummeted by 60 per cent in 1991. However, the value of convertible currency exports to the former Comecon countries actually increased to $1.8 bln. This accounts for the overall increase in convertible currency exports, even though exports to developing countries also fell sharply, by 46 per cent, due in part to Bulgaria's inability to provide hard currency credits. Exports to developed market economies fell by 24 per cent in 1991.

A similar pattern may be observed with respect to imports. Converted to US dollar equivalents, imports from the former Comecon countries totaled $6.4 bln in 1990. Out of this total, the value of imports in convertible currencies was only $108 mln. Thus, despite a 79 per cent drop in imports from the former socialist countries and a 50 per cent decrease in imports from the rest of the world, the value of imports in convertible currencies remained the same between 1990 and 1991.

3. PRESENT FORMS OF OWNERSHIP

3A. Legal framework of economic activity

Existing and planned legislation concerning property rights

The following are some of the most important legal norms concerning property rights, forms of business organization, and privatization in Bulgaria:

- Constitution of the Republic of Bulgaria;
- Law on Commerce (The Commercial Code) (SG 48/June 18, 1991);
- Law on Cooperatives (SG 63/August 3, 1991);
- Decree 56 on Economic Activity (SG 4/January 1989);
- Law on Economic Activity of Foreign Persons and on the Protection of Foreign Investment (SG 8/January 28, 1992);
- Foreign Investment Law (SG 47/June 14, 1991), repealed by the Law on Economic Activity of Foreign Persons and on Protection of Foreign Investment;
- Law on Incorporating Single-Owner Firms with State Property (SG 55/July 12, 1991);
- Law on Ownership (SG 92/November 16, 1951);
- Law on Ownership and Use of Farmlands (SG 17/March 1, 1991);
- Law on Transformation and Privatization of State and Municipal Enterprises (SG 38/May 8, 1992);
- Regulations of the Council of Ministers Concerning the Auctioning of State and Municipal Assets (SG 23/March 1991);
- Regulations of the Council of Ministers for the Establishment of the Privatization Agency (SG 12/January 1991).

Recognized forms of business organizations

STATE ENTERPRISES
While both the new Commercial Code and the 1992 Privatization Law provide for a conversion of state and municipal enterprises into joint-stock or limited-liability companies, this process has been proceeding rather slowly (see Section 5 on corporatization below), and the remaining state enterprises – 3,356 at the end of 1991 – still constitute a numerical majority in the state sector.[2] In accordance with special

---

[2] In terms of the capital involved, the corporatized part may now be greater. See Section 5 below.

interim provisions of the Commercial Code, the uncorporatized state enterprises continue to be governed by sections of the otherwise repealed transitional 1989 Decree No. 56 on Economic Activity. Although Decree No. 56 contains a number of provisions which confer an independent legal personality on state enterprises and give them control over their assets and operations, the crucial articles establishing the governance structure of the state enterprises assure that governmental agencies, such as ministries and municipalities, will continue to be firmly in control of the uncorporatized state sector.

The constitutive organs of a state enterprise are said to be the general assembly of employees (or the assembly of representatives), the management board, the supervisory board, and the general manager. The ultimate power in matters affecting a state enterprise, however, rests not with any one of its stated organs, but with the governmental body responsible for the founding of the enterprise, most commonly a branch ministry or another agency of the state. In addition to having the right to reorganize or liquidate the enterprise, the founding body also appoints 50 per cent plus one of the members of the management and supervisory boards, and has a right to dismiss the general manager before the expiration of his regular term of office.

The general assembly of the employees (or the assembly of representatives), with a two-thirds quorum requirement and an open voting procedure, has the right to elect the remaining members of the management and supervisory boards, and fulfills a few advisory functions. The setting of the overall strategy for the enterprise, as well as the determination of its organizational and managerial structure, is the task of the management board, which also approves the annual balance sheets, decides on the distribution of available funds, and appoints and dismisses the general manager (in addition to setting his salary). The general manager, who is an *ex officio* member of the management board and normally serves a five-year term, is charged with running the day-to-day operations of the enterprise, and the Decree specifically states that the management board should not interfere with his "operative work." The supervisory board of a state enterprise seems to be a weak body, charged with protecting the firm's property and assuring that the decisions of the general assembly and the management board are properly executed.

COOPERATIVES
Bulgarian cooperatives are governed by the 1991 Law on Cooperatives, which repealed the 1983 Cooperative Organizations Act. The new law

prescribed a modernized governance structure for the cooperatives, and provided for a transition from the old system to the new for agricultural cooperatives and the old cooperative unions. No transitional provisions were made, however, with respect to the other cooperative institutions, which could presumably continue in existence without any restructuring or re-registration.

As in all communist countries, Bulgarian cooperatives had been run in practice as a part of the state sector, and the individual entities had been combined into large "unions" which served as state and party instruments of control over the whole cooperative sector. In an important supplementary provision, the Law on Cooperatives abolished the old cooperative unions and redistributed their property to the constitutive individual cooperatives, although it also allowed the remaining entities to unite in new cooperative unions. The law also provided for the restitution of property confiscated or nationalized after 1944 to the existing and restored cooperatives.

Less felicitous was the law's half-hearted attempt to deal with the problem of agricultural cooperatives. These cooperatives, given their origin in a *de facto* confiscation of land from the former owners, had to be re-registered, but the law allowed their re-registration without a general meeting of the members. As a result, most agricultural cooperatives were able to reestablish themselves without much trouble and now pose a serious obstacle to the professed goal of the state, namely the restitution of the confiscated land to the former owners or their heirs. Consequently, following the October 1991 elections, the new parliament revoked the validity of the re-registration of the agricultural cooperatives and strengthened the program of land restitution (see Section 4 below). In particular, the amended Law on Ownership and Use of Farmlands established a procedure for the dissolution of the collective farms and charged special liquidation councils, appointed by the local authorities, to supervise their dismantling.

With respect to the remaining cooperatives, the Law on Cooperatives established a new structure of governance, involving a general meeting of the members, the president, the management board, and the supervisory board. The president is charged with running the day-to-day operations of the cooperative and is a nonvoting member of the management board. The voting members of the management and supervisory boards must be elected by a two-thirds majority of the general meeting, and no more than two-thirds of the members of the management board may stand for re-election. Cooperatives are also required to maintain a reserve fund equal to 20 per cent of their share capital.

Somewhat inconsistent with the regional trend toward equal treatment of all forms of property, the Law on Cooperatives promised the cooperative organizations state assistance in the form of "tax, credit, interest, custom and other economic concessions."[3]

THE COMMERCIAL CODE

All legal forms of new non-cooperative business organizations in Bulgaria are now governed by the new Commercial Code, adopted on May 16, 1991.

Bulgarian law divides all economic actors into the categories of "merchants" and "non-merchants." "Merchant" is used to denote all physical or legal persons engaged professionally in business and commercial activity, except farmers, artisans, members of the professions, and self-employed providers of services. Cooperatives (with the exception of housing cooperatives), governed by the August 1991 Law on Cooperatives, are also considered merchants. All merchants must be recorded in the commercial register and are governed by special provisions of the Code.

The Code recognizes the following forms through which merchant activity can be conducted:

- private merchant;
- (general) partnership;
- limited partnership;
- public limited partnership (also known as "limited shareholding partnership");
- limited-liability company;
- joint-stock company.

All of the above forms, with the exception of private merchants, are collectively referred to as "commercial companies." Subject to legal restrictions (such as those contained in the Law on Foreign Investment; see below), any natural or legal person, whether Bulgarian or foreign, may found a company. In a curious provision (Article 72), the Code creates very burdensome obstacles to non-cash contributions to commercial companies. Such contributions are permitted, but cannot take the form of future labor or services, and their value must be assessed by three experts appointed by the court.

---

[3] Similar remnants of the old bias in favor of state property may be noted in the language of Articles 17 and 18 of the new Bulgarian Constitution.

All banking and insurance companies must be organized as either joint-stock companies or cooperative organizations.

Private merchants Any physical person living in Bulgaria except individuals who are in the process of bankruptcy or who have deliberately caused bankruptcy leaving behind unsatisfied creditors, may register as a private merchant. An individual may only be registered once as a private merchant at any given time, and his business name must be the same as his given and family name (or another name under which the merchant is more widely known). When the business of a private merchant is transferred to another person, the new owner must add his name to the name of the business.

General partnership A partnership (denoted by the "s-te" at the end of the trade name) is formed, in writing, by two or more individuals who intend to engage professionally in commercial transactions under a joint trade name. The trade name must be the family or business name of one or more of the partners. All partners bear joint unlimited liability, and cannot engage in activities competitive to the partnership's business.

The agreement of all the partners is necessary for the appointment of a manager who is not a partner, for the acquisition and exercise of material rights with respect to real estate, and for the signing of a loan which exceeds the amount stipulated in the partnership agreement.

Limited partnership A limited partnership (denoted by the "kd" affixed to its name) is established on the basis of a contract between two or more individuals for the creation of a commercial enterprise in which at least one partner is a general partner and has personal and unlimited liability for the obligations of the partnership. General partners must contribute at least 10 per cent of the partnership capital. Limited partners, on the other hand, whose liability is limited to the value of their share (whether paid in or only pledged), are essentially passive investors who contribute capital to the partnership but do not take part in its management.

The business name of a limited partnership must contain the name of one of the general partners and must not include the name of a limited partner. (If the name of a limited partner appears in the name of the company, that partner will have unlimited liability.)

Public limited partnership A public limited partnership (identified by the "kda" in the trade name) is formed on the basis of a contract. It must have at least three limited partners, and its limited shares are issued through a public subscription in accordance with the bylaws of the partnership.

The founders of a public limited partnership are its general partners. They must contribute at least 10 per cent of the partnership's capital, draw up the bylaws, and bear unlimited liability. The general partners can freely select the limited partners from among the applicants to the subscription offer.

Unless the law otherwise stipulates, public limited partnerships are regulated by the rules applicable to joint-stock companies. The governance structure is the same as in a one-tier joint-stock company (see below), with limited partners alone having the right to vote at the general meeting, and with the management board made up only of general partners.

Limited-liability company A limited-liability company (LLC), also known as "private limited company" and identified by the "ood" at the end of its business name, may be founded by one or more individuals, all of whom are liable to the extent of their contribution to the company's capital. An LLC must have at least Leva 50,000 of capital divided into shares of no less than Leva 500 each, and its capital cannot be raised by a public subscription.

Each member of an LLC holds stock in the company's assets in proportion to his share of the capital (which, read together with the already mentioned limitations on non-cash contributions, may be quite restrictive). Stock certificates, evidencing membership, are not negotiable instruments; the interests in an LLC are said to be transferable and inheritable, but any transfer requires a unanimous resolution of the general meeting.

An LLC is governed by the general meeting, and by a managing director or a board of directors appointed and subject to dismissal by the general meeting. Employees of an LLC with more than fifty employees are represented at the general meeting, and their representative is entitled to a "deliberative" or consultative vote, as is a manager who is not a member. An unusual provision of the Code requires a unanimous resolution of the general meeting to allow the company to acquire or sell real estate. An LLC may also appoint one or more "controllers" whose task is to ensure the observance of the articles and the proper management of the company's assets. An LLC can be wound up upon a resolution of the members holding two-thirds of the company's authorized capital.

Joint-stock company   A joint-stock company (JSC) (identified by the "AD" in the company name) is a company with capital apportioned into shares which may be raised through a public subscription. The liability of the shareholders is limited to the value of their shares.

The minimum founding capital of a JSC is Leva 5 mln ($222,222, a very large sum of money in Bulgaria), if the company is formed through a public subscription, and Leva 1 mln otherwise. A joint-stock company engaged in banking must have minimum capital of Leva 10 mln.

The founders of a publicly traded JSC must publish a prospectus satisfying a number of disclosure requirements specified by the Code, and they are jointly liable for any damage caused by misrepresentation. The constitutive meeting of the subscription applicants must be attended by at least five individuals contributing no less than one-half of the subscribed capital. (This requirement may be difficult to meet in the case of widely held corporations, especially since the Code is silent on proxy powers.) At the meeting, the Articles of Association must be unanimously approved.

Shares of a JSC (which must have a nominal value of no less than Leva 100) are negotiable instruments. A JSC can issue different classes of shares, but the issuing price cannot be lower than the nominal value. (Any premium over the nominal price must be credited to the capital reserve.) Both registered and bearer shares can be issued, and both are freely transferable. Anti-dilution provisions of the Code give the shareholders an option to purchase any newly issued shares in proportion to their pre-existing holdings.

A JSC may also issue debentures (bonds), but such an issue cannot occur during the first two years of the company's operation. The debt capital raised must not exceed 50 per cent of paid-in equity. The debenture holders have their own general meetings, and each class of debenture holders appoints up to three trustees who play an advisory role at the general shareholders' meetings.

Joint-stock companies may have either one-tier or two-tier governance structure. In both types, the overarching powers are given to the shareholders acting at a general meeting, with a requirement of separate voting by each class of shareholders on resolutions which affect the rights of one class of shareholders differently from the others.

A one-tier JSC has one board of directors elected by the general meeting, with one or more of the directors charged with the management of the company. A two-tier JSC has separate management and supervisory boards. The management board, appointed by the supervisory board, operates and represents the company. The supervisory board, elected at the general meeting, is involved in the oversight but not the management of the company. The same individual cannot serve on both boards at the same time.

All joint-stock companies are required to maintain a revenue reserve. Contributions to the reserve are drawn from deposits of not less than 10 per cent of the yearly earnings until the reserve amounts to at least one-tenth of the authorized capital. In addition, any premium captured from the sale of bonds or shares is deposited into the reserve. The reserve can be used only to offset the losses of the current or the preceding year.

Regulations governing foreign ownership

The economic rights of foreign persons in Bulgaria are regulated by the 1992 Law on Economic Activity of Foreign Persons and Protection of Foreign Investment (the Foreign Activity Law). This law repeals the more restrictive Law on Foreign Investment of 1991 and certain provisions of the 1991 Law on the Ownership and Use of Farmland.

In principle, foreign citizens or entities are governed by the same legal framework as Bulgarian citizens and entities, except when specific legal regulations provide otherwise. More favorable provisions for economic activity by foreign persons, which are contained in international agreements to which Bulgaria is a party, will be applied in preference to domestic law. Existing economic activities and foreign investments are not affected by supervening normative restrictions.

Foreign persons are required to register their investments with the Ministry of Finance, but they do not need any permission to invest, except in cases specified in the law (and described below). The law also assures protection against expropriation, providing for judicial appeal and compensation (with a right to convert any award into foreign currency).

Foreign persons have the same right to purchase foreign currency from Bulgarian banks as do Bulgarian citizens, plus the right to repatriate both the principal and income from their investments. Foreign persons employed by firms with majority foreign participation may exchange up to 70 per cent of their salaries for foreign currency. (Bulgarian banks are required to assure that taxes are paid prior to the exchange and transfer of money abroad.) Foreign persons may open foreign-currency and Leva accounts in Bulgaria.

Favorable tax treatment is also extended to foreign investment: companies with 49 per cent foreign ownership and $100,000 of foreign investment are taxed at a rate of 30 per cent, while other companies are subject to a 40 per cent tax rate.

There are, however, a number of special restrictions. The most extensive of these apply to the ownership of land. The Bulgarian Constitution (Article 22 (2)) provides that foreign citizens and legal entities may not acquire property in land except by inheritance, and even in that case the land must be transferred to a Bulgarian national. The Foreign Activity Law provides additional, more specific restrictions. Foreign persons and firms with over 50 per cent foreign participation may not acquire ownership rights over agricultural land. Foreign persons can own buildings and usufructual rights over nonagricultural land, but they cannot acquire title to the underlying real estate. Moreover, even for these investments, special permission of the Council of Ministers is required if the investments are located in specially designated geographical areas. Land acquired by inheritance must be transferred within three years.

Foreign persons or firms with foreign majority participation must have special permission from the Council of Ministers in order to engage in the production or trade of weapons or ammunition, and the exploration or extraction of natural resources from the territorial sea, continental shelf, or the exclusive economic zones. These persons or firms must also apply for permission to the Bulgarian National Bank if they seek to engage in banking or insurance activity. The law specifies, however, that in cases where permission is required, the Council of Ministers and the National Bank will publish conditions which must be satisfied by the foreign applicant and will provide reasons for the denial of such applications.

A foreign natural person must have permission for permanent residence in Bulgaria in order to register as a sole proprietor, a member of a cooperative, or a general partner in any kind of partnership.

Interestingly enough, neither the Foreign Activity Law nor the Privatization Law contain any restrictions concerning the right of foreign persons to participate in the Bulgarian privatization process. Presumably, the reason for this is that Bulgarian privatization relies nearly exclusively on public sales of assets and securities, and foreign participation is an essential ingredient for the success of this type of program.

Bankruptcy and liquidation

No bankruptcies have been recorded in Bulgaria since 1951. There exists no separate bankruptcy law, although one, following Western models, is apparently in preparation (to be incorporated into the Commercial Code). Until today, the bankruptcy of a private merchant has been regulated by a few rudimentary provisions of the Code of Civil Procedure.[4] Insofar as firms are concerned, however, a set of temporary provisions is contained in Chapter 3 (Articles 65 to 81) of Decree No. 56 on Economic Activity, of January 13, 1989, as amended.

The Decree defines an insolvent firm as one unable to pay its debts for over sixty days. According to the Decree, an insolvent firm may receive aid from the state or may reach an agreement with its creditors. If its requests for aid are denied, an insolvent firm must be liquidated.

Bankruptcy proceedings begin by a declaration of insolvency, made by a bank which services the firm. This declaration may be made by the bank *sua sponte*, or at the request of the firm or of its creditors. Upon a declaration of insolvency, a conciliation proceeding will begin between the firm and its creditors (all of whom the firm must notify by registered mail fourteen days in advance). The meetings are chaired by a representative from the moving bank, and a representative of the state, appointed by a competent organ, may also take part. The meetings must be concluded within one month of their start, unless the debtor and the creditors agree to an extension.

If the parties at the conciliation meetings fail to come to an agreement, the bank representative must report the failure to the district court where the firm is registered, and the court will initiate judicial proceedings. A bankruptcy suit can also be initiated by the firm, its creditors, or the public prosecutor. Along with its decision to declare the firm bankrupt, the court will appoint a liquidator and attach the property of the debtor. (When the bankrupt is not a legal person, the court, upon the request of the creditors at the time of the declaration of bankruptcy, will also seize the personal property of the partners in the firm.) The decision is entered in the commercial register and published in the *State Gazette*, with creditors obliged to file their written claims within three months of the publication. The announcement of bankruptcy acts to terminate the economic activity of the firm, make

---

[4] There have been some mortgage foreclosures in 1992.

all its obligations due, and halt the accrual of interest on the firm's debts.

During the interim period preceding the final liquidation order, the court will attempt another conciliation agreement, drawn by the liquidator. If the creditors do not accept the proposed agreement within fourteen days, the liquidation of the firm's property must begin.

During the interim period, the liquidator can sell goods which are liable to depreciate or deteriorate quickly, negotiate the termination of contracts, and transfer contractual rights and obligations to other parties. Following the liquidation decision, the property of the debtor is sold either according to a procedure established by the court or through a specialized trading firm or public auction. State lands, forests, waters, and their underground layers which have been granted to the firm will revert to the state. If the assets of the debtor are insufficient to satisfy all of the creditors, the liquidator will give priority to wage claims, followed by compensation for unlawfully inflicted damage, taxes, and obligations secured by pledges or mortgages. The remainder of the assets is proportionally distributed to the remaining creditors. The creditors have fourteen days to raise objections with the court concerning the payment schedule proposed by the liquidator. The court's decision can be appealed within fourteen days. At the conclusion of the distribution, notice of termination of the liquidation is published in the *State Gazette* and operates to preclude any unstated and unsatisfied claims.

The Decree also specifies that the state must ensure the retraining and reemployment of the employees who have been dismissed as a result of the liquidation of a firm and that the social needs of persons left unemployed due to liquidation will be met from state funds during a period of time specified by the Council of Ministers.

3B. Structure of ownership

Measuring the size of the private sector in Bulgaria is next to impossible at this point, and only very rough estimates can be made of the changes that have occurred in the ownership structure since the fall of the old regime.

The growth of the private sector can come from essentially three sources: the creation of new private businesses, privatization of previously state-owned enterprises, and foreign investment.

The growth of the private sector due to privatization has been very limited, since delays in the enactment of the Privatization Law and the lack of an effective political leadership committed to a specific set of programs have slowed the process of the state's disengagement from the productive sector. The extent of privatization to date is described in Section 4B below.

A very large number of small private enterprises have been created since early 1990, exceeding 210,000 in mid-1992, but nearly all of these are extremely small; indeed, often even the owner, who is the only employee, does not work full time in his business.

It is also difficult to estimate the size of the private sector with the use of official employment statistics, since the official figures do not give the number of hours actually worked "on the job." But 650,000 people were listed as employed in the private sector in mid-1992, and some calculations make this equivalent to 400,000 full-time jobs. Also, many people engaged in the private sector do not register as such, partly in order to evade taxation, partly because they simultaneously receive unemployment benefits, and partly because they are working simultaneously in the public sector. Many pensioners are also employed in the private sector, but there are no official records of their number.

Overall, while the growth of the domestic private sector is still slow, it is quite significant in certain sectors. Thus, for example, prior to 1992, the number of people engaged in state-owned retail and whole-sale trade decreased by approximately 95,000, that is, by one-third. The impact of this decrease in the market was barely noticeable, however, because of the rapid development of private commerce.

There has also been some growth in foreign investment since early 1990, although the numbers are not large. Good data on foreign investment are difficult to obtain, and not much beyond the aggregate numbers is available. In the balance of payments data for 1990, the cumulative figure of foreign investment was a mere $4 mln. For 1991, it rose to $56 mln, and some other estimates put it between $50 mln and $80 mln. The number of joint ventures was put at 240 in mid-1991, most of them with very small capital. As of June 1992, a new tax register of joint ventures was created in the Ministry of Finance, but it contains very incomplete data so far.

4. THE PRIVATIZATION PROCESS

Introduction: the politics of privatization legislation

The progress of privatization in Bulgaria has been extremely tortuous and subject to sharp political controversies. As a result, Bulgaria has not yet even begun to implement any comprehensive privatization program, and, except for some special pieces of legislation, the first major law on the subject, the Transformation and Privatization of State and Municipal Enterprises Act (the Privatization Law), was not passed until April 1992.

Little, if any, progress was achieved on fundamental economic reorganization in 1990, the first year after the downfall of the Zhivkov communist regime. The Bulgarian Socialist Party (BSP), the former communist party under a new name, succeeded in retaining its control of the government (with Andrei Lukanov as the prime minister) as a result of having obtained a majority in the first postcommunist general election in June 1990. The noncommunist opposition, organized under a loose framework known as the Union of Democratic Forces (UDF), refused to enter a proposed broad coalition under BSP leadership, and the BSP's moral authority to govern was contested by a continuing wave of demonstrations, protests, and industrial action. The BSP government finally resigned in late November 1990.

One of the most important criticisms of the BSP government by those who later emerged as the leading economic figures in the UDF government, I. Pushkarov and I. Kostov, concerned the government's reliance on monetary measures rather than privatization in the program of economic stabilization. According to these influential critics, privatization should have been one of the principal initial elements of the process of reform.

A more radical program of economic reform, including much greater emphasis on privatization, was expected to be one of the most important priorities of the new transitional coalition government, formed in December 1990 under the non-party leadership of Dimitur Popov. Pending Bulgaria's second postcommunist general election (eventually held in October 1991), the new government negotiated a set of reform measures with the International Monetary Fund and the World Bank, which included a commitment to a rapid privatization program. In its memorandum to the IMF, the government stated that it was drawing up a comprehensive privatization program and expected substantial sales to be effected in the first quarter of 1991. Sales of gas stations were to initiate the process, with foreign companies to be invited to participate in the auctions. The State Budget Law, passed in February 1991, anticipated that the revenues from "transactions with state and municipal property" would amount to Leva 214 mln – 0.34 per cent of all revenues.

The goals and intentions announced by the Popov government were never realized. Although a special Privatization Agency was established, the transitional government failed to enact a comprehensive privatization bill. Even the modest small-scale privatization program, involving mainly some sales of gas stations, was halted after three months, when the newly passed comprehensive Law on Commerce of June 1991 required that privatization be governed by a comprehensive act of legislation, setting out appropriate standards and procedures.

The general election of October 1991 resulted in the victory of the UDF alliance and the relegation of the BSP to the role of opposition. One of the most important political issues in the election campaign was the formulation of a new comprehensive privatization legislation. The new UDF government, led by Philip Dimitrov, took office in November 1991, and announced again that accelerated privatization was a major element in its economic reform program. Still, the framing of the necessary legislation remained highly contentious. In November 1991, even before the Dimitrov government was formed, three UDF parliamentary activists, including the chairman of the Parliamentary Commission for Economic Policy, Mr. Assen Michkovski, submitted their own draft of a privatization law to the National Assembly. The BSP (now in opposition) announced its support for an amended version of a privatization bill presented to the previous parliament in 1990. The government's own plan was submitted in December 1991.

The controversy reflected two completely different approaches to the privatization process. The government proposed to proceed on the basis of an amendment to the existing law of July 1991 on Incorporating Sole-Ownership Companies with Limited Liability which would have empowered the ministries, on behalf of the government, to initiate, conduct, and supervise the whole privatization process. This proposal was unacceptable both to a part of the UDF parliamentary fraction and to the BSP, which criticized the government bill as a palliative measure that would delegate enormous discretionary powers to state-owned enterprises and the Ministry of Industry and Trade. It was also objected that the bill made no provision for workers' participation in the privatization process and relied exclusively on the technique of sale by public tender. The Michkovski draft, on the other hand, was criticized for proposing an excessively high level of preferences for employees, since it envisaged that workers could acquire (through an ESOP plan) up to 49 per cent of each company's shares at a 50 per cent discount (with the amount of discount granted to each employee limited to the amount of his or her annual salary). The government also claimed that the Michkovski draft unnecessarily slowed the legislative process, that it gave an excessive degree of autonomy to the Privatization Agency, and that it too lacked provisions for important privatization techniques, such as management contracts with buy-out clauses.

The conflict between the government and the Parliamentary Commission for Economic Policy intensified further when one of the two most influential labor unions, the Labor Confederation "Podkrepa" (Support), itself a founding member of UDF, backed the Michkovski draft with its generous treatment of workers. In a growing factional split within UDF, Podkrepa demanded the resignation of the two most influential economic ministers in the Dimitrov government (I. Kostov and I. Pushkarov). The government also became an object of increasing attacks by the other big trade union, the Confederation of Independent Trade Unions, and the Socialist Party, which accused the government of having achieved nothing in its first 100 days in power.

In the spring of 1992, amid mounting political tension, the government, with some prodding from the World Bank, revised its proposed draft of the privatization law to take account of the criticisms of its earlier proposals. The new bill provided for a greater role of the Privatization Agency, although it still made it subordinate to the Council of Ministers. It also provided for some employee preferences, but on a significantly reduced scale as compared with the Michkovski draft. The bill was finally passed, with some amendments, on April 23, 1992.

The Privatization Law covers, essentially, the sale of state and municipal companies, often following their transformation into joint-stock or sole-ownership companies. Insofar as the law also regulates this prior requirement of corporatization, it supersedes the previous law of June 1991 on Incorporating Single-Owner Firms with State Property, and the regulations issued thereunder. (See Section 5 on corporatization below.)

The law also provides for the preparation of comprehensive annual privatization programs, to be drafted by the Privatization Agency, approved by the Council of Ministers, and passed by the National

Assembly simultaneously with the National Budget Act. Annual reports on the progress of privatization are also to be presented to the Assembly together with the national budget report.

4A. Organizational structure of state regulation of privatization

Prior to the enactment of the Privatization Law, the only privatization activity outside of the area of housing and agriculture occurred during March–June 1991, when an attempt was made to sell some small-scale enterprises. The process was quite centralized, with the Ministry of Industry, Trade, and Services and the larger municipalities in charge of the operation. The Ministry and the municipalities chose the objects to be sold, and while the management of the selected companies was authorized to handle the sale, the method of tender was prescribed for all transactions, and the management decisions were supervised by the branch ministries and municipal councils.

While there is so far no experience with privatization under the new legal regime, the Privatization Law sets up a very centralized process for the proposed privatization of Bulgarian enterprises. Except for municipally-owned property, a single Privatization Agency is charged with implementing all transactions concerning assets valued at more than Leva 10 mln ($444,444). Moreover, when the value of assets exceeds Leva 200 mln ($8.9 mln), the transaction must be approved in advance by the Council of Ministers. Even the privatization of small businesses with the value of less than Leva 10 mln is to be handled by a body designated by the Council of Ministers, which is likely to be one of the ministries.

The privatization of municipal assets is to be handled by the municipal councils themselves, but the procedure is rigidly laid down in the Privatization Law, and no public offering of shares can be made without a clearance from the Privatization Agency. The municipal authorities can retain 50 per cent of the proceeds to be used for debt repayment and for investment purposes, but not for current expenses.

The Privatization Agency

The Privatization Law mandates the creation of a new Privatization Agency, financed from the budget. The Agency is governed by a Supervisory Board of eleven members, appointed for four-year terms, with five members appointed by the Council of Ministers, and six by the National Assembly. The day-to-day operations of the Agency are managed by the Executive Director elected by, and responsible to, the Board (which will have the power to dismiss him). The Agency is charged with preparing an annual privatization program, to be approved by the Council of Ministers, including minimum privatization targets for the coming year, the list of enterprises to be privatized, and the privatization guidelines for local authorities. The program will be annually debated in the parliament and passed together with the National Budget Act.

The Privatization Agency created under the new Privatization Law is a new institution, distinct from the body of the same name set up in February 1991 by the Popov government. The old Agency had no authority to conduct any actual privatizations, and was largely confined to personnel training, methodological preparation and discussions of privatization schemes, collecting relevant information, preparing rules for the valuation of enterprises, and establishing and maintaining contacts with foreign organizations as well as with local and foreign consulting firms. The new Agency, by contrast, is charged with overseeing the whole privatization process and conducting the sales of individual enterprises.

The new Agency is still being formed and its mode of operation is not yet fully established. At this point, the Agency has two sectoral divisions. The first, Division of Programs and Methods of Privatization, consists of departments dealing with the licensing of property valuators; methods of privatization; analysis, prognosis and programs of privatization; and information services. The second is the sectoral Division of the Organization of the Privatization Process, which consists of departments dealing with financing and privatization transactions. The Agency also has a number of administrative, legal and public relations departments accountable directly to the executive director. It is also envisaged that eleven regional offices will be set up in major cities in the country.

In early October 1992, the Agency employed approximately seventy people, but the projected staff will grow to 262.

Other state organs

In addition to the institutions described above, there are several other state or semi-state bodies which are called into existence in connection with the privatization process. They include the Ministry of Agriculture, which supervises the redistribution of land, and the Mutual Fund, created under Article 8 of the Privatization Law, as a special purpose repository for a portion of the privatization proceeds. See the subsection on sales programs in Section 4B, below.

The Act on. Restoring Ownership of Nationalized Land and Property, passed in early April 1992 to amend the Law on Ownership and Use of Farmland, also calls for the creation of special liquidation councils, appointed by the local authorities, to supervise the dismantling of collective farms and the distribution and sale of the land to new owners (see the subsection on cooperatives in Section 3A above).

4B. Overview of privatization programs

As already indicated, the Bulgarian experience of actual privatization is very limited so far, consisting only of the small-scale privatization program launched and aborted between March and June 1991, some measures for property restitution, especially in agriculture, and the informal or *nomenklatura* privatization which is sometimes referred to in Bulgaria as "quiet" and "illegal" privatization. The only area in which privatization has been significant is that of housing. While the new Privatization Law sets out an ambitious program of sales of existing state enterprises, its future is still rather uncertain.

The sales programs for state-owned companies and enterprises

The 1992 Privatization Law takes a rather conservative approach to the privatization of most state enterprises, relying exclusively on sales and the use of relatively traditional methods of privatization.

The law prescribes the corporatization procedure for most existing state enterprises (see Section 5 below). It then provides that all sales of state-owned commercial companies with assets valued at more than Leva 10 mln ($444,444) must be preceded by a formal valuation performed by an independent foreign or Bulgarian expert firm licensed by the Privatization Agency. The method of sale of any company in this category is to be determined by the Privatization Agency (with the approval of the Council of Ministers for all companies with assets valued at more than Leva 200 mln), but the choice is limited to a public offering, a public auction of shares, a publicly invited tender, or a publicized private placement, with the initial or reservation price established by the prescribed valuation procedure.

For all commercial companies with assets exceeding Leva 10 mln, the law also provides for preferential sales to employees and retirees of up to 20 per cent of the shares. Each employee or retiree is to be entitled to a 50 per cent discount up to an amount equal to between eight and twelve months' salary, depending on the length of employment. The employee shares are to have no voting rights for the first three years.

The strictures of the traditional sales are only minimally relaxed with respect to commercial companies with assets below Leva 10 mln and those state enterprises which had not been transformed into commercial companies (as well as with respect to assets remaining after bankruptcy proceedings). Sales of these smaller units need not be preceded by a formal valuation, but they must be offered at public auctions or tenders, with the general terms and procedures for such auctions or tenders to be determined by the Council of Ministers. If more than 30 per cent of the employees declare that they intend to bid in the auction or tender for their company, they may empower a special representative for this purpose, and, if such representative wins the auction or tender, the price will be reduced by 30 per cent, provided that the discount does not exceed the aggregate maximum preferences allowable under the procedures described above for companies with assets exceeding Leva 10 mln. The law also provides for the possibility of installment sales and long-term leasing arrangements with an option to purchase.

No juristic person which is more than 50 per cent owned by the state may participate as a buyer in the privatization process without the permission of the Privatization Agency or the appropriate municipal authority (for municipal enterprises). Similarly, debt-for-equity swaps in the context of privatization must be approved by the Council of Ministers.

Twenty per cent of the shares of the privatized enterprises (or a monetary equivalent thereof) must, according to the Privatization Law, be deposited in a specially created Mutual Fund. The resources from this fund may then be allocated (by the Council of Ministers) for the purpose of capitalizing the social security fund, funding schemes of free share distribution to Bulgarian citizens, and compensating former owners. The law also mandates additional contributions toward the capitalization of the social security fund, the maintenance of an Agriculture Assistance and Development Fund (10 per cent of total proceeds), a State Fund for Reconstruction and Development, and other purposes.

Small-scale privatization

The legal basis of the March–June 1991 small-scale privatization was the amendment, by the Council of Ministers, of Article 13 of the 1989 Decree No. 56 on Economic Activity and the regulations issued under that Decree on tenders for state and municipal property. The intention was to launch a program of privatizing a large number of state and municipal establishments, such as tourist facilities, shops, restaurants, workshops, gas stations, offices, and storage facilities. As explained earlier, the program was halted because the newly passed Law on Commerce required that privatization operations be governed by comprehensive legislation with appropriate standards and procedures. (Transactions already under way at the time of the enactment of the Law on Commerce were permitted to proceed.)

The sales program was drawn up by the Ministry of Industry, Trade and Services and by the larger municipalities. The management boards of the companies were authorized to handle the sales under the supervision of their branch ministries and municipal councils. Tender was the only authorized method of sale.

The initial price of the properties offered for sale was fixed by the management of the privatized enterprises on the basis of evaluations made by independent experts selected from a list of 1,517 persons specially authorized for this purpose by the Ministry of Finance and the Ministry of Justice. The companies involved in the program were to retain 40 per cent of the sale proceeds; 30 per cent was to be channeled to a State or Municipal Investment Fund; and 30 per cent was targeted for the settlement of foreign debt.

As implemented, the program produced modest results. Altogether sixty-five public tenders were held, with the property initially valued at Leva 75 mln ($3.33 mln); no comprehensive information has been released about the total proceeds from the sales. While more than 300 gas stations were initially earmarked for privatization, only ten were put up for public auctions in June 1991, of which only three were sold. In September, three additional gas stations were offered, but only one was sold, and the total value of gas stations sold amounted to Leva 8,192,200 ($508,820). In the field of trade and services six auctions were held, covering sixty-six properties, of which fifty-six were sold, with the total sales amounting to Leva 9,668,000.

The sales program was widely considered a failure. The process lacked clear procedures, and the valuation criteria were considered inadequate. The businesses offered for sale were poorly marketed, the gas stations were not located on important traffic routes, and no serious efforts were made to attract foreign investors.

Privatization of housing

The traditional pattern of housing in Bulgaria has been based on individual ownership, rather than rental, and this remained the case even under the communist regime: 85 per cent of the housing stock was still in private hands in 1985. The state did own, however, a sizeable portion of the urban housing stock. According to a decree dating back to 1968, the state and the municipalities had a right to sell the houses and apartments they owned, but for many years the law did not produce any significant changes in the pattern of housing ownership. Then, in 1990, the Lukanov government launched a program to privatize the remaining stock of housing in order to raise revenues for the budget. The prices of the units sold had not been adjusted to reflect anything approaching their market value, with the average price ranging between Leva 15,000 and 20,000 ($800–1,000), and the interest rate as low as 2 per cent. (The market rate or cost of construction for the same units was estimated to have been up to Leva 1 mln, or $44,444.) After the start of the economic reform program in 1991, the interest rate on new sales went up to 45 per cent (with old mortgages adjusted to 10 per cent), but prices were not correspondingly adjusted, and people continued to take out loans for home purchases, especially since housing prices on the free market were increasing at a pace still higher than the interest rate.

It is difficult to give an accurate quantitative assessment of the scope of housing privatization because Bulgarian statistics only record housing ownership patterns when a full census is conducted. According to unofficial expert estimates, however, only 300,000 out of a total of 3,300,000 dwellings (9.5 per cent) are now owned by the state or municipalities.

Restitution of land to former owners

The process of land restitution began in February 1991, when the National Assembly was still dominated by the BSP, with the passage of the Law on Ownership and Use of Farmlands. This law provided for restitution to the former owners and their heirs of the land forcibly collectivized in the 1950s. The law aimed to re-establish the land ownership structure as of 1946. Provisions have also been made, however, for auctioning off some 400,000 hectares of state lands to peasants who have never owned land.

As originally passed, the law was considered inadequate, and a number of amendments were introduced in March 1992. Also, the UDF government quickly introduced new regulations under the law, designed to facilitate the reprivatization process. Still, progress has been rather slow, and many problems remain unresolved.

Among the most important difficulties with the law have been the obstacles in verifying titles, since the existing land register (the *cadastre*) has not been properly maintained,[5] and many titles came to be contested among neighbors or among the heirs of the original owners. Also, the process of land restitution was originally not conceived in parallel with the dismantling of the collective farms which continued to own agricultural machinery, buildings, and other facilities. As a result, private farmers could not obtain the wherewithal necessary for working their land. While the new amendments were aimed at decentralizing and accelerating the dismantling of the cooperatives, the issue is highly political and progress is slow.

The original law further limited the effectiveness of private farming by restricting private agricultural holdings to 20 hectares per household in areas of intensive farming and to 30 hectares per household in other areas. Although the old ownership structure made it unlikely that many large farms would result from the restitution process (according to the last census before 1946, 63.1 per cent of farms were of five hectares or less), the restrictions on the size of private farms were seen as limiting the scope for farm enlargement in response to market forces. Consequently, the new amendments have eliminated the size restrictions.

In addition to these problems, private agricultural business operations face a very high cost of credit (with interest rates of 60 per cent per year), low farm gate prices paid by monopolistic wholesale purchasing and procurement agencies, and high costs for animal feed. As a result, the majority of the former owners and their heirs, many of whom have become city dwellers, did not come forward to resume their ownership – despite the new law's extension of the original deadline for the filing of claims, only 50 per cent (approximately 1 mln persons) of the former owners have applied. As of August 1992, approximately 10 per cent of the land has been returned to the former owners, and additional 20 per cent is expected to be returned this fall.

Despite the slow progress of the land restitution program, its economic effect may be considerable. The output of private farms is

---

[5] Instances have been reported of intentional destruction of maps and archival materials by the communist-dominated local authorities in 1990 and 1991.

reported to have increased by 30 per cent in 1991, apparently account-ing for a relatively smaller decline of agricultural production (7 per cent), as compared with other sectors (23 per cent of GDP and 27 per cent of industrial production).

Restitution of other property

A number of laws on restitution of nationalized property, passed after the UDF election victory of late 1991, regulate the restitution of confiscated factories, warehouses, apartment houses, buildings, shops, etc. if they exist in their former shape. However, such cases are said to be rare. The 1992 Privatization Law also provides special procedures for the restitution of the still existing immovables and land nationalized between 1946 and 1962 and incorporated into the fixed assets of state or municipal enterprises. The previous owners must file their claims within one year of the entry of the law into force, and they will be entitled to receive a proportionate part of the shares or interest of the transformed enterprises into which their property had been incorporated.

Spontaneous ("quiet" and "illegal") privatization

As in many other Eastern European countries, members of the depart-ing communist *nomenklatura* in Bulgaria, especially in the last months of communist rule, have attempted to divert to their private ownership a part of the state property under their managerial control. In Bulgaria, such transactions are sometimes referred to as "quiet" and "illegal" privatization. "Quiet" privatization usually involves no formal illegality, but relies on normative acts (mainly Council of Ministers' regulations) which do not provide for open, public, and competitive sales of state property. "Illegal" privatization, by contrast, refers to transfers of state property which breach the existing legislation.

An example of "quiet" privatization was provided by transactions under Regulation 17/1989 of the Council of Ministers which allowed home trading outlets to be leased to insiders without public auction. Leases to insiders under this arrangement generally resulted in substantially lower rents, as compared with cases when auctions were held. Another regulation (Regulation 36/1990), governing the leasing and sale of businesses in trade, tourism, and the service sector, provided vague and inadequate auction and valuation procedures, and enabled the insiders to conclude a number of unfair transactions. Still another regulation (Regulation 2/1989), this time issued by the Ministry of Transport, allowed for sales of second-hand state-owned vehicles and farm machinery (including tractors, harvester combines, etc.), and many "quiet" transactions have resulted in sales at very low prices.

Perhaps the most egregious cases of "quiet" privatization occurred under the amendments to Article 13 of Decree No. 56 on Economic Activity, which were in force between May and August 1990, when a special moratorium was announced. In accordance with these amendments, the management boards of state-owned companies were empowered to make sales of "fixed assets to physical and juridical bodies" without any clear-cut auction procedures, and much state property was transferred at that time to private firms or individuals belonging to the circles of the *nomenklatura*.

Most cases of "illegal" privatization occurred when shares in state companies were sold to insiders in violation of the existing laws and regulations. Thus, for example, the Law on Incorporating Single-Owner Firms with State Property, which regulated the process of corporatization of Bulgarian state enterprises, specifically prohibited any transfer of shares prior to the enactment of the Privatization Law. Nevertheless, a number of companies illegally sold shares to their insiders, often on preferential terms or at prices reflecting the value of the company's assets before the required inflation adjustments. Similarly, state assets sometimes continued to be sold according to the defective auction procedures, even after they had been invalidated by the Law on Commerce.

While a number of cases of "quiet" and "illegal" privatization (especially in the case of sales of shares in two state banks) have received extensive coverage in the Bulgarian press, most of the transactions remain undiscovered, and it is very difficult to determine the extent of this form of privatization.

5. CORPORATIZATION

The corporatization of state-owned enterprises is the process by which firms are converted into commercial companies with a structure familiar in the capitalist systems. Prior to their ultimate privatization, the state or the appropriate municipality remains the single owner of the transformed state enterprises. This has necessitated special legal provisions, where the law would otherwise require more than one owner for a particular form of business organization (such as the joint-stock company, for example).

The initial legal framework that could be used as a basis for corporatization was created in January 1989 by Decree No. 56 on Economic Activity, re-establishing for the first time since 1951 (when the old Commercial Code had been repealed) the company structure in Bulgaria. While a spate of conversions occurred between October 1989 and January 1990, the speed of corporatization decreased after February 1991, and the relevant portions of Decree No. 56 were superseded in June 1991 by the new Commercial Code, which contains special provisions allowing for the establishment of single-owner commercial companies. In the following month, a new legislative basis for corporatization of state-owned enterprises was set out in the Law on Incorporating Single-Owner Firms with State Property, together with the Regulation Guidelines concerning the management of the converted enterprises. The same law also prohibited transactions involving the shares of such companies, pending the approval of the Privatization Law. Finally, the Privatization Law of April 1992 superseded the Law on Incorporating Single-Owner Companies and consolidated the legal provisions concerning the corporatization and privatization of state enterprises in Bulgaria.

The Privatization Law provides a simple set of rules for the transformation of state enterprises into commercial companies. It basically leaves the process to the discretion of the Council of Ministers, allowing the Council to delegate its powers to another body (most likely a sectoral ministry) in the case of enterprises with book value of assets below Leva 10 mln ($444,444), and requiring it to consult the Privatization Agency with respect to all enterprises above this threshold. The shares of all corporatized state enterprises must be offered for sale within five years from the date of conversion.

Only a few aggregate figures are available concerning the size of the corporatization to date. As of May 1992, there were 547 wholly-owned state joint-stock companies with assets valued at Leva 15 bln ($670 mln), while the reported number of state-owned limited-liability companies stood at 1,151 and the number of remaining state enterprises at 3,356. These figures should be treated with some skepticism, however, since the process of registering new companies is decentralized, and data from the regional courts have not been fully entered into the national statistics. Even more questionable are the data concerning the value of the converted companies, since their assets had often been entered according to the old book values, without any adjustments for inflation.[6] But some independent sources estimate the value of the capital of the corporatized sector as between 60 and 70 per cent of the total state sector.

While corporatization was often combined with the splitting of existing state enterprises and the creation of separate companies out of individual plants, preliminary results from a still incomplete survey of managers in the state sector conducted by the Center for the Study of Democracy in Sofia indicate that little change has occurred in the corporatized enterprises in terms of their management and operations.

---

[6] Thus, for example, the new state Electricity Company, valued at $100 mln, owns all power stations in the country (one of them nuclear), producing 45 bln kWh per year, as well as all of the transmission lines and local stations.

CZECHOSLOVAKIA

CONTENTS

1. INTRODUCTION

Main points of the reform program

The Soviet-led invasion of Czechoslovakia in 1968 cut short the formulation of the Hungarian-style reforms, which were being developed during the 1960s. After the invasion, the structure of the classical command economy was reimposed in Czechoslovakia. As the Czechoslovak economy gradually degenerated, the Communist Party and the government recognized the need for the reform of the system. Toward the end of communist rule, limited reform measures were carried out.

In 1990, a radical transition and austerity plan was passed by the parliament and implemented through laws and government decrees in a step-by-step preparatory phase. The first impact of the new macro-economic policies began to be felt in 1990, but it was not until January 1991 that a complete set of transition policies came into effect. The main policy measures were:

- restrictive monetary and fiscal policies;
- privatization program;
- liberalization of prices combined with limited price controls;
- internal convertibility with a sharp devaluation of the currency and import protection through import surcharges.

The cost of these transition measures has much been higher in Slovakia than in the Czech part of the country. This has strengthened the separatist and anti-reform forces in Slovakia, which resulted in the strong showing by the party seeking Slovak independence in the June 1992 elections. A political agreement had already been made concerning the separation of the Republics, while the legal details are being worked out.

2. ECONOMIC ENVIRONMENT

The structure of output

In 1991, the gross national product (GNP) of Czechoslovakia, in current prices, was Kcs 979.4 bln ($33.2 bln).[1] The structure of the net material product has remained largely unchanged between 1988 and 1991, with industry retaining about a 60 per cent share.

Table 2.1 The structure of net material product (per cent of the total)

	1988	1991
Industry	61	63
Agriculture and forestry	7	7
Construction	11	9
Transport and communication	5	4
Trade and other	16	17

Source: PlanEcon

Czechoslovak industry is extremely concentrated. The largest 100 companies in 1990 accounted for 26 per cent of industrial employment and over 50 per cent of the total assets of the state sector.

Table 2.2 Concentration of industry in 1990

	The biggest 100 companies	The biggest 200 companies
Total employment (thousands)	878,503	1,250,941
(as per cent of labor force)	26	38
Total book value of assets (Kcs mln)	753	942
(as per cent of total assest of industrial enterprises)	51	63

Source: Computations based on the data of the Federal Ministry of Finance

---

[1] The koruna–dollar exchange rate used here is the average rate for the year as calculated by *PlanEcon Review*. For the period covered by this report, these rates were as follows: 1988, Kcs 14.3; 1989, Kcs 14.3; 1990, Kcs 18.0; 1991, Kcs 29.5; 1992, Kcs 29.2 (estimate).

Output

In 1990 and 1991, the gross domestic product (GDP) declined by 0.4 per cent and 15.9 per cent, respectively. The corresponding declines in the net material product (NMP) were 0.6 per cent and 19.9 per cent. The drop in NMP in 1991 was led by a 28 per cent fall in construction and a 21 per cent decline in industry. The output of agriculture and forestry, transportation, and trade decreased by 13.6 per cent, 18.7 per cent, and 12.4 per cent, respectively. During the first quarter of 1992, industrial production has remained about 35 per cent below the pre-reform levels of 1989. Since the drop in industrial production was greater than the decline in employment, average productivity in industry fell by 14.4 per cent in 1991.

Table 2.3 Industrial production (1989 monthly average = 100)

	Jan	Feb	Mar	Apr	May	June	July	Aug	Sept	Oct	Nov	Dec
1991	89.1	83.2	79.2	84.9	72.7	72.1	62.6	60.1	63.5	76.1	70.9	53.7
1992	55.1	64.6	62.8									

Source: PlanEcon

Investment

After a 3.7 per cent rise in 1990, gross investment in fixed capital fell sharply by 28.8 per cent in 1991.

Household savings

There is no reliable estimate of total household savings. According to the International Monetary Fund (IMF) monetary survey, the total amounts of time and demand deposits officially held by households, as of September 1991, were Kcs 188.1 bln ($6.4 bln) and Kr 92 bln ($3.1 bln), respectively. In addition, households held foreign currency deposits totaling about $711 mln. As of the end of June 1992, the Federal Statistical Office estimated the total household savings in domestic currency at Kcs 319.1 bln, and in hard currencies at $2 bln.

Price liberalization

On January 1, 1991, the government liberalized about 85 per cent of all retail prices. Other prices were increased substantially and are being gradually freed. By the end of 1991, the share of products with prices that were still regulated was only about 5 per cent of GDP.

Price jumps after liberalization were higher than expected, but prices stabilized by June 1991 and remained virtually unchanged from June until October 1991.

Inflation

The Czechoslovak government has had considerable success in controlling inflation. After a sharp rise in the first months of 1991, the industrial wholesale price index stabilized in April 1991.

There was also a significant increase in the retail price index in early 1991; in January 1991 alone the index rose 25.8 per cent. The index stabilized in April 1991. The resulting annual increase was 58.9 per cent.

Table 2.4   Retail price index (month-to-month per cent changes)

	Jan	Feb	Mar	Apr	May	June	July	Aug	Sept	Oct	Nov	Dec
1991	25.8	6.9	5.0	1.8	2.0	1.8	0.1	0.1	0.2	−0.1	1.5	1.2
1992	1.0	0.5	0.4	0.5	0.5	0.5						

Source: PlanEcon

The average prices of food items increased 31.2 per cent in January 1991, but only 38.1 per cent for the entire year. January 1991 also saw a 68.2 per cent increase in the average prices of non-food items; however, they rose at the rate of 78.3 per cent for the entire year. The overall GDP deflator rose by 42 per cent in 1991.

Behavior of wages

Wage setting in Czechoslovakia is governed by a government decree issued in 1990. The decree defines twenty-one compensation classes. Total allowed compensation in each class consists of the base level and a supplementary increase, which depend on the wage rate, various rewards, bonuses, and other extra payments. For example, in 1990 the base wage level of the highest class was Kcs 7,700 ($428) per month, and the supplementary monthly payment ranged between Kcs 300 ($17) and Kcs 2,200 ($122).

In addition to the levels of individual compensation, the government also regulates the growth of the enterprise wage bill. The enterprises exceeding the centrally set limits are required to pay an excess wage tax.

Wages and incomes have not increased at the same rate as prices. Nominal wages rose 15 per cent in 1991. Pensions and other social benefits, typically low, were allowed to increase 20 per cent due to strong social pressure. Incomes in the agricultural sector dropped 24.2 per cent in 1991, relative to 1990. Real wages dropped 25.3 per cent in 1991, while the real wage index in industry rose by 8 per cent between January and December of 1991.

Nominal wages, in current US dollars, also increased from $128 per month, in January 1991, to $163, in March 1992.

Table 2.5 Real wage in industry (January 1990 = 100)

	Jan	Feb	Mar	Apr	May	June	July	Aug	Sept	Oct	Nov	Dec
1991	70.9	62.4	70.1	66.6	65.9	68.9	68.7	63.1	66.0	73.9	80.7	76.6
1992	70.0	64.4	76.2									

Source: PlanEcon

Table 2.6 Average monthly industrial wage (in current US dollars)

	Jan	Feb	Mar	Apr	May	June	July	Aug	Sept	Oct	Nov	Dec
1991	128.7	123.0	137.4	127.6	128.0	132.8	132.1	123.3	131.4	147.8	167.8	164.6
1992	153.0	139.3	163.3									

Source: PlanEcon

Unemployment

With the acceleration of economic reform in 1991, unemployment gradually began to rise to significant levels. By the end of 1991 the total number of registered unemployed increased to 523,700, representing

Table 2.7   Unemployment rate (as per cent of labor force)

	Jan	Feb	Mar	Apr	May	June	July	Aug	Sept	Oct	Nov	Dec
1991	1.5	1.9	2.3	2.8	3.2	3.8	4.6	5.1	5.6	6.0	6.3	6.6
1992	7.1	6.9	6.5	6.0								

Source: PlanEcon

6.6 per cent of the labor force. However, the recovery of industrial production during the first quarter of 1992 resulted in the gradual reduction of the unemployment rate between January and April of 1992.

While the unemployment rate in the Czech region of the country declined during the first quarter of 1992, unemployment in Slovakia continued to increase. Slovakia suffered considerably more than the Czech republic. In July the average unemployment rate in Slovakia was 11.1 per cent, four times higher than the rate of 2.7 per cent in the Czech region of the country.

Table 2.8   Recent unemployment rates in the republics

	Czechoslovakia	Czech Republic	Slovak Republic
1992			
April 30	6.0	3.2	11.8
May 31	5.6	2.9	11.3
June 30	5.5	2.7	11.3
July 31	5.4	2.7	11.1

Source: Ministry of Industry and Trade

Unemployment benefits are paid at a rate of 60 per cent of the previous average monthly salary for the first three months of unemployment and 50 per cent for the rest of the first six months. After that, an unemployed person in 1991 received a fixed amount of Kcs 1,500 ($51) per month. Persons without previous employment (including graduates and women after maternity leave) were also paid Kcs 1,500 a month. During 1991, the total payments for unemployment benefits exceeded Kcs 4.45 bln ($151 mln).

State budget

At the end of 1991, the federal budget posted a slight surplus of Kcs 6.4 bln ($217 mln). Republican governments (Czech and Slovak) did not succeed in balancing their budgets in 1991. The Czech republic ended 1991 with a deficit of Kcs 14.7 bln ($498 mln). Slovakia's deficit was Kcs 10.2 bln ($346 mln).

Following the protracted debate, in 1991, over the division of powers between the republics, the role of the federal budget has been considerably curtailed in favor of the Czech and Slovak governments. Parliament decided in April 1992 to allocate some of the federal surplus to offset the republics' deficits. Kcs 1.3 bln ($44.5 mln) was earmarked for the Czech republic and Kcs 934 mln ($32 mln) for the Slovak republic. The 1992 budget allows for a Kcs 3.3 bln ($113 mln) deficit in the Czech republic and a Kcs 2.7 bln ($92.5 mln) deficit in the Slovak republic. Both deficits are to be covered by the surplus in the federal budget.

TAXATION

A tax reform bill was approved by the Czechoslovak parliament in April 1992 and is scheduled to become effective in January 1993. The new law consolidates corporate tax rates at 45 per cent, although an extra 5 per cent may be added by republican governments. The republics can also give companies tax breaks and other preferences. However, the federal government is not permitted to grant such preferences. It is clear that this and other provisions of the new tax law will have to be modified if the Czechoslovak federation dissolves before the beginning of 1993.

The current system of taxation, valid until December 1992, contains the following provisions. Employee income tax is payable monthly. Wages up to Kcs 2,400 ($133) are taxed at a progressive rate ranging from 5 to 20 per cent, while a rate of 20 per cent is applied to wages between Kcs 2,400 and Kcs 10,000 ($342) per month. The rate of 33 per cent is used for salaries above Kcs 10,000. In contrast, the Tax Reform Act scheduled to become effective in 1993 introduces individual income tax rates that range from 15 to 47 per cent, with the highest tax rate applying to incomes above Kcs 1 mln ($34,246) per annum. Entrepreneurial income tax is payable annually. A rate of 15 per cent is applied to income up to Kcs 60,000 ($2,055) per annum. Incomes between Kcs 60,000 and Kcs 200,000 ($6,849) are taxed at the rate of

25 per cent, while a rate of 35 per cent is applied to incomes between Kcs 200,000 and Kcs 540,000 ($18,493). Higher tax rates apply to incomes over Kcs 540,000. Individuals and their employers pay 50 per cent each of the required contribution to the social security fund. Entrepreneurs pay this tax monthly. Their monthly contributions range from Kcs 500 ($17) to Kcs 2,500 ($85).

Corporate income tax is payable at a rate of 20 per cent on annual income up to Kcs 200,000 ($6,849), and at a 55 per cent rate on income above Kcs 200,000. This taxation rate is reduced to 40 per cent for joint ventures with over 30 per cent of foreign participation. Joint ventures and foreign investors may also be entitled to other reductions in the corporate income tax.

In addition, enterprises pay 50 per cent of the total wage bill for "social insurance." Under the new tax regime scheduled for 1993, this tax rate will be reduced to 30 per cent for health and social insurance, and 2 per cent for the unemployment fund. This levy is, moreover, deductible for corporate income tax purposes.

Since May 1991, three turnover tax rates have been used. These include an 11 per cent rate for building materials, 20 per cent for manufactured goods, and 29 per cent for cosmetics and cars. Fuels, energy, basic foods, and exports are exempted from turnover taxes. In January 1993, these rates are to be replaced by two value-added taxes (VAT): a 5 per cent tax on essential items and a 23 per cent tax on other goods and services.

Monetary policy

INTEREST RATES AND CREDIT
The State Bank implemented a restrictive monetary policy on January 1, 1991. The policy involved sharp increases in interest rates, with a maximum rate of 24 per cent, and introduction of credit ceilings. The average annualized short-term interest rate was about 15 per cent in 1991.

Table 2.9 Short-term interest rates (in per cent annualized)

	Jan	Feb	Mar	Apr	May	June	July	Aug	Sept	Oct	Nov	Dec
1991	14.7	14.7	14.7	15.3	16.3	15.2	14.9	15.0	14.9	14.8	14.9	—

Source: PlanEcon

Although real interest rates were negative, credit ceilings were not reached by commercial banks, which sharply restricted the supply of credit to enterprises hit by the liquidity crunch. Commercial banks also began to charge the maximum interest rate on working capital loans, and, in some instances, when loans were not repaid, the overdraft rate of 36 per cent was applied. These loans, totaling Kcs 170 bln ($5.8 bln), amounted to nearly one-third of all commercial credit.

INTER-ENTERPRISE DEBT

Sharply higher prices during the first four months of 1991 and the consequent revaluation of inventories increased the paper profits of enterprises by 137 per cent to Kcs 95.4 bln ($3.2 bln). However, contraction of domestic and foreign demand led to declining sales revenues and increasing payment difficulties experienced by debtor enterprises. As late payments increased and insolvency became wide-spread, enterprises resorted to the so-called inter-enterprise credits.

Table 2.10   Enterprise indebtedness (in Kcs bln)

Date	Debt to banks	Inter-enterprise debt
1989		
December 31	530.8	6.6
1990		
June 30	533.5	14.5
December 31	536.0	46.8
1991		
June 30	611.3	123.5
December 31	646.8	170.6
1992		
March 31	654.0	170.2
June 30	628.7	n/a

Source: Federal Statistical Office

Debt

In the fourth quarter of 1991, Czechoslovakia's gross hard currency debt increased by $500 mln, to reach $9.4 bln by the end of 1991. The increased hard currency borrowing coincided with the current account surplus of more than $300 mln. This surplus helped to strengthen

Czechoslovakia's foreign trade position and made the hard currency debt more manageable. The country's hard currency reserves amounted to $3.3 bln at the end of 1991.

In early 1992, Czechoslovakia and Russia reached a tentative agreement concerning the repayment of Soviet debt. Total Soviet indebtedness to Czechoslovakia is $5 bln. $1 bln is to be repaid in the form of natural gas deliveries, while another $2 bln will be repaid in the form of trade credits. Settlement of the remaining $2 bln was still under discussion in 1992.

The IMF granted Czechoslovakia an annual credit of $322 mln to support its privatization program in 1992. In June 1992, the World Bank approved a $246 mln loan for pollution control and modernization of existing power generating facilities.

In addition to foreign borrowing, foreign direct investment represented an important part of hard currency inflows. In 1991, it totaled slightly more than $600 mln.

Foreign trade

Foreign trade used to be conducted almost exclusively by specialized and highly concentrated foreign trade enterprises. In early 1991, participation in foreign trade was made easier. In addition to specialized foreign trade companies, a large number of state enterprises, private companies, and individuals are now engaged in foreign trade transactions. Except for trade in armaments and pharmaceutical products, it is no longer necessary to obtain a special foreign trade permit from the Federal Finance Ministry. Imports, particularly of consumer goods, are restricted by high import duties designed to protect the government's hard currency reserves. Liberalization of trade has been accompanied by the limited convertibility of the Czechoslovak koruna. Following a devaluation at the end of 1990, the koruna became internally convertible. Commercial and tourist exchange rates were also unified at that time.

Czechoslovak convertible currency exports and imports in 1991 were $10.1 bln and $9.2 bln, respectively, while the corresponding figures in 1990, in current US dollars, were $6.2 bln and $6.8 bln.

Exports to Western markets increased by 13 per cent, while exports to developing countries fell slightly. Following the breakdown of Comecon trading arrangements, Czechoslovak exports to the former socialist countries fell by 36 per cent. However, the remaining exports to this group of countries were paid for in convertible currencies, thus contributing to a substantial increase in the Czechoslovak convertible currency exports in 1991.

Imports from the Comecon countries remained the same between 1990 and 1991, which, in turn, contributed to a substantial increase in convertible currency imports. Imports from developed market economies and developing countries declined 14 per cent and 1 per cent, respectively.

3. PRESENT FORMS OF OWNERSHIP

3A. Legal framework of economic activity

Existing and planned legislation concerning property rights

The following is a list of the more important laws concerning property rights, forms of business organizations, and privatization in Czechoslovakia:

— Act No. 103/1990   Amendments to the Economic Code, Act No. 98/1988, which amended Act No. 109/1964;
— Act No. 104/1990   On Joint Stock Companies;
— Act No. 105/1990   On Private Business;
— Act No. 111/1990   On State Enterprises;
— Act No. 112/1990   On Enterprises with Foreign Capital Participation, amending Act No. 173/1988;
— Act No. 113/1990   On Economic Relations with Foreign Countries, amending Act No. 42/1980;
— Act No. 298/1990   On Regulations of Property Relations of Religious Orders and Congregations and the Archdiocese of Olomouc;
— Act No. 403/1990   Mitigation of Property Related Injustices ["Small-Scale Reprivatization Act"];
— Act No. 427/1990   About the Transfer of State Property and Some Goods to Other Legal or Physical Persons ["Small-Scale Privatization Law"];
— Act No. 458/1990   Amendment of Act No. 403/1990;
— Act No. 528/1990   The Foreign Exchange Act;
— Act No. 87/1991   On Out-of-Court Rehabilitations [The "Large-Scale Reprivatization Law"];

— Act No. 92/1991   On Conditions and terms Governing the Transfer of State Property to Other Persons ["Large-Scale Privatization Law"];
— Act No. 229/1991   On Regulation of Ownership of Land and Other Agricultural Property;
— Act No. 328/1991   On Bankruptcy and Settlement;
— Act No. 455/1991   The Entrepreneurial Act;
— Act No. 513/1991   The Commercial Code;
— Act No. 42/1992   On Regulation of Property Relations in Cooperatives;
— Act No. 248/1992   On Investment Corporation and Investment Fund.

Recognized forms of business organizations

Prior to 1989, there existed four principal types of economic enterprises in Czechoslovakia: state enterprises, cooperatives, foreign trade enterprises, and municipal enterprises. Czechoslovakia also had three different legal regimes regulating commercial relations. The Civil Code governed the relations between private individuals and enterprises. The Economic Code regulated interactions among enterprises. The International Trade Code governed relationships arising in the context of international trade.

In the wake of the collapse of the communist regime, a wholesale reform of the legal framework of economic activity has been accomplished within a period of less than two years. The Economic Code was first amended (in April 1990), and subsequently superseded as of January 1992 by the new Commercial Code. In addition, a special Law on State Enterprises was passed in April 1990 and transformed the rules governing the operation of state enterprises. Another law, the Law on Private Business of April 18, 1990, abolished the old system of permits, established an individual right to perform private economic activities without any limitation on the number of employees, and set up a system of registration of individual business enterprises.

STATE ENTERPRISES
Unlike Central European countries, such as Hungary and Poland, in which the process of decentralization conferred a considerable measure of autonomy on state enterprises, the Czechoslovak state managed until the fall of the communist regime to retain its historically commanding role in the socialized sector. Although Czechoslovakia

had been preparing a decentralizing reform package in the late 1960s, the process came to an abrupt halt in the wake of the Soviet invasion of 1968, and the state reasserted its administrative powers over the enterprises, effectively preventing the emergence of powerful insiders. The survival of this system until 1989, and the weakness of the special interests nourished by the communist economic reforms in other Eastern European countries, may have enabled the postcommunist Czechoslovak government to proceed more rapidly with certain aspects of the transformation process than was possible in other countries in the region.

The communist state enterprise in Czechoslovakia was headed by the managing director. The director could be nominated by the founding organ (usually the relevant sectoral ministry) or elected by the workers' council, but even in the latter case, the government retained the right to approve or reject the choice of the council. The ministry also approved the compensation of all employees, including top management, and retained the right to interfere with current production decisions.

The 1990 Law on State Enterprises changed the legal structure of the state enterprises in Czechoslovakia and adapted them to the new economic environment. The law created an intermediate form between the "classical" state enterprise and the regular corporate form of business organization. Most of the new state enterprises are not supposed to be permanent entities: they are expected to go out of existence with the progress of privatization. In accordance with the dismantling of the central planning system, the law defines a state enterprise (SE) as "a producer of goods which performs its entrepreneurial activity independently" and "accepts an appropriate business risk." While an SE is thus given substantial managerial autonomy, the state preserves its ownership rights and ultimate control. To be sure, even with respect to the privatization process, Czechoslovak insiders are not left without input; along with any other interested parties, they can (indeed must) prepare their own privatization projects (see below, subsection on large privatization in Section 4B). However, the decision as to which to implement is left to the Federal Ministry of Finance (in the case of banking institutions) or an agency of one of the republican administrations; neither managers nor workers retain the effective last word over the SE.

SEs are divided into two categories:

- *Basic State Enterprises.* These are SEs involved in commercial activity. The principal officers of the Basic State Enterprise are the managers, nominated by the founding organ, and the Supervisory Council.
- *Public Interest Enterprises.* These enterprises are involved in the provision of public-oriented services. They have no supervisory councils, and their founding agencies (usually government ministries) are directly involved in the running of the enterprise.

An SE, registered in the Company Register, is a legal person acting in its own name, bearing full responsibility for its activities. The activity and operation of the SE can only be limited or interfered with in the manner stipulated by law, and the founding organ is obligated to provide compensation to the SE for any losses incurred due to its intervention in the running of the SE.

SEs do not have ownership rights in the objects and property entrusted to them at the time of their foundation; instead, these objects remain the property of the state. They can be taken away, however, only in accordance with the procedures stipulated by law.

After paying taxes on profits, state enterprises are required to maintain four special funds to cover: (1) research, development, and modernization costs; (2) losses and risks from business activities; (3) employee bonuses; and (4) certain social services for the workers. State enterprises have considerable discretion with respect to the use of the four funds, and the funds cannot be confiscated by the state. The SE, moreover, has complete discretion with respect to the use of the remaining profits.

The governing organs of an SE are the manager and the Supervisory Council. The manager is appointed and may be dismissed by the founding organ (usually a ministry or another governmental agency) after consultation with the Council. The powers of the manager are significantly greater than in a traditional corporation, since he not only runs the day-to-day operations of the SE, but also, after consulting with the Council, approves the accounting statements and distributes the available profits. The Supervisory Council, therefore, is primarily an advisory body, with no direct powers. It is authorized to review the accounting statements and the distribution of profits, to discuss the major issues concerning the development of the SE, and to recommend the dismissal of the manager. The founding organ determines the number of members of the Council, of whom half are appointed by the founding organ and half elected by the employees. Until

December 31, 1990, the founding organ could transform the SE into a joint-stock company, transferring to it all property entrusted to the SE, with the new company taking over all the right and liabilities. After that date, all transformations of SEs into commercial company form are connected with the privatization process described in the subsection on large privatization in Section 4B.

COOPERATIVES

The problems of transition Like all communist countries, Czechoslovakia had a very large pseudo-cooperative sector, especially in agriculture (with 650,000 employees and two-thirds of agricultural production). Cooperatives were also active in the manufacturing of small durable goods, retail trade, services, and housing. The share of the cooperative sector in the NMP in 1989 was 12.6 per cent, and its share of employment was 12.8 per cent.

The future of communist pseudo-cooperatives posed a serious political problem for the new Czechoslovak authorities. The old pseudo-cooperatives were not voluntarily formed and were run much like the rest of the state sector. Consequently, some have proposed to treat them as state-owned entities that should be dismantled and privatized. On the other hand, a large number of people working in pseudo-cooperatives, especially in agriculture, do not want them dismantled.[2] These people often also resisted any attempts at the transformation of the existing cooperatives, fearing that the process would deprive them of their position. This fear was especially acute in the agricultural cooperatives, since over half of the people working in them had no title to the land going back to the time before collectivization, and thus faced the prospect of total disenfranchisement in favor of the previous owners. The legal situation with respect to the cooperative land could only strengthen their apprehensions, since the land had remained formally private even in communist times; although landowners had been forced to enter into cooperatives, they remained *de jure*, if not *de facto*, owners. Since most of the old owners chose to leave the land, approximately 50 per cent of the land used by the cooperatives was now formally owned by absentee landlords, who were not members.

---

[2] According to some estimates, only 2–3 per cent of farmers want to go private. See J. Kostrohoun: "Peasants are not asked" *Rudé právo*, 30.4. 1991, No. 101, pp. 1 and 3.

In 1991, the parliament passed the Law on Regulation of Ownership of Land and Other Agricultural Property, which made it possible, until the end of 1992, for individuals to establish private farms with the property of former agricultural cooperatives. However, since public response to this opportunity was very small, this law did little to solve the problem of how to transform agricultural pseudo-cooperatives into genuine cooperatives. The question was not how to divide the land, which had always been "de jure" private, but how to divide the other farm assets (capital, livestock, seed, etc.) among those who contributed land, labor and capital to the creation of the cooperative's net asset value.

Outside of agriculture, a special issue was also raised by the claims of old, precommunist cooperatives to the property taken over by their communist successors in 1952. In fact, a large share of Czechoslovak cooperatives had prewar antecedents: in 1948, cooperatives were responsible for 2.6 per cent of the Czechoslovak NMP. The current reprivatization laws, however, do not allow the prewar cooperatives to pursue their claims.

A comprehensive solution to the problem of the old pseudo-cooperatives was provided in the new Law on Regulation of Property Relations in Cooperatives, which entered into effect at the end of January 1992. The law provides guidelines for the transformation of all kinds of cooperative institutions, and requires that all of them be made to conform with the governance structure prescribed for cooperatives by the new Commercial Code or transform themselves into ordinary commercial companies. The whole process is to be completed within a year, and any cooperative which fails to approve a transformation plan by the end of January 1992 will be subject to liquidation proceedings.

With respect to agricultural cooperatives, the law seeks to balance the interests of the non-member owners of the cooperative land with those of the non-owner members. In determining the form of the cooperative's transformation, the law gives one vote to each landowner member and non-member, as well as to each "landless" member.

The new cooperative legal regime The Commercial Code provides a legal framework for a modern system of cooperatives. It defines the cooperative as an association of an open-ended number of individuals, established to undertake business activities or provide for the economic, social, or other needs of its members. Cooperatives must have at least five members and must be capitalized at a minimum of

Kcs 50,000. Cooperatives are legal entities held liable for their obligations up to the total value of their property, while individual cooperative members have no personal liability.

The basic capital of the cooperative comprises the total contributions pledged by the members. A constitutive meeting, which sets the level of basic capitalization, approves the bylaws, and elects the statutory organs, is a prerequisite for the establishment of a cooperative. Any individual who votes against the adoption of bylaws that were subsequently adopted is required to withdraw his application from the cooperative.

Provided the bylaws do not stipulate otherwise, a member can transfer, subject to approval by the Board of Directors, his rights and obligations to another member of the cooperative. The transfer of rights and obligations connected with membership in a housing cooperative, however, is not subject to the approval of the Board of Directors.

All cooperatives are required to create an indivisible fund. The initial contribution to the fund must be at least 10 per cent of the recorded basic capital; the fund must be subsequently augmented by at least 10 per cent of the net profits annually, until the fund has a value equal to not less than one-half of the capitalization of the cooperative. The indivisible fund may not be used for distribution during the existence of the cooperative.

The profits of a cooperative are distributed to the members in proportion to their paid-in contributions, unless the bylaws stipulate another method of distribution.

The organs of a cooperative are the Membership Meeting, the Board of Directors, and the Auditing Commission. In a cooperative with fewer than fifty members, the Membership Meeting may perform the functions of the Board of Directors and the Auditing Commission. All cooperative organs are validly convened if they are attended by more than 50 per cent of the individuals entitled to be at the meeting.

The Board of Directors oversees the activities of the cooperative and decides all matters relating to the cooperative not specifically assigned to another cooperative body. The Auditing Commission is authorized to investigate all activities of the cooperative and handle the complaints of the members.

COMMERCIAL COMPANIES – GENERAL PROVISIONS
All organized business activities other than state enterprises are now governed by the Commercial Code. In addition to individual private

entrepreneurship and cooperative activity, the Code recognizes four types of legal entities organized for the purpose of engaging in entrepreneurial activity:

- general commercial companies;
- limited partnerships;
- limited-liability companies;
- joint-stock companies.[3]

The general term used in the Code to refer to all these entities is "commercial company." All commercial companies must be listed in the Commercial Register.

A characteristic feature of the Commercial Code is that, more than the corresponding legal acts in the other East European countries, it tends to leave the parties engaged in economic activity the freedom to set their own rules in the appropriate bylaws and other founding statutes. While a large number of the Code's provisions are mandatory, other provisions often serve as "defaults" in those cases in which the parties do not regulate their own relations.

General commercial company (partnership) A General commercial company (denoted by "v.o.s." or "a spol." in the trade name), which can be created by two or more natural persons, is the name the Code gives to what is known in other countries as a partnership. All partners are jointly and severally liable, and private persons may only be partners with unlimited liability in one commercial company at any given time.

The rights and obligations of the partners are governed by the partnership agreement, and changes in the agreement require the unanimous consent of all partners. Unless the partnership agreement provides otherwise, profits are distributed in equal shares to the partners; partners are also entitled to receive interest on their paid-in contributions.

Limited partnership A limited partnership (identified by "kom. spol." or "k.s." in the trade name) is a partnership with one or more "general partners," who are liable for the obligations of the company to the full

---

[3] The Code eliminated the following, previously existing, forms of business organization: private company limited by shares, partnership limited by shares, and silent partnership.

extent of their assets, and one or more "limited partners," who are liable to the extent of their contributions. Unless otherwise stipulated, limited partnerships are regulated by the rules for general commercial companies, and the legal status of limited partners is regulated by the laws applicable to limited-liability companies. The partnership agreement may permit limited partners to transfer their membership to a third party without the approval of the other partners.

Only general partners can manage the commercial activity of the company. Unless the partnership agreement provides otherwise, the profits of the company are distributed equally between the limited and general partners, with the general partners sharing their portion equally and the limited partners receiving a portion proportionate to their paid-in contribution. In the case of a liquidation, limited partners have priority over the general partners for a refund of their contribution.

Limited-liability company A limited-liability company (LLC) (denoted by "spol. s r.o." or "s.r.o." in its name) is a familiar Central European form of business organization. Although an LLC is not publicly traded, it provides investors with the shield of limited liability (the member's liability extends to his pledged contribution). While a member is statutorily entitled to a share of the profits of the company – determined by the ratio of his paid-in contribution to the assets of the company – the shareholders' agreement may provide otherwise. An LLC may be established by a single person and can have no more than fifty members. The minimum contribution of each member must be Kcs 20,000 and the minimum capitalization of an LLC is Kcs 100,000.

While an LLC is free to set the rules for the transferability of its shares, the statutory default rule is that a member may contractually transfer his share to another member with the approval of the general meeting.

The highest organ of the LLC is the General Meeting. Members may also make decisions outside of general meetings through votes taken in writing on circulated written proposals. LLCs are required to have agents who are appointed by the General Meeting and act in the name of the company. An LLC may also establish a Supervisory Board, made up of at least three members elected by the General Meeting, responsible for overseeing the actions of the agents.

An LLC must set up a reserve fund at the time it is established. The initial contribution to the fund may not be less than 5 per cent of basic capitalization, and the fund must be augmented by at least 5 per cent of the net annual profits until it reaches a minimum size of 10 per cent of the basic capitalization. The reserve fund can only be used to cover corporate losses or to mitigate the damages caused by poor management decisions.

Joint-stock company A joint-stock company (JSC) (identified by "akc. spol." or "a.s." in its name) is a company with limited liability, the shares of which may be publicly traded. Its basic capitalization involves a specific number of shares with a set nominal value. A JSC must have a minimum capital of Kcs 1 mln, and may be established by a single legal entity.

The share capital of a JSC is created through a subscription of shares. The establishment of a JSC is deemed to have failed if all the shares have not been pledged by the subscription deadline. The Constitutive Assembly of subscribers must be called within sixty days after the end of the subscription period, with subscribers to at least one-half of the shares in attendance (which may be difficult in the case of a widely held corporation). The Assembly may depart from the provisions of the founders' agreement only with the unanimous approval of the subscribers present.

A JSC may issue both registered and bearer shares, both of which are freely transferable. Different classes of stock may also be issued, but preferred stock can make up no more than one-half of the capital stock. The company can also issue employee stock certificates. These shares, the value of which cannot exceed 5 per cent of basic capitalization, are restricted, and can be transferred only among employees and retired employees of the company. Unless the bylaws of the company provide otherwise, upon death or termination of employment the company will repurchase an employee's shares for their nominal value, or, if the company's shares are traded on a stock market, for the proportionate value of the restricted shares. Unless otherwise provided in the bylaws, employee shareholders enjoy the same rights as other shareholders. The Code provides for a mandatory employee bonus plan, specifying that the employees must share in the distribution of profits, but no size of the bonus is specified. The bylaws of the company may stipulate that the employees' share of the profits must be used only to acquire employee shares.

The General Meeting of shareholders is the highest organ of the company. It must have a quorum of shareholders with at least 30 per cent of the company's capitalization. The number of votes assigned to each shareholder is determined by the nominal value of the shares, but the bylaws may restrict the exercise of voting rights by specifying the highest number of votes any one shareholder can cast. Decisions affecting the rights of a class of shareholders require a two-thirds majority vote of the holders of that class. Existing shareholders have preemptive rights to purchase a *pro rata* portion of any new share issue.

A JSC is required to have a Board of Directors, at least three members of which must be elected by the General Meeting or the Supervisory Board. The Directors manage the company and act in its name. A JSC must also have a Supervisory Board comprised of at least three members. Supervisory Board members are elected by the General Meeting, but in all JSCs with more than fifty employees at least one-third (but not more than one-half) of the Supervisory Board must be elected by an assembly of company employees. No person shall serve simultaneously on both the Board of Directors and the Supervisory Boards, and members of either board are subject to specific conflict-of-interest provisions.

The Code mandates that all JSCs maintain a reserve fund. The initial amount to be placed in the reserve fund will be no less than 10 per cent of the basic capitalization. The fund will be annually augmented by not less than 5 per cent of the net profits of the company until the fund reaches at least 20 per cent of basic capitalization. The fund may be used only to offset company losses or mitigate the damage caused by poor management decisions.

Regulations governing foreign ownership

Since January 1, 1992, foreign investment in Czechoslovakia has been regulated primarily by the Commercial Code. The repatriation of profits from foreign investments is governed by Act No. 528/1990, the Foreign Exchange Act, and the implementing regulations concerning profit repatriation are contained in the Announcement of the State Bank of Czechoslovakia No. 15, Regarding Transfers of Income from Nonresident Investments in the Czech and Slovak Federative Republic.

The Commercial Code repealed the old joint venture law, which contained a number of restrictive provisions, including cumbersome permit requirements. Under the Code, foreign persons – defined as including Czechoslovak citizens residing abroad – may engage in business activity on the Czechoslovak territory under the same conditions, and to the same extent, as Czechoslovak nationals, except where the law stipulates otherwise. The process of registration is essentially the same for foreign persons as for domestic entities. A foreign person may establish a joint venture with a Czechoslovak entity or participate as a partner or member in an existing legal entity. Foreign persons may also found wholly-owned limited-liability companies (the most common form of foreign investment) or single-person joint-stock companies.

The usual protections against confiscation are provided by the Code, and provisions concerning foreign investment contained in international agreements entered into by Czechoslovakia take precedence over contrary domestic law. Bilateral agreements of this kind have been concluded with, among others, Austria, Belgium, Canada, Denmark, Finland, France, Greece, Italy, Netherlands, Norway, Spain, Sweden, Switzerland, and the United Kingdom.

A foreign investor may convert and repatriate all income from investments, including profits, interest, capital gains, income from securities, and fees from intellectual property, although a transfer of funds abroad by a foreign investor requires a foreign exchange license issued by the Czechoslovak State Bank upon the presentation of proper proof of the origin of the funds. Wages and salaries of foreign persons may be freely repatriated, and their employers may transfer funds for, among other purposes, their social security payments and pension plans. Foreign investors are also permitted, when authorized by the State Bank of Czechoslovakia, to keep foreign currency accounts in Czechoslovak banks. However, the earnings of all Czechoslovak businesses, including foreign-owned ones, must be converted into local currency.

Among the significant restrictions on foreign investment, the following are particularly noteworthy:

(1) A foreign investor domiciled abroad (referred to as a "foreign exchange expatriate" by the Foreign Exchange Act) may not acquire land in Czechoslovakia, except by descent and special legal provisions (primarily the restitution laws). A Czechoslovak business entity, however, even if wholly owned by a foreign exchange expatriate, or a foreign person with a registered domicile in Czechoslovakia[4] may purchase land without any limitations.

---

[4] Domestic business entities owned by foreign persons and foreign persons residing in Czechoslovakia are referred to by the Foreign Exchange Act as "foreign exchange nationals."

(2) Foreign persons are not entitled to take part in the first round of public auctions held under the Small Privatization Act.
(3) Licenses must be obtained from the State Bank of Czechoslovakia for businesses in the banking sector, and other restrictions apply to businesses engaged in the defense sector, utilities, and cultural institutions.
(4) State approval must be obtained to form a joint-venture with a business entity created before July 1, 1988, i.e. with all state enterprises.
(5) When a foreign investor wishes to purchase the assets or shares of a state-owned enterprise, the purchase must be incorporated into the privatization plan for the enterprise and approved by the appropriate ministry (see Section 4B below).

As of the summer of 1992, businesses with over 30 per cent foreign participation enjoy a number of tax advantages. Qualified businesses can be given a tax holiday for up to two years, with a one-year holiday now given automatically to new companies with tax liabilities up to 1 mln Kcs ($34,000). A one-year holiday may also be given, at the discretion of the Republican Finance Ministries, for taxes over that amount, provided that the profits covered by the holiday are reinvested in the company, and not distributed.[5] In addition, companies with over 30 per cent foreign participation pay smaller taxes than domestic companies, with the top rate (applicable to income over 200,000 Kcs ($6,800)) of 40 (instead of 55) per cent. According to the new tax law, effective as of January 1993, however, all incorporated businesses will pay the uniform tax with the maximum rate of 45 per cent (with an additional 5 per cent at the discretion of the republics). Also, the special tax concessions will no longer be granted, although previously negotiated holidays will be honored.

Bankruptcy and liquidation

The present Czechoslovak Law on Bankruptcy and Settlement (Bankruptcy Law), Act No. 328, went into effect on October 1, 1991. The law applies to individual entrepreneurs and legal entities –

---

[5] The rules summarized here apply in the Czech Republic, and are somewhat different in Slovakia, where the automatic exemption is for two years for up to 700,000 Kcs. Some activities are excluded from the automatic holidays in both republics.

including commercial companies, state enterprises, and cooperatives – but not to natural persons who are not entrepreneurs. The law vests very considerable powers in the courts, and is relatively harsh to creditors.

The Bankruptcy Law specifies two distinct procedures for resolving the insolvency situation: bankruptcy proper, with a subsequent sale of the assets of the debtor; and a settlement procedure allowing the debtor to reach an agreement with the creditors, while remaining in (limited) control of the business. The definition of bankruptcy provided by the law is extremely vague. A debtor is defined as bankrupt if "he has several creditors[6] and has been unable to repay his obligations, which are due, over a long period of time." An individual entrepreneur, or a legal entity, is considered bankrupt if "insolvent." Also, neither the Bankruptcy Law nor other regulations force the debtor or the creditors to file a bankruptcy petition. Given the uncontrolled growth of inter-enterprise credit in Eastern Europe (including Czechoslovakia, see subsection on inter-enterprise debt in Section 2) and the tendency of banks to continue their lending to state enterprises regardless of their solvency, the Bankruptcy Law is unlikely to provide a serious hardening of the enterprise budget constraint. In this respect, the emphasis of the Czechoslovak authorities seems to be on rapid privatization, rather than the effects that the threat of bankruptcy has on the behavior of a state economic organization.

BANKRUPTCY PROCEEDINGS

A bankruptcy petition may be brought by the debtor, a creditor, or a liquidator of a legal entity. Only a court with appropriate jurisdiction has the power to make the declaration of bankruptcy, and the debtor must have sufficient assets to defray the costs of the proceedings. Upon the filing of a bankruptcy petition, a trustee is appointed from among the list of qualified persons maintained by the court. The court then convenes a meeting of all of the bankrupt's creditors, who may elect a Creditors' Committee to oversee the work of the Trustee. If the Court determines that the conditions for declaring bankruptcy have been met, it will make the formal declaration. The declaration of

---

[6] Apparently, bankruptcy proceedings are seen as appropriate if there are conflicting claims of several creditors. Sole creditors can presumably obtain satisfaction in other proceedings.

bankruptcy has, among others, the following effects:

- control and right to dispose of assets is transferred to the Trustee;
- all claims and obligations to the bankrupt's assets become due;
- preferential rights to assets acquired by creditors within two months preceding the declaration are voided;
- legal proceedings related to claims on the assets of the bankrupt are either halted or, if the claims are secured by particular assets, continued against the Trustee;
- ongoing privatization procedures are halted.

All creditors must assert their claims within thirty days of the public announcement of bankruptcy. The claims are then reviewed by the Trustee and the court. In order to satisfy the approved debts, the debtor's assets are sold through court-approved procedures, including non-auction sales administered by the Trustee, and the court issues a distribution decree.

The distribution priorities are the following:

- expenditures of the Trustee, including remuneration and the commitments undertaken in the administration of the bankrupt's estate;
- claims of secured creditors to revenues from the sale of the assets that secured the debts owed to them;
- workers' secured and unsecured wage claims;
- taxes, duties, fees, social insurance payments;
- other claims.

Prior to the issuing of the distribution decree, the bankrupt can propose a so-called "forced settlement," i.e. an alternative payment schedule that may prevent the liquidation of the bankrupt's assets. Any such proposal must be heard by representatives of the debtor's creditors holding not less than 75 per cent of all claims filed against the debtor (not including claims of secured creditors). The proposed payment schedule must then receive approval from the representatives of these creditors holding not less than 50 per cent of all claims filed against the debtor.

SETTLEMENT PROCEDURES
As an alternative to bankruptcy proceedings, a debtor who fulfills the conditions of bankruptcy but has not yet been declared bankrupt may petition the court to undertake settlement procedures. During these proceedings, subject to a number of restrictions (which include

prohibitions against alienation or encumbrance of assets and against taking any legal actions that might harm the interests of creditors), the debtor remains in control of his assets and is protected against liquidation proceedings. Interest payments on debts owed by the debtor are also suspended, which may provide a significant advantage to the debtor's business. Among the conditions for allowing settlement are that the debtor not have been in bankruptcy (or settlement) within the past five years and that unsecured creditors be offered a payment equal to at least 45 per cent of their claims accruing within the preceding two years.

If the court accepts the petition for settlement it appoints a Trustee to review the list of creditors and permits creditors to file additional claims. The settlement proceedings must take no longer than ninety days, although the court may extend this time limit "in the event the settlement involves an economically important enterprise and if the public interest requires that the deadline be extended." The proposed settlement, after satisfying secured creditors, must give priority to claims related to the cost of the settlement proceedings, followed by taxes, wage claims, and the claims of other creditors.

During the proceedings, the court must determine which creditors are willing to consent to the proposed settlement, whether the rights of preferred creditors are adversely affected, and whether some creditors are not unjustly treated. Within these parameters, however, the court has broad discretion, including the right to confirm the settlement without the agreement of any specific proportion of the creditors. The court may also refuse the settlement, even if all creditors agree, if it determines that "there are no reasons for permitting settlement" or the advantages accruing to the debtor as a result of the settlement are "in considerable conflict with his ascertained economic conditions." At the conclusion of the proceeding, the court issues a decree confirming or rejecting the proposed settlement; the decree may be appealed by the debtor, in case of rejection, or by creditors who did not expressly agree to the settlement.

According to government sources, eighty-nine bankruptcy proceedings have been opened until the end of 1991 concerning state enterprises. No further data on the results of these proceedings were available as of October 1992.

3B. Structure of ownership

Pending implementation of the large-scale privatization program, the structure of the Czechoslovak economy remains overwhelmingly dominated by state-owned enterprises. Data on the exact size of different ownership categories are fragmentary, however, particularly concerning output and the value of capital. Some information is available about the number of firms and levels of employment in different categories.

Table 3B.1 Number of economic organizations by ownership category (as of January 1, 1992)

Ownership category	Number of organizations
State	27,460
Municipal	1,118
Cooperative	5,879
Private	1,151,546
Foreign	3,225
Joint ventures	4,894
Total*	1,210,087

*Note: Data are reproduced directly from the original source, where the individual categories do not sum exactly to the total.

Source: Federal Statistical Office

Small privatization and reprivatization have resulted in rapid growth in the number of small private firms in the retail trade and services sector. While the number of registered privately-owned units grew from 157,547 at the end of 1990 to 1.152 mln at the end of 1991 and to 1.423 mln in May 1992, these figures tend to overstate the economic impact of this phenomenon due to the presence of a large number of registered entrepreneurs who run their businesses only on a part-time basis.[7]

An analysis of 8,201 medium and large economic units in June 1991 reveals that state enterprises still accounted for 80 per cent of the total

---

[7] Estimates of the proportion of registered entrepreneurs engaged full-time in running their businesses range from 10 per cent to 30 per cent.

NMP produced by these units, while cooperatives accounted for 6 per cent and municipal enterprises made up 4 per cent. Joint ventures and those classified as private accounted for well under 1 per cent combined, while 10 per cent of NMP was contributed by "others," including mixed ownership forms. These figures, based on Federal Statistical Office information that excludes private firms employing fewer than twenty-five people, and state and municipal enterprises and cooperatives employing fewer than one hundred, probably understate the contribution of private enterprises.

In 1991, the private sector's production was estimated to be Kcs 79 bln, representing 8 per cent of GNP. The state sector is expected to shrink rapidly following the current wave of voucher privatization, which should put in private hands state firms employing 1.258 million people. This would increase the official count of non-state employment to 3.5 mln, or 52 per cent of the total, with an estimated additional 15 per cent of the work-force to be added by the end of the second wave. The size of the unreported "shadow" economy, estimated at up to 10 per cent of the labor force, means that official statistics consistently understate the extent of private ownership.[8]

Data on the distribution of private business activity by sector can only be obtained from the registration entrepreneurs are required to file with municipal authorities, in which they must list their principal activity.[9] Table 3B.2 shows the number of registered private establishments at the end of 1990 and the end of 1991, with their distribution by field of activity. It reveals that, as of the end of 1991, over two-thirds of the 1.3 mln registered private concerns were in industry, trade, or construction, but that the fastest growth was in private sector trade. According to Benacek, 46 per cent of reported retail sales came in private shops, and the actual proportion is probably considerably higher than this official count. Section 4B below contains an account of the small privatization program, targeting the trade sector in particular.

The number of units under municipal ownership increased during

---

[8] "Review of Some Czechoslovak Economic Indicators for 1991 in Comparison with 1990." Compiled by Vladimir Benacek, Center for Economic Research and Graduate Education, June 14, 1992.

[9] Progress on compiling a company register, requirements of disclosure of activities for tax purposes and new legislation on collection of statistics should all contribute to an improvement in this information.

Table 3B.2 Private sector growth by branch: number of registered units

	Dec. 1990	Dec. 1991
Total Registered Private Sector Units	488,361	1,338,353
Percent distribution:		
Agriculture, forestry and water works	1.7	3.3
Manufacturing industry	27.8	24.8
Construction	27.3	21.0
Transportation and telecommunications	2.9	3.5
Trade	12.6	21.5
Research and development	0.2	0.1
Housing services	0.0	0.0
Services related to tourism	2.1	2.0
Municipal services	9.1	7.2
Education, culture, health and social care	2.9	2.5
Other and non-identified	13.4	14.1

Source: Federal Statistical Office

1990 and 1991 as property formerly under local ownership, the bulk of it small businesses and residences, was returned by the republican governments. Accordingly, enterprises under municipal ownership are concentrated in construction, domestic trade, housing services, utilities, transport, and small municipally based service establishments. The number of state enterprises also increased, reflecting the division of large concerns into smaller units. Finally, the number of cooperatives grew by more than 25 per cent in 1991, perhaps due, in part, to changes in reporting standards. Cooperatives are especially concentrated in agriculture, but a large number are concerned with construction and domestic trade.

The extent of direct foreign ownership and joint ventures[10]

There are no official data about joint ventures or foreign investment in Czechoslovakia because these entities are permitted to register in

[10] Unless otherwise indicated, the data used to support this section were provided by the Federal Ministry of Finance and include the period between May 1990 and April 1991. As there is currently no official procedure for gathering statistical information on joint ventures in Czechoslovakia, these figures should be treated with caution. The new Commercial Code provides for more rigorous collection of such data.

Table 3B.3 Number and capital of joint ventures in the CSFR

Number of joint ventures	2/91	5/91	7/91	8/91
Czech Republic	1,638.0	2,222.0	2,261.0	2,266.0
Slovak Republic	486.0	665.0	676.0	680.0
Total CSFR	2,124.0	2,896.0	2,937.0	2,946.0
Capital (Kcs bln)				
Czech Republic	7.4	20.7	22.7	22.9
Slovak Republic	1.9	3.4	3.7	3.5
Total CSFR	9.3	23.9	2.0	26.4
of which foreign capital	4.8	10.3	11.8	–

Note: There are no official data about joint ventures in Czechoslovakia as there is no "official" place for their registration and they can register in different ministries.

Source: Federal Ministry of Finance

various ministries. The Federal Statistical Office has information about registered organizations, probably including those that are non-economic, and some evidence about the growth of the non-state sector activities comes from observing the increase in the number of organizations with foreign ownership. By the end of 1991, there were 3,225 companies registered as having solely foreign ownership and an additional 4,984 joint-ventures.[11] Three-quarters of wholly foreign-owned companies were in either social care (39 per cent) or trade (36 per cent), with significant numbers operating in publishing (3 per cent), insurance (3 per cent), and construction (2 per cent). Joint ventures are distributed similarly across sectors, with trade (41 per cent), social care (27 per cent), and construction (6 per cent) being the most common areas of activity.[12]

Table 3B.3 shows the cumulative growth of joint-ventures in the Czech and Slovak republics. Through mid-1991 (the most recent data obtained), the large majority of these joint ventures were small (capital of less than Kcs 1 mln ($34,000)) and only twenty-two involved capital of more than Kcs 100 mln ($3.4 mln).

---

[11] According to the table in the *Monthly Statistical Bulletin*, May 1992, on p. 4. The table on p. 7 indicates a total of 4,894 joint ventures, although the numbers for all the other categories are identical. Neither set of numbers adds up to the (identical on both pages) reported total for all business units.

[12] Here the source is more comprehensive data collected by the Federal Statistical Office, including all entrants in the register of organizations.

Table 3B.4 Origin of foreign investment in Czechoslovakia (July 1991)

Countries with largest number of joint ventures	Number	Countries with largest value of investments	Value (mln CSK)
Germany	865	Germany	5,711
Austria	825	Netherlands	911
Switzerland	197	Belgium	853
Italy	134	Austria	824
USA	132	USA	797
Netherlands	92	Switzerland	749

Not surprisingly, the largest numbers of joint ventures come from Germany and Austria, as shown in Table 3B.4. In terms of capital, by far the largest investor is Germany (due to the Volkswagen–Skoda deal). According to Benacek, about 80 per cent of the nearly 4,000 joint ventures in 1991 came from Germany and Austria, which also dominated in terms of the value of capital, but other sources, particularly the United States, have become increasingly significant during 1992.

Again according to Benacek, there was a total of $607 mln of foreign investment in 1991, which is expected to increase to $1.5 bln in 1992. Total commitments from the US over the entire 1990 to May 1992 period are approximately $1.4 bln.

4. THE PRIVATIZATION PROCESS

Introduction

Rapid privatization of the economy is one of the most important components of Czechoslovakia's economic reform program. Rather than delaying privatization to carefully prepare enterprises and build institutions for the market, the Czechoslovak strategy has been to plunge ahead to change the ownership structure as quickly as possible, leaving most restructuring to the new, private owners and developing new legal frameworks and institutions only when the need becomes pressing. Implementation of the privatization program itself began when few of the particulars, or arguably many of the important features, had been worked out: the commonplace argument in Prague is to draw an analogy with a chess game, where in the opening, one can only have a vague idea of the shape of the middlegame and little notion whatsoever of the eventual endgame.

In the period immediately following the "velvet revolution" of November 1989, political camps developed around two basic approaches: the "radical" approach to rapid transition to a market economy just described, and an alternative, "gradualist" approach that emphasized the importance of preparation for the transition and of mitigating social costs. It was the radical approach, particularly associated with the former Federal Finance Minister and leader of the Civic Democratic Party (ODS), Vaclav Klaus, that eventually won the support of the parliament; this direction was strongly confirmed by the elections in early June, which gave the Civic Democratic Party a sturdy plurality, and Klaus the premiership.

At least in the Czech Republic, therefore, political developments are favorable for a continuation of the current reform course. The situation is, however, less clear in Slovakia, where the hand of Vladimir Meciar, leader of the new Movement for a Democratic Slovakia (HZDS) and Slovak Prime Minister, was strengthened in the June 1992 election. Although the recent agreement on an interim Federal Government between Klaus and Meciar included the declaration of commitment from both sides to the privatization program, opposition to it is clearly stronger in Slovakia, and includes elements within the HZDS. "Competence" quarrels among the Czech, Slovak, and Federal governments, together with the protracted disputes over property restitution in 1990 and 1991, have already slowed parliamentary decision-making and have almost certainly acted to discourage foreign, and even domestic, investors. These problems may be exacerbated, at least in the short run, by the impending in the Federation. Nonetheless, to a large extent the process is irreversible in both republics: only the immediate outcome, whether it be rapidly increasing prosperity or widespread bankruptcy, is still open to question.

Basic legislation on corporatization and privatization

Privatization programs in Czechoslovakia are being implemented under laws and governmental decrees adopted step-by-step in a preparatory phase in 1990, as well as under the relevant aspects of a more comprehensive economic transition program that came into effect on January 1, 1991. Corporatization is described in Section 5 below.

The privatization process has three principal elements: wide-ranging reprivatization measures, a small-scale privatization program, and large-scale privatization. The main legislation for reprivatization includes Acts No. 298 ("On Regulations of Property Relations of Religious Orders and Congregations and the Archdiocese of Olomouc") and No. 403 of 1990 ("Mitigation of Property Related Injustices"), and Act No. 87/1991, "On Out-of-Court Rehabilitations" (the Large-Scale Reprivatization Law), as well as Act No. 229/1991 "On Regulation of Ownership of Land and Other Agricultural Property." Concerning small-scale privatization, the relevant law is Act No. 427/1990 ("About the Transfer of State Property and Some Goods to Other Legal or Physical Persons"). With regard to large-scale privatization, the principal laws are Act No. 92 of 1991, "On Conditions and terms Governing the Transfer of State Property to Other Persons," and the follow-up legislation in the Czech Republic Act No. 171 setting up the Czech Republic Property Fund.

The programs themselves are described in Section 4B below.

4A. Organizational structure of state regulation of privatization

The main organs of government involved in regulating the Czechoslovak privatization process are the Czech and Slovak Privatization Ministries, the Federal Finance Ministry, and the Federal and Republican Funds of National Property.

The organization of the process of large privatization in Czechoslovakia is characterized by decentralization in the proposal of privatization plans ("projects"), most of which come from managers or prospective buyers, contrasted with a relatively centralized procedure of final approval. Founding ministries play an intermediary role, formally submitting all projects proposed to them, along with their own recommendations or comments, to one of the Republican Privatization Ministries or the Federal Finance Ministry, where the most important decisions are made about which alternative method of privatization is accepted.

The **Federal Finance Ministry** approves privatization projects of enterprises founded by federal ministries; this amounted to no more than a few dozen enterprises, or 10 per cent of total book value among voucher projects in the first wave. Through the ministry's Center for Coupon Privatization (CCP), the Federal Finance Ministry is also solely responsible for organizing the demand side of the voucher program,

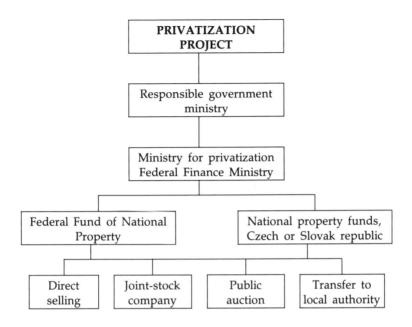

Chart 4A.1   Process of large-scale privatization in Czechoslovakia

overseeing the distribution and registration of voucher booklets to the 8.5 mln participating Czechoslovak citizens. A committee of ministry officials oversees the bidding process in voucher privatization, setting the initial share price in the first round, processing bidding information, adjusting the share price in subsequent rounds, deciding when bids are successful, and publishing the results of each round. Parliament rejected an alternative proposal under which a special commission would have been set up to supervise voucher privatization. Furthermore, the Finance Ministry plays a key role in coordinating the work of other government bodies in the process of voucher privatization, particularly in determining the timetable.

The republican **Ministries of National Property Administration and Privatization** (commonly known as the "Privatization Ministries"), play the most influential role in both the selection of enterprises to be privatized and the exact methods of privatization. They decide which enterprises to include in each privatization wave, and which privatization project is accepted for enterprises in their respective jurisdictions.

Decisions regarding the approval of projects are concentrated in the hands of a relatively small number of individuals in the privatization ministries; the Czech Privatization Ministry had a total staff of twenty initially, which had grown to only 160 by mid-1992. The only cases in which the decision of the Privatization Ministries is not final are certain exceptional projects (for example, enterprises with more than 3,000 employees) and direct sales, which must be approved by the responsible government, either republican or federal.[13]

Founding ministries, though they have a formal role in the process, have been less influential than the Privatization Ministries. Under Act No. 92/1991 "On Conditions and terms Governing the Transfer of State Property to Other Persons" (the "Large Privatization" Law), founders are responsible for preparation of privatization projects of their enterprises and may either directly prepare a project, although this happened in only twenty-two cases in the first wave, or, as in the rest of the cases, require that enterprise management prepare it. Founding ministries must pass on all projects proposed to them, including those they do not recommend, to the relevant government organ (Republican Privatization Ministry or Federal Finance Ministry) along with their recommendations. Following the government changes in the middle of 1992, founding ministries may play an increasingly active role in the approval process.

Three **National Property Funds** (FNP) were set up under Act No. 92 of 1991 and subsequent legislation in the two republics, namely the Federal Fund of National Property (FFNP), the Fund of National Property of the Czech Republic (FNPCR) and the Fund of National Property of the Slovak Republic (FNPSR). These funds hold the shares not yet sold of corporatized enterprises and are themselves legal entities appearing in the Company Register, mutually independent, with jurisdiction over a precisely defined sphere of enterprises.

The funds are supposed to privatize the shares remaining after voucher privatization within the next five years. In the meantime, the FNPs act as shareholders, appointing the Supervisory Board and Board of Directors and, after partial privatization, participating as owners. The funds are also charged with overseeing the sale process in the case of approved projects calling for public auction, public tender, or direct sale. Once a project has been approved by the Privatization Ministry and the enterprise has been registered with the FNP, the funds are

---

[13] Technically, the relevant government can intervene in any project decision, but this right has never been exercised.

formally responsible for disposing of shares as specified in the project.

While there is a legal and organizational distinction between the Privatization Ministries and the FNP, in practice the funds are under the direct supervision of these ministries, notwithstanding the formal parliamentary oversight provided for in the law. Each of the funds is governed by a nine-member presidium; by law, the republican Privatization Ministers preside over their respective FNP, and the other eight presidium members are elected by the republican parliament, while all nine members of the presidium of the FFNP are elected by the federal parliament. A member of the presidium of the FFNP cannot be a member of the federal or republican governments or parliaments. These presidiums appoint the ten-member Executive Committees of each fund, comprising employees of the fund, which direct the funds' activities within the framework of instructions from the presidiums. Governmental oversight of the funds is performed by five-member Supervisory Boards elected by the respective parliaments; the board members cannot be fund employees. The members of all fund bodies serve a five-year term.

In the **Small Privatization** process (governed by Law No. 427/1990, the Small Privatization Law), the Privatization Ministers appoint twenty-member **local privatization commissions** for each of the seventy-five local districts. These commissions are charged with selecting enterprises for auctions and collecting and publishing data on the property of these enterprises. Founding ministries assess whether to include these enterprises in small privatization or to reserve them for large privatization. Final approval of enterprises to be auctioned off under the Small Privatization Law is given by the privatization ministries.

The Privatization Ministries also have the key role in **reprivatization** of small businesses under Act No. 403/1990, "Mitigation of Property-Related Injustices," deciding on the validity of claims for restitution and awarding compensation based on a valuation of the property claimed. Restitution claims arising within the context of privatization projects, involving larger enterprises, are settled by the Ministry of Finance in accordance with Act No. 87/1991, the Large-Scale Reprivatization Law.

4B. Overview of privatization programs

Czechoslovakia has given considerable priority to wide-ranging reprivatization, returning property expropriated under the communist regime. The program has proven controversial to enact, and problematic, costly, and time-consuming to administer. In 1990 and 1991, it was feared, partly as a result of the difficulties encountered with restitution and partly due to uncertainty over the future of the Czech and Slovak Federation, that other privatization measures would be delayed. However, a small-scale privatization program was prepared in 1990 and carried through with some success in the succeeding year. Preparations for the ambitious large privatization scheme, including an innovative use of vouchers, were meanwhile continually underway, and the first rounds of bidding for shares in state companies began in the summer of 1992. This section contains summaries of these programs, as well as brief accounts of privatization in agriculture and housing; more detailed analysis will appear in future CEU Privatization Project Reports.[14]

Reprivatization

Czechoslovakia has the largest reprivatization program of any of the former socialist central and Eastern European countries outside former East Germany. Under three separate laws, the state has sought to return to resident Czechoslovak citizens and the Catholic Church property that was nationalized after the communist coup in February 1948. This process has helped in the rapid creation of private property that could be used by the private retail trade sector,[15] but it has also delayed small and large privatization while claims on nationalized property have been processed and assessed. Although the share of

---

[14] Throughout, we attempt to provide data about the progress of these programs in each of the Czech and Slovak Republics, as well as in the Federation as a whole. In some cases, however, we have been able to obtain data for only one republic. So far, implementation of these programs is very similar in the two republics, but this could change with a split in the Federation.

[15] According to most estimates, restitution and small privatization together resulted in roughly 40 per cent of the retail trade and services sector being privatized by the end of 1991. See Dusan Triska, "Political, Organizational, and Legislative Aspects of Mass Privatization – Czechoslovakia" in *Privatization in Central & Eastern Europe 1991*, M. Simoneti and A. Bohm. (eds.), Central and East European Privatization Network, 1992.

private firms was not high in 1948, a large number of enterprises (one government estimate is 30 per cent) have at least some part of their property subject to reprivatization.

The first reprivatization law (Act No. 298 of 1990 "On Regulation of Property Relations of Religious Orders and Congregations and the Archdiocese of Olomouc") returned to the Catholic Church seventy-four properties (with an additional 176 expected to be returned later). Most of the properties were monasteries nationalized after 1950. Reprivatization to individual citizens began with the passage on October 2, 1990 of Act No. 403/1990 "Mitigation of Property Related Injustices" (the Small-Scale Reprivatization Act), authorizing the return of, or compensation for, the 80,000 or so small retail and service establishments nationalized during the latest wave of nationalization beginning in 1955. The program was broadened in 1991 under Act No. 87/1991 "On Out-of-Court Rehabilitations" (the Large-Scale Reprivatization Act) which authorized the return to former owners of all physical property, excluding land (described below), nationalized or expropriated from Czechoslovak citizens after February 25, 1948. The law also offers compensation to those who lost their jobs, were imprisoned, served in work camps or special military units, or were not allowed to finish their education. But the selected cut-off date meant that other groups, notably Jews whose property was seized by the Nazis and Sudeten Germans forced to leave the country just after the war, were excluded.

In all cases, the government attempts to provide restitution in kind, but in many cases this will probably be impracticable and financial restitution will be necessary. In these cases, former owners receive up to Kcs 30,000 in cash and the rest in shares in the investment Money Market Privatization Fund. This fund, managed by institutions sub-contracted by the republican National Property Funds, will invest in privatized enterprises using vouchers representing 3 per cent of the value of each privatized enterprise.

Small privatization

Czechoslovak small privatization began with plans to sell between 100,000 and 120,000 restaurants, shops, and small businesses in an effort to revitalize the small private sector in an economy that had experienced an extraordinarily high proportion of state ownership, even relative to other socialist countries.

Act No. 427 of 1990, About the Transfer of State Property and Some

Things to Other Legal or Physical Persons (the "Small-Scale Privatization" Law) provided for the sale or lease of these properties, requiring that they be sold by public auction, and established procedures for these auctions. Any person could propose any business unit that was not subject to restitution for small privatization by submitting a proposal to the regional privatization office. There was no official limit to the size of business units eligible for the program, but units that had been designated for large privatization could not be proposed for small privatization auctions. Proposals approved by the local privatization boards were confirmed by the republican Ministries of Privatization and designated for auction.

Lists of the units to be privatized, including basic information about the business and the real estate on which it rests, the starting price (based on appraisals of real estate, capital equipment and other assets), and details about the auction itself, were made public at least thirty days in advance of the public auction. The owner of the property involved (usually a larger enterprise) was entitled to raise a claim against privatization if it could show that sale of the unit would threaten the activity of the parent enterprise. This provision constituted a partial obstacle to the program, as parent enterprises generally resisted attempts to auction off their subsidiary units and assets.

Concerning eligibility for participation, initial auctions were open only to Czechoslovak citizens (or those who held citizenship for some period after February 1948). Units which were not sold in first round auctions were re-auctioned later in a second round in which foreign participation was allowed. Following a spirited debate over the issue of employee preferences, the law ultimately provided no special privileges to workers or managers of the privatized enterprises.

About three-quarters of the units auctioned in the small privatization program did not include the real estate on which they rest. Therefore, the buyer typically received the right to lease the premises from the owner, usually the state or municipality, initially for two and later extended to five years. The guaranteed lease period was extended to increase the incentives for new operators to invest; this also resulted in increased proceeds from higher auction prices.

The first auction took place on January 26, 1991. By the end of that year, over 21,000 enterprises had been sold for proceeds of Kcs 25.5 bln ($860 mln), with two-thirds of the sales and revenues coming from the Czech Republic. In October 1991, however, the Czech Privatization Minister, Tomas Jezek, announced that the small privatization

Table 4B.1 Small privatization in the Czech and Slovak republics

Czech Republic, 1991	number of units	starting price (bln CSK)	sale price (bln CSK)
Scheduled	21,940	22,096	
Sold in auction	14,726	11,549	18,122
of which:			
including real estate	3,814	10,490	14,000
rental rights only	10,912	1,059	4,122

Slovakia, through Nov. 24, 1991	units sold	starting price (bln CSK)	sale price (bln CSK)
Sold in auction	6,723	6,134	7,486

Sources: Fund of National Property, Czech Republic. *Telegraf*, Feb. 5, 1992

program in the Czech lands would be terminated after the sale of 23,000 units. The remaining enterprises originally targeted for the program are to be folded into the large privatization program, which offers the advantage of allowing the state to require the buyer to assume an enterprise's liabilities. While the process has slowed considerably, the actual number of sales in the Czech Republic has slightly exceeded Jezek's figure; as of March 1992, the total had reached 25,584.[16]

Proceeds from small privatization auctions were deposited in the Fund of National Property of the respective republic. These monies are frozen for two years and may be used only as deposits in the banking system and not for budgetary purposes.

Large privatization

The Czechoslovak "large privatization" was established in April 1991 through Act No. 92 "On Conditions and terms Governing the Transfer of State Property to Other Persons." The program has both decentralized aspects, such as the right of anyone to submit a proposal for privatization ("privatization project") specifying the use of any of a

---

[16] Czech Fund of National Property.

large number of privatization methods and the right of individuals to choose whether to participate and on which enterprises to bid, and highly centralized aspects, such as the forced pace of the process and the concentrated power of project approval in the Privatization and Finance Ministries. Essentially all state enterprises intended for privatization are obligatorily included, except those small businesses and shops auctioned under the rubric of "small privatization." Several dozen enterprises for which any form of privatization was considered inconceivable were, however, selected for liquidation.

The program occurs in two overlapping waves: the first will finish near the end of 1992, and the second is presently (summer 1992) in its initial stages and will probably finish by the end of 1993. Enterprises included in the program were divided between the two waves by the Privatization Ministries of the two republics and the Federal Ministry of Finance, for property belonging to the republics and the federation, respectively.

It is important but little understood in the West that vouchers are only one part of the Czechoslovak large privatization process. The other methods that the law stipulates as permissible, and that are used for different enterprises as well as combined together for single enterprises, include sales of assets (whole or parts of enterprises) through auctions, tenders, and direct sales; sales of shares by auction, tenders, and direct sales; and transfers to municipalities and pension and health care institutions.[17] In addition, at least 3 per cent of the shares of each enterprise are reserved for restitution, more when there is a chance that some of the property must be reprivatized.

To begin the process of determining the methods of privatization that would apply, the management of each enterprise included in a wave submits a plan or so-called "basic project." The deadline was October 31, 1991 for the first wave. Anyone else, for instance other managers or foreigners, may submit an unlimited number of plans called "competing projects," for which the first wave deadline was January 20, 1992 (extended from November 31, 1991 to give more time for competing projects to be developed). Most came from various management groups. All projects must include basic information about

---

[17] Some health care and pension institutions have actually expressed disinterest in receiving shares in companies because they do not have the skills to manage them. It seems these shares will be held by the National Property Funds until those "institutional investors" are ready to assume their new role.

the enterprise, the methods of privatization, and a business plan. The project that is approved for a particular enterprise determines how its property will be privatized and whether it remains intact or is somehow divided; thus, the distribution of shares and, therefore, the new ownership structure as well as the amount of disintegration varies across enterprises.[18]

The number of competing projects multiplied rapidly in the last weeks and days before the January 20, 1992 deadline. Some enterprises had as many as twenty or thirty competing projects (the highest number was 126 for the milk processing factory Lacrum Brno). In all, there were 2,884 basic or obligatory projects and 8,065 competing projects submitted to the Czech Ministry of Privatization, the latter forming 73.7 per cent of the total. Among the basic projects, conversion to joint stock form (leading to share sales, meaning mostly voucher privatization[19]) predominated; among the competing projects, direct sales predominated.

In the case of direct sales, the rules for the projects stipulate that citizens may pay the book value, while foreigners must pay market value, according to some "independent" valuation. Although foreigners thus normally have to pay much more than book value, it must be recognized that market value can, in fact, be more or less than book value. There were, therefore, cases of both foreigners and Czechoslovak citizens offering to pay less than book value in their projects. Citizens might have been inclined to offer more under the presumption that the projects were competing with one another on the basis of price.

Theories abound as to the intentions of the parties proposing projects. It may be supposed that managers' preferences are the following: first, buyout at a low price; second, find a sweetheart deal with a foreign buyer; third, if neither of these is possible, create a dispersed ownership structure so that little effective control over the manager is exercised. It may be for this reason that many basic projects proposed a high proportion of vouchers and/or that significant shares go to the health care and pension institutions. Many projects, both basic and competing, but especially the latter, proposed direct sale to a new company, sometimes formed by a group of insiders.

---

[18] Otherwise, restructuring is left almost completely to the new owners.
[19] Among 1,491 Czech and Slovak companies in the program, only forty-nine, or 3.29 per cent, have sales of shares (as opposed to assets, or the whole company) to foreigners.

Direct sales to domestic investors at book value are often alleged to hide the real buyer: a foreigner.

Projects were first evaluated by the founder (branch ministry, local authority, etc.), which then sent them on, accompanied by their recommendations[20] and the opinion of the company management, to the appropriate Czech or Slovak Privatization Ministry or to the Federal Finance Ministry for the final decision. The criteria for evaluation, however, were never clearly spelled out: aside from having to meet the formal requirements for the project, no official regulations were promulgated as to the preferences of the ministry over different kinds of projects. The new Czechoslovak constitution declares the "equality of different forms of ownership before the law" (paradoxically during a period of unprecedented change of ownership), and the "equality of methods of privatization" has often been asserted. Thus, the game was really played "without knowing the rules."[21] The same person or group sometimes submitted multiple projects for the same enterprise because of uncertainty about the priorities of the ministry.

But some principles for selection of projects were generally known. In the case of asset sales, auctions were preferred to tenders, which were preferred to direct sales. In the case of vouchers versus sales, the question was less clear-cut. Sales have the advantage of producing revenue, but there was a strong political commitment to ensure that a certain amount of property would go to vouchers. With respect to employee shares, the ministry let it be known that it would oppose more than a 10 per cent total stake.

Because of the deadline at the end of March 1992 for final ministry approval of voucher projects, those projects that included vouchers were analyzed on a priority basis. The number of individuals with registered vouchers soared in early 1992 far beyond any earlier forecast, which also led to a higher proportion of projects with vouchers receiving approval, in an attempt to prevent the average voucher value from falling excessively. Thus, data from early 1992

---

[20] In the first wave, there was no clearly-specified time for the founders to accomplish this evaluation; in the second, they have a two-month period, possibly implying a stronger role in the process. The decision of the appropriate Privatization or Finance Ministry is final, except for enterprises with more than 3,000 employees, however, or where the project proposes a direct sale (either to a foreign or a domestic buyer): the approval of the project by the Ministry then also requires the endorsement of the relevant government as a whole.

[21] J. Havel and E. Kukla, "Mass Privatization Programs in Czechoslovakia, 1991–1992," unpublished paper of the CEU Privatization Project, April 1992.

Table 4B.2 Approval of basic and competing projects in the Czech Republic (status as of June 1992)

	Basic	Competing	Total
Number submitted	2,906	8,257	11,163
Number approved	782	266	1,048
Book value approved (billion CSK)	313.55	104.11	417.66
% of approved	74.62	25.38	100
% approved of those submitted	26.91	2.88	9.39

Source: Unpublished data from the Czech Ministry of Privatization, June 1992

show a high proportion of voucher projects in all approved projects. Since March, however, there has been a disproportionate increase in other privatization methods, especially direct sales. The delay in completing evaluation of voucher projects from the end of January to the end of March 1992, however controversial at the time, in retrospect seems reasonable in having provided a small amount of additional time to study the projects responsibly.

In fact, only about 7,000 of 11,000 projects in the first wave have been evaluated so far by the Czech Privatization Ministry. The remaining projects probably propose mostly non-voucher methods; those approved with vouchers will be put into the second wave. Table 4B.2 shows the approval of projects thus far. Although competing projects outnumber basic projects by a factor of almost three, the ratio is reversed for the number approved: nearly three-quarters of the approved projects are basic projects.[22] The 1,048 approved projects in the Czech Republic correspond to 2,154 business units, so there will clearly be some significant disintegration of large enterprises as part of this process.

With regard to voucher projects, Table 4B.3 shows the number, total book value, book value of all shares, and book value of shares

[22] This ratio is gradually shifting more towards competing projects, probably because projects with vouchers were, for the most part, considered first, and basic projects tended to favor vouchers more than did competing projects, which had a greater proportion of direct sales. See A. Buchtikova, A. Capek, and E. Macourkova, "Statistical Analysis of the Privatization Projects," Institute of Economics of the Czechoslovak Academy of Sciences, Prague 1992.

Table 4B.3 Voucher privatization in Czechoslovakia

	Czech	Slovak	Federal	Total
number of enterprises	943	487	62	1,492
total book value	362.2	133.6	2.8	568.6
total equity (book value of all shares)	323.1	114.4	25.4	463.0
book value privatized through vouchers	200.8	85.1	13.5	299.4

Source: Data from the Czech Ministry of Privatization, June 1992, quoted in M. Mejstrik (ed.), *Privatization Newsletter* No. 7, June 1992

distributed through vouchers of all the enterprises in the first wave voucher program. Only 53 per cent of the total book value of these enterprises will go to vouchers (about 10 per cent of the book value of all productive assets in Czechoslovakia), the rest being privatized by sales of assets or sales of shares or held in the FNP. As a percentage of total equity (all shares) in these companies, vouchers account for 65 per cent in the CSFR, but this ratio is 74 per cent for Slovak, 62 per cent for Czech, and 50 per cent for federal enterprises. Analysis of data for the 943 units in the Czech voucher program reveals that the remaining 38 per cent of equity is accounted for by shares held temporarily by the National Property Fund (16 per cent), those transferred at no charge, those reserved for restitution, and those sold directly to foreign or domestic buyers, in declining order of importance.

Of the companies using the voucher method, 81 per cent of those in Slovakia use vouchers exclusively, aside from the 3 per cent reserved for restitution.[23] In the Czech Republic, only thirty-two companies have over 90 per cent of their shares going to vouchers, accounting for only 4.6 per cent of all voucher property; 813 companies have over 50 per cent in the program.

Turning to the demand side of the Czechoslovak voucher privatization program, each resident citizen over the age of 18 in October 1991 was eligible to purchase a voucher booklet for Kcs 35 ($1.20) and could register it for Kcs 1,000 ($34, or about 25 per cent of the average

---

[23] These results in Slovakia are often interpreted to mean that there was little alternative for these enterprises; there were no interested buyers. But it could also mean that the Slovak Ministry of Privatization is actually following more closely the original policy of Federal Finance Minister Vaclav Klaus, which pushed for a much larger share of vouchers.

monthly wage). This voucher is divisible into 1,000 points that can be invested in companies directly or in intermediaries. Although the response early on was meager, participation soared in January and February of 1992, and the total number reached 8.57 mln, 79 per cent of the eligible population, by the deadline at the end of February 1992. This growth was astounding when compared with the under one-half mln registered in late December 1992. Participation was 5.98 mln in the Czech Republic and 2.59 mln in Slovakia.

The allocation process of shares may be characterized as a "discrete-time tatonnement." In the first round, all shares have the same price in terms of voucher points, calculated by dividing the total book value by the total number of points, three shares for 100 points. Thus, initially, each enterprise has a number of shares proportional to its value. Individual voucher holders and intermediaries then have a two-week period to register their demands for various enterprise shares at that price. If excess demand is less than 25 per cent higher than the total share supply, then the demand is satisfied, with priority going to individuals over intermediaries. In a situation of excess supply, the demand is satisfied at the given price, and the remaining shares go to a second round at a lower price. The shares of enterprises for which demand exceeds supply by 25 per cent are not sold but all proceed to the next round at a higher price.

The price adjustment rules after the first round of the first wave were as follows. In the case of excess demand (greater than 25 per cent), prices were raised by the same factor as the ratio of excess demand to supply. Under the presumption of unitary demand elasticity, this would result in market clearing for these enterprises. For cases where this rule implied a price increase of more than nine times (so that the implied new price would be over 300 points per share in the second round), a price adjustment committee met to adjust the price "manually" (with a maximum increase to 400 points-per-share in the second round). If the price rises as high as 1,000 points per share in some future round, so that no individual would have enough points to buy even one share, those shares will be removed from voucher privatization and sold separately. The price adjustment function after the first round was more complicated in the case of excess supply: rather than specifying some overall rule, various ranges of degree of excess demand corresponded to different prices, with some of them set so that the market cleared overall. The lowest price of shares going into the second round was ten points per share.

Price adjustment rules after future rounds may differ from those after the first. As with virtually all aspects of the program, the Czechs and Slovaks wait to see the results of one decision before making the next. It is still unknown even how many rounds there will be; the expectation has been that the process ends when a certain proportion of shares have been sold, in perhaps three to seven rounds.

The Czechoslovak program has thus assigned an unusually active role to individuals, who must decide whether to participate, which companies to invest in, and how many of their points to invest in intermediaries. The intermediaries, which can bid for shares with the voucher points that individuals have invested with them, have grown from a mere vague possibility in the original planning to one of the most important aspects of the whole program. It was their offer to repurchase shares from individuals at prices ten to fifteen times the original Kcs 1,035 investment (and even more, although the largest offers met with so much public distrust that few individuals risked their vouchers) that created a mania to participate in early 1992. Two-thirds of all voucher holders invested 100 per cent of their points in the intermediaries and others invested some of their points, so that by the end of the so-called "zero round," which denotes the time period during which individuals had to decide what proportion of their points they would invest in intermediaries, these funds controlled 72 per cent of all points.

But this same success in generating interest in the program makes it much more difficult to keep the commitment to repurchase shares at the promised price: the larger number of participants lowers the expected value of each voucher. Originally, with an expected participation of under 2 mln, the book value of assets in the program was over Kcs 150,000 per voucher; with 8.6 mln vouchers, this value became only about Kcs 34,000. Of course, this is unlikely to equal exactly the market value, and some calculations suggest that on average it is likely to be an overestimate.[24] Furthermore, this market value should be some long-run estimate of the present discounted value of future profits. In the short run, the price of shares could fall significantly as liquidity-constrained individuals seek to cash in their voucher

---

[24] Oldrich Kyn calculates a market value of about Kcs 30,000 (standard deviation of Kcs 7,500) per voucher booklet assuming no risk premium, and a value of Kcs 15,000 (standard deviation of Kcs 3,500) with a risk premium. See O. Kyn, *Trh, Kupony a Investicni Fondy*, transcript of lecture at CERGE, 1992. Any such attempt to estimate market value in the post-socialist economies obviously requires heroic assumptions.

holdings. The riskiness of all shares in the short run will also greatly lower their value. Consequently, the average value of a voucher's worth of shares may well fall below Kcs 15,000 in the short run. It may thus be impossible for the funds to honor their commitments.

There is, moreover, a legal reason that the option contracts may not be valid. The intermediaries were originally organized as closed-end funds, meaning that they would not be obliged to redeem their own shares. They may be made open in the future, but until then the legal status of these contracts is dubious. There may also be good economic reasons for them not to be open: there is no stock market on which their shares could trade; although one is planned, it will probably not function effectively for some time. Furthermore, the funds themselves will certainly have very low liquidity initially.

Intermediaries are not organized directly by the state, and they were supposed to be a purely private activity. But state-owned joint-stock companies are allowed to establish intermediaries, and the largest banks took advantage of this possibility, together with the chance to use their networks of information and facilities, to attract investors. The Czech Savings Bank set up the largest intermediary with about 800 mln points, or 10 per cent of the total. Other large state-owned banks that established intermediaries include the Czech Investment and the Commercial Bank. Foreigners are also allowed to establish intermediaries, and the Austrian Creditanstalt became one of the largest. Among the large intermediaries, the only private one is Harvard Capital and Consulting, which began the voucher mania with its repurchase promises. A total of 437 intermediaries are operating in the first round, but the largest thirteen control 40 per cent of all voucher points.

The lack of regulation of intermediaries is generally considered to be one of the weaknesses of the whole Czechoslovak privatization process. Originally, the investment company that administers the fund was required to have a small founding capital of Kcs 1 mln, and the fund itself needed only Kcs 100,000; the capital requirement of the fund was increased to one mln after January 1, 1991, but it is still low even by Czechoslovak standards. To establish an insurance company, for instance, requires Kcs 10 mln.

Since March 28, 1992, regulation has become more extensive as a result of Act No. 248/1992, "On Investment Corporations and Investment Funds." New rules on disclosure, conflicts of interest, operation, and diversification were included. With respect to diversification, no fund is allowed to hold more than 20 per cent of the shares in any privatized enterprise, and if an investment company administers several funds, there can be no more than 40 per cent of any company in the entire portfolio. Funds are not allowed to engage in either commercial or investment banking. Compensation of the investment company by the intermediary is limited to 2 per cent of the book value of the intermediary's assets at the close of the first wave, when the shares are received.[25]

Although there are thus far no restrictions on the tradeability of shares or on futures and option contracts, it is widely rumored that such restrictions will be included in a forthcoming Securities Law. The possible restrictions include a one-year period of complete non-tradability, restrictions only on sales to foreigners, restrictions only on the shares in particular enterprises, or sale of shares only at the "price of the officially agreed stock market." Any such restrictions could create discomforts and legal ambiguities for the funds, for they have not only promised the repurchase option, but it is also widely suspected that they have futures contracts with foreigners that would be awkward to break.

The first round of the first wave finished in mid-June 1992, and the results were announced at the end of the month. One concern that had been voiced earlier was the possibility that this procedure would permit various kinds of speculation, for instance holding back points for later rounds when prices may have fallen.[26] Although early on in the first round the data seemed to indicate that this may in fact have been happening, towards the end of the round there was a rush of orders, so that 92 per cent of all vouchers were used to place bids (95 per cent of the funds' vouchers and 84 per cent of individuals'). Whether this represented an attempt at skillful speculation that was hindered by government jaw-boning, as some rumors have it, or simply procrastination, as occured with voucher registration, is an open question.

About 30 per cent of all shares were sold in the first round, twice as much as expected; over three-quarters of successful bids came from

---

[25] Thereafter, determination of the compensation of fund managers is left to the shareholders.

[26] The advantage of this waiting strategy is, paradoxically, a direct consequence of a policy designed to achieve just the opposite: by issuing shares to investors in under-subscribed companies and then lowering the offering price in future rounds, rather than waiting to let the market clear at the equilibrium price, the government hopes to accelerate the process; but rational investors will prefer to postpone placing orders for shares whose future price may fall.

funds. The shares available for vouchers in forty-eight firms were sold completely, while 1,022 firms were undersubscribed (although it is interesting to note that every firm received some bid), and 421 were oversubscribed.[27] Thus, at least some shares were sold from 1,070 firms. Regarding cross-republican boundaries investment, half the total and 28 per cent of the satisfied demand of Slovak funds and individuals were for Czech enterprises, but the proportions were only 4 per cent in the other direction. The ratio of the book value of property in the first wave voucher program to the number of participants was, according to plan, roughly equal across the two republics, so that no fairness issues would arise (at least insofar as book value bears the same relation to true value across the two). In the event of a split, appropriate legislation concerning foreign ownership would be required.

The second round took place from July 8 to 28, 1992, and the results are due to be published in mid-August 1992. It is still unknown how many further rounds will follow, or even what the criteria are for ending the process. According to some rumors, the end may be announced *ex-post*, perhaps already after the conclusion of the third round.

The review by branch ministries of basic and competing projects in the second wave was supposed to be completed sometime between June 16 and August 16, 1992, after which the republican Privatization Ministries were to make the final choice. As noted above, the branch ministries are likely to have a strengthened role in the second wave for at least two reasons: the allocation of two months' time for them to comment on projects, and, in the Czech Republic, the creation of a new privatization commission that will be composed of branch ministry officials and chaired by the Privatization Minister (Jiri Skalicky, who replaced Tomas Jezek) and which is supposed to adjudicate disputes between project authors and the Privatization Ministry.[28] Another probable change in the second wave is the result

27 Oversubscription was common among breweries, banks, hotels, and companies that had already received the attention of foreign investors. The undersubscribed included many of the large state enterprises, such as the utility company. Data come from *The Prague Post*, July 7–13, 1992.

28 On the one hand, the branch ministries may be regarded as relative experts in the areas of technology and potential market power, so that they may complement the emphasis placed by the Privatization Ministry on restitutional clarity and the formal and legal aspects of projects. On the other hand, it must be recognized that branch ministry officials tend to be quite close to enterprise managers, since, under the old system, the latter were appointed by the former, and the former were usually promoted from the ranks of the latter.

of expectations of a split in the federation: the plan calls for each republic to conduct its voucher program separately, so that no cross-border investment will be allowed. The Slovak Republic may also modify its privatization policy to diminish the prevalence of direct sales and to grant special preferences to employees.

Privatization of agriculture

The issue of transformation of the country's 1,660 agricultural cooperatives, which accounted for two-thirds of agricultural production and employed over 600,000 workers in 1989, has been included in the Law on Regulation of Property Relations in Cooperatives (January 1992), a general law covering cooperatives of all types. Further information on cooperatives appears in Section 3A. The privatization of state farms will begin in 1993, following the resolution of reprivatization issues.

Privatization of housing

Housing is another area in which privatization to date has come only through the reprivatization program. In mid-1991, approximately 25 per cent of the country's 5.32 mln residences were state apartments, 20 per cent were cooperatives, 45 per cent were family homes and 10 per cent were owned by companies. The government is considering various means of privatizing housing that will give current residents the first opportunity to buy and will not force people to leave their homes. One possibility is continued rent subsidies in some cases, or subsidies for the construction of low-income private housing.

Rents are still strictly controlled and in many cases have changed little since before the Second World War. On July 1, 1992, the Government raised rents in all state-owned, company-owned, and private rent-controlled apartments by 100 per cent and planned to impose an additional 40 per cent increase by the end of 1992. Before the increase, the average national apartment rent was Kcs 115 monthly, representing less than 4 per cent of average income, and finance ministry officials say apartments rarely cost more than 10 per cent of a tenant's income. Consumer prices of goods and services related to housing also increased in 1992, fueled by the liberalization of utility prices. Despite these price increases, the state still subsidizes residents by providing free maintenance through municipal authorities, though recently these funds proved to be insufficient to cover rising materials costs.

5. CORPORATIZATION

Corporatization, the process of turning "socialized enterprises" into joint-stock companies wholly owned by the state, was launched as a special program in Czechoslovakia under Act No. 111 of 1990, "On State Enterprises." The main intention was to give units greater financial independence and full control of their own disposable profit under continued state ownership. Under this plan, corporatization proceeded in two distinct steps. The first step was conversion into a so-called "state enterprise," as defined in Act No. 111/1990, with a governance structure giving effective control to the founding organ (see Section 3A above). The second step was conversion into a state-owned joint stock company as defined in Act No. 104/1990, "On Joint Stock Companies."

This program was abandoned, however, after it had been applied to roughly 100 enterprises, in favor of an approach in which transformation comes only in preparation for at least partial privatization and where corporate governance is supposed to be exercised by the National Property Funds. Those enterprises whose projects have been approved within the context of large privatization are converted to joint-stock companies and entered in the company register. Their shares are immediately transferred to the appropriate National Property Fund,[29] which prepares the enterprise for privatization and may hold a packet of shares for some period of time. The funds are supposed to privatize the shares remaining after voucher privatization and the sales now in progress in the next five years. How exactly this will be accomplished is still unclear, but this aspect of the Czechoslovak privatization has received comparatively little attention.

In the meantime, the FNP act as shareholders, appointing the first supervisory board and board of directors and, after partial privatization participating as owners. In practice, the "goal is not to administer but to privatize," but the implication is a further period of weak governance and even less outside control over insiders' activities. Critics claim that asset stripping and transfer pricing schemes are rampant; while this cannot be proven, it does seem clear that there are few

---

[29] The enterprises were thus removed from the control of their founders, the branch ministries.

incentives for efficient operation during this period. To prevent spontaneous privatization, the enterprises are supposed to be "frozen," with all activities beyond normal business prohibited; they cannot sell except for output and cannot invest in new firms. Indeed, investment in state enterprises has fallen by 30 per cent compared to 1989. This period of FNP control will be two or three years for nearly every enterprise, and it could be still longer until the new private owners start to exercise their rights vigorously.[30]

Even before the wave of corporatization that accompanied the first wave of privatization, the number of state-owned enterprises registered as joint-stock companies grew considerably, from 67 (3.5 per cent of all state enterprises) in June 1990 to 419 (5 per cent of all) one year later. The first privatization wave saw a rapid increase in joint-stock companies under at least partial and temporary state ownership, with the creation of 943 new ones in the Czech Republic as of June 1992.[31] Most of the shares of these companies were to be privatized immediately through the voucher program, but a significant number of shares (representing an estimated 16 per cent of the property of the 943 enterprises in the voucher scheme, or some 37 bln Kcs) will be held by the Czech FNP for an unspecified, "temporary" period.

---

[30] The FNP receives the revenue from the sale of shares, but not from asset sales. This allows it to fulfill another function: to clear some of the debts accumulated by enterprises to banks. Interfirm debts have also grown especially rapidly since the revolution. In return for banks clearing these debts, the FNP issued them bonds paying the discount rate plus 2 per cent. The banks can exchange the bonds for shares in privatized companies, or have them repurchased by the FNP with revenues from sales.

[31] *Privatization Newsletter* no. 7, June 1992, M. Mejstrik (ed.).

HUNGARY

CONTENTS

1. Introduction

Brief history of reforms

Substantial economic reforms in Hungary began in 1968. They were intended to replace the economic system based on bureaucratic control with the so-called "New Economic Mechanism," relying instead on enterprise autonomy, the profit motive, and market coordination. The reforms were also intended to improve the ability of Hungarian enterprises to compete in foreign markets and thus accelerate the substantial opening of the economy already evident in the early 1960s. However, many of the central foreign trade controls were retained, and a significant proportion of exports remained directed to the East European and Soviet markets.

By the early 1970s, it had become clear that the results of the 1968 reforms fell short of expectations. At the same time, favorable conditions in the Western capital markets opened the possibility of substantial hard currency borrowing. In an attempt to boost living standards, the central authorities used the borrowed funds to engineer a consumption and investment boom. However, subsequent adverse developments in world capital markets, combined with the inability of Hungarian enterprises to generate sufficient convertible currency revenue and the orientation of the Hungarian trade toward the Soviet economy, led to an acute balance of payments crisis by the end of the 1970s. The authorities responded with tough austerity measures and further decentralizing reforms in the 1980s, but these again failed to revitalize the Hungarian economy.

In 1989, the Communist Party lost its monopoly on political power, following a split within its own ranks. After free elections were held in 1990, the first postcommunist government accelerated the gradual reforms begun under the previous regime. Despite the apparent continuity of reforms, the announced goal of the new government is the transition to a capitalist market economy rather than the further pursuit of a socialist market system.

Main points of the reform program

In March 1991, the Finance Minister, Mihaly Kupa, presented to Parliament a five-year program of conversion and development of the Hungarian economy. This long-term economic strategy included measures to accelerate trade liberalization and rapid redirection of trade away from the former Comecon region to Western markets. The program also envisages increasing the pace of privatization and aims to reduce state ownership in the economy to less than 50 per cent by 1994.

In addition to setting out the longer-term strategy, other measures introduced during 1991 include the reform of accounting rules, the restructuring of the banking system, and the establishment of guidelines for compensating owners of property confiscated by the former communist regime.

In February 1991, Hungary signed a three-year agreement with the International Monetary Fund. The agreement provided for around $1.6 bln in new lending, $68 mln of which was available for drawing in 1991. Based on Hungary's 1991 results and 1992 targets, the IMF approved a second tranche of the credit program in March 1992. Hungary's positive prospects on the current and capital account, however, make it unlikely that full recourse to the available IMF credit will be necessary.

2. Economic environment

The structure of output

Gross National Product (GNP), as reported by *PlanEcon*, was Ft 2,540 bln ($34 bln)[1] in 1991. The structure of GDP in 1988 and 1991 shows the decline in the share of industry over this period. This change is evidently associated with the restructuring of the state sector.

Table 2.1   The structure of GDP (in per cent of total, in current prices)

	1988	1991
Industry	31	28
Agriculture	15	14
Services	19	20
Other	35	38

Source: PlanEcon

One of the characteristic features of communist economies has been the extreme concentration of industrial production. As shown in Table 2.2, the 100 biggest enterprises in 1990 accounted for 13 per cent of the work force and 48 per cent of the total assets of the state sector.

Table 2.2   Concentration of industry in 1990

	The biggest 100 companies	The biggest 200 companies
Total revenue (Ft bn)	2,160	2,660
Total employment (thousands) (as per cent cent of labor force)	575	762
	13	17
Total book value of assets (Ft bn) (as per cent of total assets of state enterprises)	916	1,107
	48	58

Source: Figyelo

[1] The forint–dollar exchange rate used here is the average rate for the year as calculated by *PlanEcon Review*. For the period covered by this report, these rates were as follows: 1987, Ft 47.0; 1988, Ft 50.4; 1989, Ft 59.1; 1990, Ft 63.2; 1991, Ft 74.7; 1992, Ft 81.0 (estimated).

Output

Following a 4 per cent decline in 1990, real GDP dropped by 11 per cent in 1991. Gross industrial output declined 19.1 per cent in 1991, after falling 9.6 per cent in 1990. The most severe decreases were in the metallurgical, building materials, and machine building industries. Output of the construction sector fell 17–18 per cent. Gross agricultural output dropped another 17.9 per cent, after a 3.8 per cent fall in 1990.

Table 2.3 Industrial production (1989 monthly average = 100; seasonally adjusted)

	Jan	Feb	Mar	Apr	May	June	July	Aug	Sept	Oct	Nov	Dec
1991	81.9	80.1	75.4	74.3	70.4	68.3	69.4	64.0	63.6	62.4	62.2	60.6
1992	58.3	58.5										

Source: *PlanEcon*

Investment

After a 7 per cent decline in 1990, gross investment in fixed capital fell by 20 per cent in 1991. The share of gross fixed investment in final domestic demand, in 1981 prices, also declined from about 21 per cent in 1990 to 19 per cent in 1991. Official Hungarian investment figures probably underestimate aggregate investment because they do not appear to include investment by unincorporated businesses.

Household savings

There is no reliable estimate of the total stock of household savings. A significant proportion has probably been kept outside the official banking system. Savings of the population have been reported to total Ft 557 bln ($7.5 bln) at the end of October 1991. About 19 per cent of total savings were held in foreign currencies, an almost 50 per cent increase compared to the value at the end of 1990, while the value of savings held in securities represented about 30 per cent of the total, an almost twofold increase since the end of 1990.

Price liberalization

Unlike most other countries of Eastern Europe, price liberalization did not come suddenly in Hungary, but was already one of the important features of the New Economic Mechanism introduced in 1968. However, formal and informal methods continued to be used to regulate price setting by state enterprises. Profits were controlled, and most input prices, interest rates, and prices of capital goods were fixed by the authorities. Exchange rates and export prices were also heavily regulated.

After the 1972–73 agricultural and oil price shocks, the government's policy of maintaining low food and energy prices amplified the distortions in the price system. The resulting subsidies proved unsustainable and necessitated another round of price reforms in 1980. Most energy and raw material prices were linked to the world market prices and, where possible, prices of manufactured goods were calculated according to the convertible export prices.

During the 1980s, formal intervention in enterprise price setting was gradually replaced with informal pressures and controls. For example, enterprises had to report planned price increases if they exceeded 7 per cent or concerned basic foods. However, the liberalization of imports in 1989 rendered many of the price controls obsolete, and, by 1990, only 16 per cent of prices were fixed by the state (public transport, fuels, rents, some basic food remained in that category).

Inflation

Consumer price inflation averaged 35 per cent in 1991, substantially above the 1990 level of 29 per cent. By March 1991, the rate of increase of retail prices slowed to about 2 per cent. During the third and fourth quarters, the monthly increases fluctuated between 0.2 and 1.6 per cent. Retail price increases were somewhat higher during the first six months of 1992.

Table 2.4 Retail Price Index (month-to-month per cent changes)

	Jan	Feb	Mar	Apr	May	June	July	Aug	Sept	Oct	Nov	Dec
1991	7.5	4.9	3.7	2.4	2.2	2.1	0.9	0.2	1.5	1.3	1.4	1.6
1992	3.2	2.7	1.9	1.3	1.0	1.0						

Source: PlanEcon

Behavior of wages

Real wages stagnated during the second half of the 1980s. Hungary avoided the build-up of a price–wage spiral typically associated with the loose monetary discipline and weak external enterprise control in the Eastern European economies.

Before 1990, there existed a fundamentally centralized system of wage setting, with the state setting wage ranges for each category of workers. Wage regulation served as a tool of macroeconomic policy and as an indirect control device over the activity of state enterprises.

Since 1990, Hungary has had a modified, liberalized system of wage setting. A new group, the Negotiation Council, was set up in order to provide a formal method of organizing talks among representatives of employees, employers, and the government. Participants in the Council discuss the terms of wage regulation, minimum wage rules and desirable employment policy. There is no automatic indexation of wages.

In order to induce enterprise managers to grant only moderate wage increases, the excess wage tax was introduced in 1991. If the company's wages grew by less than 18 per cent, they were untaxed; if the rate of growth in wages was between 18 and 28 per cent, then the excess part of the increase in wages over 18 per cent was taxed as additional profit; if the rate of growth in wages was over 28 per cent, then the total increase in wages was taxed as additional profit. There were, however, exemptions from these rules: companies with a wage bill under Ft 20 mln ($267,774) and companies where the foreign stake was over 20 per cent or over Ft 5 mln ($66,934) were not taxed.

The excess wage tax was modified in 1992. Under the new tax scheme, if the increase in the economy-wide average wage in 1992 is higher than 23 per cent (according to the Central Statistical Office), those companies that increase wages more than 28 per cent must add their wage increase to pretax profit. If the increase in the economy-wide average wage in 1992 is less than 23 per cent, then no company (even those with wage increases larger than 28 per cent) will have to pay the excess wage tax.

Nominal wages increased at an average annual rate of 25 per cent in 1990, and 18 per cent in 1991.

Table 2.5 Average monthly industrial wage (in current US dollars)

	Jan	Feb	Mar	Apr	May	June	July	Aug	Sept	Oct	Nov	Dec
1991	209.7	210.3	219.4	213.1	222.7	221.7	230.4	249.9	243.5	241.6	255.1	281.4
1992	229.3	234.1										

Source: PlanEcon

Table 2.6 Real wage in industry (January 1990 = 100)

	Jan	Feb	Mar	Apr	May	June	July	Aug	Sept	Oct	Nov	Dec
1991	96.4	93.4	98.2	96.4	99.1	98.4	101.8	108.7	103.3	100.8	107.8	116.3
1992	92.0	92.5										

Source: PlanEcon

Unemployment

The number of registered unemployed has been steadily rising since the beginning of 1990, except for a small temporary decline during the summer of 1991. The unemployment rate increased from about 2 per cent at the beginning of 1991 to 10.1 per cent in June 1992.

Unemployment benefits are 70 per cent of the former pay for up to one year and 50 per cent for up to an additional six months, with a cap of two times the minimum wage.

State budget

The state budget, plus local spending and social security transfers, accounted for 62 per cent of GDP in 1991. The government aims to reduce this to 57 per cent by 1994.

The most important recent change in the structure of the state expenditures has been a decline of subsidies from 13 per cent of GDP in 1989 to 7 per cent in 1991. The authorities plan to reduce subsidies to below 4 per cent of GDP in 1993.

At the end of 1991 Hungary had a budget deficit of Ft 114.2 bln ($1.5 bln), about 4.5 per cent of GDP, after a minor deficit, Ft 0.7 bln, in 1990. The main reason for the unexpectedly large deficit of 1991 is that the tax revenues from industry were below target.

The budget deficit for 1992 reached Ft 66.7 bln ($823 mln) by the end of April. Tax refunds to companies that made less than expected profits in 1991, low first quarter profits in 1992 and decisions by the larger banks to bolster reserves rather than record profits hit revenues hard in the first four months of 1992. The government now expects the deficit to reach Ft 115 bln by the end of 1992 – 65 per cent more than originally planned, but the same in nominal terms and roughly 20 per cent less in real terms than in 1991.

TAXATION

Hungary introduced the foundations of a western-style tax system on January 1, 1988. Hungary has three value-added tax (VAT) rates: 0, 15 and 25 per cent. There are plans to introduce a two-rate system, with the higher rate of 20 per cent.

Income tax is progressive, with the highest marginal rate at 40 per cent on incomes above 500,000 Ft ($6,200) per annum. Child support and government transfers are not counted as income.

The government imposes a tax on profits of 40 per cent. Since 1990 state enterprises have had to pay a dividend tax on their state assets. This tax is equivalent to an additional 25 per cent profit tax. The taxed profits are net of depreciation allowances. However, the currently allowed depreciation allowance is too low. The government plans to increase this allowance to reflect more closely real rates of depreciation by 1994.

In addition, companies pay social security contributions on the wages of their employees at a rate of 44 per cent. There is also a levy of 4.5 per cent on the previous year's taxable profit which is payable to the Central Technical Development Fund.

As of January 1, 1991, the profit tax rate can be reduced if the company meets one of the following conditions:

- start-up capital exceeds Ft 50 mln ($669,344);
- foreign participation is greater than 30 per cent;
- over 50 per cent of income is derived from the operation of a hotel which the company either built or renovated.

For the first five years, tax payable is reduced by 60 per cent, and for the next five years tax is reduced by 40 per cent. If a company's activities are in a designated priority sector, there is no tax payable for the first five years, and for the next five years, tax is reduced by 60 per cent.

Monetary policy

MONEY SUPPLY
For 1991, the Hungarian National Bank set the target rate of growth of broad money (M2) at 24–26 per cent. The nominal GDP was also projected to grow at the same rate. Although the actual growth of money was within the target range, the nominal GDP increased by only 12.9 per cent. Since the actual inflation rate was close to the projected rate, the unexpectedly low rate of growth of the nominal GDP was due to the much deeper than anticipated drop of the real GDP. It is also evident that velocity experienced a sharp decline.

INTEREST RATES
After the launching of the two-tier banking system in 1987, commercial banks were permitted, within limits, to set their own lending rates. At the beginning, the newly constituted Central Bank was the main provider of funds to the banks. It also determined the maximum premia between its "refinancing" rate and various lending rates charged by the commercial banks. Thus, the National Bank of Hungary has had a dominant influence on the economy-wide lending rates.

The average refinancing rate was 30 per cent in 1991. During the same period, the average lending rate charged by banks on credits with maturity of less than one year has stayed above 35 per cent, slightly above the inflation rate in 1991. Nominal rates on longer-term credits were negative, in real terms, but were somewhat higher after mid-1991.

Projecting a lower inflation rate for 1992, the Central Bank gradually lowered the refinancing rate during the first six months of the year. The rate was set at 24 per cent in June. The interbank credit rates also declined during the same period. However, the average lending rate charged by commercial banks on longer-term credit was higher in May than in January 1992.

INTER-ENTERPRISE DEBT
Hungary has recently experienced a sharp growth in the so-called "inter-enterprise" debt. This debt, often involuntary, is used as a substitute for payments between enterprises and from the enterprises to the Social Security Fund and other components of the state budget. It lessens the severity of tight monetary policy being pursued by the Central Bank in its attempt to harden the budget constraints faced by

Table 2.7 Interest rates (in per cent per annum)

	Refinancing	Interbank credit rates		Lending rates	
		one week	three months	for less than one year	longer term
1991	24				
Jan				33.1	27.8
Feb				34.2	27.9
Mar				34.8	27.4
Apr				35.2	28.7
May				34.9	30.6
June				35.0	28.8
July				35.7	31.4
Aug				35.8	32.0
Sept				36.2	32.2
Oct				35.7	30.0
Nov				35.7	33.5
Dec				35.5	34.3
1992					
Jan	29			36.0	31.5
Feb		29.5–30	34–35	36.1	33.5
Mar	28	24.5–25	31–31.5	35.5	29.5
Apr		23.5	30–30.5	35.5	32.5
May		23–23.5	27.5–28	35.6	33.0
June	24	16	22		

Source: Monthly Bulletin of the National Bank of Hungary

the enterprises. In 1990, the ratio of inter-enterprise debt to the total indebtedness of enterprises to banks was about 16 per cent. As reported by the National Bank of Hungary, the inter-enterprise debt grew from Ft 90.4 bln ($1.2 bln) in December 1990 to Ft 159.8 bln ($2.1 bln) by November 1991.

The figures in Table 2.8 underestimate the amount of the inter-enterprise debt because the enterprises do not have to report it to the National Bank. According to local experts, the actual amount is close to Ft 300 bln ($4 bln).

Table 2.8 Inter-enterprise debt (Ft bln)

1990	
Dec	90.4
1991	
Jan	116.3
Feb	115.4
Mar	119.4
Apr	128.6
May	137.8
June	144.1
July	137.1
Aug	139.8
Nov	159.8

Source: *Monthly Bulletin of the National Bank of Hungary*

Debt

The Hungarian Government continues to promise that it will abide by all its financial agreements with foreign lenders. The current account surplus in 1991 should make the timely servicing of the external debt easier.

Hungary's hard currency debt decreased slightly from $22.658 bln at the end of 1991 to $21.617 bln in February 1992. Net debt fell by even more as hard currency reserves (not including gold) rose from $1.166 bln at the end of 1990 to $4.095 bln in February 1992. The large inflows of direct foreign investment in 1991 ($1.538 bln) eased Hungary's borrowing requirements.

Foreign trade

Until 1989 all imports required permission from the Foreign Trade Ministry. Tariffs remained moderate, on the average about 16 per cent, but rose for some goods to 60 per cent.

A three-year foreign trade liberalization program was introduced on January 1, 1989. In the first wave, about 40 per cent of the 1988 hard currency imports were liberalized – mostly machinery and certain kinds of consumer electronics. In the second stage, implemented in 1990, most of the imports of the chemical and metallurgical products were freed. At the beginning of 1991, energy resources, some foodstuffs, copper, cellulose, cotton, and other products were added to the list of liberalized goods.

Also in 1991, a "global quota" system for non-liberalized consumer goods was instituted. This system set the aggregate value of imports of some products (mainly shoes, textiles, clothes, detergents, tobacco, and some kinds of foodstuffs). For example, the maximum amount of money that could be spent to import shoes in 1991 was $2.4 mln. The system also prescribed the distribution of the quota over the exporting countries. For instance, 38 per cent of the total quota of imports of household detergents was allocated to German suppliers, 16 per cent to imports from Austria and the rest to various other countries. The would-be importer of the products affected by these restrictions had to obtain permission from the Foreign Trade Ministry, which it gave on a "first come first served" basis. In 1991, most of the quotas were binding, that is the demand for import permissions was higher than the supply, and there was an informal secondary market for the permissions. This quota system is estimated to have affected less than 10 per cent of the value of total imports. However, most of these import restrictions were eliminated in 1992.

The elimination of the barter and payment systems linked with Comecon trade caused a significant change in the external trade position of Hungary in 1990 and 1991. In 1990, about 46 per cent of the value of Hungarian exports was directed toward the Eastern European region. This proportion fell to 23 per cent in 1991. At the same time the proportion of exports to the countries with developed market economies increased from 47 per cent in 1990 to 70 per cent in 1991.

Although exports to the former Comecon countries dropped by 54 per cent in 1991, the convertible part of these exports actually increased by $804 mln. This together with a $1.9 bln increase of exports to the developed market economies accounted for a 38 per cent increase in the Hungarian convertible currency exports in 1991.

A similar pattern emerged for imports. Hungarian imports from the former Comecon countries plummeted by 64 per cent, while imports from the developed market economies increased by 62 per cent. However, the convertible currency imports increased by over $5 bln, resulting in a trade deficit of nearly $1.5 bln.

The forint is not a fully convertible currency. However, commercial buying and selling of the forint for business purposes and for the repatriation of investments and profits by foreign investors is not restricted. Private individuals can buy only a limited amount of foreign currency ($50 per annum). Nevertheless, the black market premium on hard currencies ranks below 10 per cent. Hungarian citizens are allowed to have bank accounts in foreign currency and the origin of the money is not investigated. New rules on exchange controls are to be implemented in 1993, and full convertibility of the forint is planned for 1994–95.

The Hungarian National Bank sets the official exchange rate for the forint against a basket of ten currencies, weighted according to the structure of Hungarian foreign trade. In December 1991, the National Bank began to fix the rate for the same day, rather than for the next day, as had been the case.

Since 1989, all of the banks have been allowed to collect hard currency deposits. Since 1990, transactions related to foreign trade have been liberalized. Domestic companies are permitted to buy foreign currency to pay for imports at the current exchange rate as long as the import is on the list of liberalized goods or the permission to import has been secured.

3. PRESENT FORMS OF OWNERSHIP

3A. Legal framework of economic activity

Existing and planned legislation concerning property rights

The following laws are the most important legal norms defining property rights (including acts relating to privatization) and existing forms of business organization in Hungary:

— Law No. 33 of 1984 on Enterprise Council, amending Law No. 6 of 1977 on State Enterprises;
— Law No. I of 1987 on Lands;
— Law No. VI of 1988 (as amended) on Business Societies, Associations, Companies and Ventures (Company Law);
— Law No. XXIV of 1988 on Foreign Investment in Hungary;
— Law No. XIII of 1989 on the Transformation of Economic Organizations and Business Associations (Transformation Law);
— Law No. VII of 1990 (as amended) on the State Property Agency and on the Management of State Property in State Enterprises;
— Law No. VIII of 1990 on the Protection of Property Entrusted to State Enterprises;
— Law No. LXXIV of 1990 on the Privatization, Alienation, and

Utilization of State-Owned Enterprises Engaged in Retail Trade,
Catering and Consumer Services (Preprivatization Law);
— Law No. XXV of 1991 on Partial Compensation for Damages
Unlawfully Caused by the State to Properties Owned by Citizens in
the Interest of Settling Ownership Relations;
— Law No. XXXIII of 1991 on Transferring Certain State Properties
into the Ownership of Local Governments;
— Law No. I of 1992 on Cooperatives;
— Law No. II of 1992 on the Entry into Force of Law I of 1992 and the
Rules of Transition (Cooperative Transition Law).

Recognized forms of business organizations

STATE ENTERPRISES
The standard unit of the communist economy was the state or
"socialized" enterprise (SE). While a multitude of laws and other
normative acts regulated the behavior of these units, the authorities
never considered it very important to give a precise legal meaning to
the ownership of the SEs. In theory, their being "socialized" meant
that they belonged to the people as a whole. In practice, during the
"classical" period of communist rule, they were more akin to
administrative units of the state apparatus (the sectoral ministries)
than to legal entities similar to Western corporations. In particular, the
questions of state regulation, managerial discretion, and ownership
control were never separated from one another, leaving no clear boundaries between the ministries, the state budget, the banks, and the
enterprises themselves. The special feature of the Hungarian economy
under communism was the fact that, beginning in 1968 and increasingly in the 1980s, the socialized enterprises were given much greater
autonomy than in other countries in the region. An important
milestone in this progression was the 1984 Law on Enterprise Councils, which still largely determines the legal status of the socialized
enterprises.

The Law on Enterprise Councils divided the state enterprises into
three categories. The first category contained those units, such as
utilities and other strategic enterprises, which were to remain under
direct state control. These units (altogether approximately one-third of
all the enterprises), referred to as "enterprises under state supervision," continued to be subordinated to the responsible sectoral
minister. In the remaining two categories of state enterprises, however,
the law introduced a self-management system, which gave the insiders

effective control over a number of crucial decisions, including the appointment of the chief executive and such structural reorganizations as mergers, subdivisions, and joint-ventures. Small SEs with up to 500 employees were grouped in a separate category, and their governance was placed in the hands of a council elected by the employees. In all medium and large enterprises, grouped in the third category, the role of the state was to be taken up by newly created enterprise councils, with 50 per cent of the council membership elected by the workers, 33 per cent coming from the higher level of management, one person appointed by the sectoral ministry, and the rest designated by the managing director. While a casual observer might conclude that the Law on Enterprise Councils gave the employees a major role in the governance of Hungarian socialized enterprises, knowledgeable local observers agree that they have exerted only minor influence on key enterprise decisions, with the managers retaining most of the control.

COOPERATIVES
In addition to state enterprises, the productive assets of the communist economies were also organized in the form of cooperatives. Cooperatives were particularly numerous in agriculture and services, but they were also common in commerce, housing construction, and a section of the banking sector. According to available estimates, some five million Hungarians were cooperative members in 1991. Despite their designation, however, during much of the communist period, the cooperatives were in fact run much like state enterprises, with membership bearing little relation to genuine ownership. While the Hungarian Constitution (Art. 12, paragraph 1) pledges state support for voluntary cooperatives, the old cooperatives needed to be completely restructured before they could become an integral part of the new legal order.

At the beginning of 1992, the Hungarian parliament adopted a comprehensive package of legislation designed to provide the new legal framework for the operation of cooperatives and for the transition to the new cooperative regime. The basic principles are set down in the Law on Cooperatives, which establishes a governance structure for cooperatives, comprising a General Assembly of members, a Board of Directors (who manage the day-to-day business), and a Supervisory Board (which represents the interests of the members as owners). A two-tier equity structure is also established, distinguishing between "shares" (nontransferable and voting) and "quotas" (transferable, subject to preemptive rights, and nonvoting).

The interim rules are laid down in the Cooperative Transition Law, which required all cooperatives existing at the beginning of 1992 to follow a prescribed transformation procedure and to complete the transition process, depending on the type of cooperative, by July 1992 or the end of the year. Recognizing the involuntary nature of most Hungarian cooperatives, the law provides each member of an existing cooperative with a right of withdrawal. The cooperatives themselves may be dissolved, transformed into joint-stock or limited-liability companies (with savings, credit, and insurance cooperatives limited to joint-stock companies), or restructured in conformity with the Law on Cooperatives.

The bulk of the Cooperative Transition Law is devoted to establishing a workable procedure for the division of cooperative assets – a very complex problem involving asset valuation, the need to separate divisible from indivisible assets, and the formula for the distribution of property among the withdrawing members. In all cases in which more than 10 per cent of members choose to withdraw, the law provides for a two-stage auction. The first stage is open only to members who bid for the cooperative assets with the securities distributed by the cooperative. The second stage is open to the public, and disposes of the remaining assets for cash.

THE COMPANY LAW

The legal basis of business activity has been dramatically changed since January, 1989, when a new law, the 1988 Act on Business Societies, Associations, Companies and Ventures (also known as the Act on Economic Associations and referred to here as the Company Law) came into force. This law regulates the formation, organization and operation of all business entities in Hungary with the exception of cooperatives, sole traders, and businesses created by international treaties. A few well-known companies which escaped nationalization in the 1950s are also unaffected by the Company Law.

The Company Law provides for six types of business organizations:

- ordinary partnerships;
- limited partnerships;
- business unions;
- joint companies;
- limited-liability companies;
- joint-stock companies.

Of these forms, all but ordinary and limited partnerships have legal personality.

Ordinary partnership Ordinary partnerships are formed by a Contract of Association, and can be identified by the "kkt" designation in the name of the firm. Partnerships can consist of legal or natural persons, and all members are jointly and severally liable for all obligations of the partnership.

Limited partnership A limited partnership is formed when partners undertake to carry on a common economic activity and when the liability of at least one partner is unlimited (jointly and severally with the other general partners) and the liability of at least one of the partners is limited to the extent of his (its) capital contribution. Full partners are obligated to participate actively in all business activities.

Business union A business union (denoted by the "egyesules" in the firm name) may be established only by legal persons for the purpose of enhancing the profitability of, and harmonizing, their business activities, as well as to represent their business interests. A business union is a non profit making organization and is governed by a Council of Managers. The members of the union have full joint and several liability for the debts of the union.

Joint company A joint company (denoted by the "kv" in the firm name) is a profit-oriented business formed by two or more legal entities. If the property of the company does not cover its liabilities, the members of the company are liable jointly as collateral guarantors in proportion to their contributions.

A joint company is governed by a Council of Managers. Each member, regardless of the amount of its contribution, appoints one representative to the Council. Profits are divided among members in proportion to their contributions.

Limited-liability company The limited-liability company (LLC) (denoted by the "Kft" or "Ltd." in the firm name) is a business organization shielding its stakeholders from personal liability and providing them with considerable flexibility in structure and management. It is also one of the two major types of economic entities into which a state-owned enterprises may be converted. (See Section 5 on corporatization below.)

The minimum capitalization of an LLC is Ft 1 mln. An LLC is formed with capital divided into so-called "quotas," or participation certificates, of a stated amount (but not less than Ft 100,000). Liability of a quotaholder is limited to the payment of his capital contribution. Quotaholders cannot be publicly solicited, and the existing quotaholders have preemptive rights with respect to the purchase of quotas put up for sale and new quotas issued to increase the capital of their LLC.

The governing body of the LLC is the Quotaholders' Meeting, while the day-to-day operations are controlled by managers. The LLC must also appoint a Supervisory Board (elected by the Meeting) if the company has capital of over Ft 20 mln, if there are more than twenty-five quotaholders, or if the number of employees exceeds two hundred.

Joint-stock company A joint-stock company (denoted by the "rt" in the firm name) is a familiar European business organization formed with capital divided into shares of a stated nominal value. The minimum share capital of a joint-stock company is Ft 10 mln. The liability of each shareholder is limited to the value of his shares.

While a joint-stock company may have different classes of shareholders, all shareholders of the same class must have the same rights, and the nominal value of all shares of a given class must be equal. A joint-stock company can issue bearer or registered shares, but foreigners may purchase only registered shares.[2] Shares with full rights can be issued to the workers for no consideration or at a discount, but they must be issued from the assets of the company which exceed the existing share capital, and they must not exceed 10 per cent of the total share capital after the issue. Also, the shares issued to workers must be registered shares freely transferable among the employees and the pensioners of the company.

The share capital of a joint-stock company can be secured by a public subscription based on a prospectus issued by the promoter, which includes information prescribed by law about the proposed company. Among the mandatory disclosure requirements are the privileges of the promoters, the identification and value of any contribution in kind, and the number of shares to be given for such contribution.

As an alternative to public subscription, the promoters of a joint-stock company who are not natural persons can also arrange for all the

---

[2] A company owned totally or in the majority by foreigners also cannot obtain a majority interest in another company.

shares to be purchased by themselves. (This technique is termed a "private formation".) A joint-stock company can also be formed with a single shareholder if the shareholder is a state-financed organization or a financial institution.

The governance structure of the joint-stock company follows the pattern common in Central Europe. The supreme governing body is the General Meeting of the shareholders, which has extensive authority on most important questions. The management body is the Board of Directors, elected by the shareholder meeting, while the oversight functions are performed by the Supervisory Board.

Joint venture See the next subsection for the discussion of joint ventures.

Regulations governing foreign ownership

Foreign companies have been able to establish joint ventures with Hungarian enterprises since 1974. The basic legislation governing foreign economic activity today is Law No. XXIV of 1988 on Foreign Investments in Hungary. This law regulates the establishment of foreign business in Hungary, the operation of wholly or partly foreign-owned businesses, and the acquisition of shares in existing businesses by foreign investors.

Under the law, foreign investment must be registered, but no special permission is required for a foreign investor to set up a business (whether wholly owned or a joint venture), or to buy shares (including, in most cases, acquiring a majority stake) in an existing business association.[3] The procedure for the initiation, selection, and approval of foreign investments and joint ventures does not differ from the procedures for domestic private investment. There are also no restrictions on the repatriation of profits or capital.

The Hungarian Constitution contains guarantees against confiscation of private property, and the Law on Foreign Investments contains specific provisions on the protection of foreign investment. The law prescribes full and prompt indemnification, in the currency in which the investment was made, for any loss due to nationalization or expropriation.

---

[3] Foreigners cannot purchase bearer shares, however, and must covert them to registered shares within one year of acquisition by gift or inheritance. Also, foreign-owned companies cannot purchase a majority of another Hungarian company.

Foreign ownership in the financial sphere is subject to certain restrictions. Most important among them is the requirement of permission from the Ministry of Finance for a foreign investor's acquisition of a majority stake in a bank, or a foreign person's purchase of the state interest in commercial banks, financial institutions, and insurance companies. (There is, however, a significant foreign participation in the Hungarian financial sector, amounting to over 11 per cent of the banking system.)

There are also restrictions on foreign ownership of land. Foreign-owned businesses or joint ventures with foreign participation are allowed to purchase real estate, without any special permits, in connection with the economic activity specified in their articles of association. However, in any other context, the 1987 Law on Lands stipulates that companies and organizations not legally domiciled in Hungary, as well as foreign individuals, cannot acquire real estate (whether by purchase, gift, or exchange) without obtaining prior permission from the Ministry of Finance.

Except in special cases, foreign investors are also excluded from participation in the preprivatization program designed to sell state-owned retail outlets, catering, and consumer services (see subsection on preprivatization in Section 4B). While the restrictions under this law prevent foreigners from buying these types of property (including shops) directly from the state, they are free to purchase them in the secondary market from the Hungarians who have bought them from the state.

Other, less formal restrictions on foreign ownership, principally relating to the purchase of companies enjoying a monopoly position, public utilities, and traditional trade names, are contained in the initial Property Policy Guidelines issued by the parliament for the State Property Agency. In light of the vagueness of the Guidelines and the parliament's failure to reissue them on an annual basis, as required by law, the restrictions involved here may have lost some of their legal significance.

Companies with foreign participation of at least 30 per cent enjoy significant tax privileges, if they are involved in certain types of activities (high-tech industries, including semiconductors and consumer electronics, transport vehicle manufacturing, and hotel construction) and if their founding capital exceeds Ft 50 mln. The tax reductions range from 40 to 100 per cent and extend up to ten years. Reinvestment of dividends by foreign citizens is also tax exempt, and no duty is imposed on means of production brought into the country as in-kind contributions, or purchased with the funds from the convertible currency cash contribution, of the foreign partner of a business association.[4]

Bankruptcy and liquidation

The Hungarian bankruptcy regime was radically altered by the enactment of Law IL of 1991 on Bankruptcy Procedures, Liquidation Procedures and Final Settlement ("Bankruptcy Law"). This law, which went into effect on January 1, 1992, supplants the 1986 bankruptcy law, which itself was amended in 1990. It applies to all business organizations and creditors with the exception of banking institutions.

The Hungarian law envisages bankruptcy (as opposed to liquidation), somewhat analogously with Chapter 11 proceedings in the United States, as a process temporarily shielding the debtor from his creditors, and allowing him an opportunity for restructuring and reorganization. At the same time, by forcing the debtor himself to declare bankruptcy even in the absence of strong pressure from the creditors, the drafters clearly intended to "harden" the "soft budget constraint" characteristic of the state-owned business organizations.

A debtor may declare bankruptcy as long as it has not done so within the previous three years. Interestingly enough, the debtor is forced to file for bankruptcy if it is more than ninety days behind in the payment of its debts, and managers who fail to take this step are made personally liable for the losses originating from the delay. Clearly, among the intentions of the drafters was to break the chain of forced inter-firm indebtedness endemic in the postcommunist countries. (For inter-firm credit in Hungary, see subsection on inter-enterprise debt in Section 2). The important question concerning the law's effectiveness in this respect is whether the offending state enterprises will be able to obtain additional sources of credit from their accommodating bankers and suppliers, thus remaining nominally solvent and escaping the strictures of the law.

Within fifteen days of the debtor's announcement, the court commences the bankruptcy procedure and its writ is published in the

---

[4] For more information on the treatment of foreign investment in Hungary, see Tivadar Faur, "Foreign Capital in Hungary's Privatization," in J. Earle, R. Frydman and A. Rapaczynski (1992), (eds.), *Privatization in the Transition to a Market Economy* (Pinter Publishers and St. Martin's Press, 1992).

Firm Registry Gazette. Publication acts as a ninety-day automatic stay on pecuniary claims against the debtor except those based on wages, alimony, annuities, and similar claims.[5] Upon a petition from the creditors, the court also appoints a bankruptcy trustee who exercises supervision over the property of the debtor. In this role, the trustee may attack the contracts entered into within one year before bankruptcy which, in the trustee's opinion, were entered into with insufficient consideration.

A debtor in bankruptcy is charged with preparing a compromise plan for restoring solvency and presenting it to the creditors for approval. If a compromise is reached with all of the creditors,[6] the court declares the procedure at an end. If no agreement is reached during the moratorium period, the debtor must report this failure to the court, and liquidation procedures begin within fifteen days.

The liquidation procedure, leading to the company's potential dissolution and the distribution of its assets among the creditors, may be initiated at the unsuccessful conclusion of bankruptcy proceedings, at the request of the debtor, or at the request of a creditor.

Upon the designation of insolvency, the court appoints a liquidator responsible for winding up the business and protecting any balance remaining after the satisfaction of the outstanding debts. In the event that all creditors cannot be satisfied from the assets of the debtor, a payment priority list has been established, with the costs of liquidation (including wages), mortgage claims, other benefits of the employees, and taxes to be satisfied first, followed by payments to secured and unsecured creditors, and penalties for unpaid taxes to the budget and the Social Security Fund. The lowering of the priority of the penalties for unpaid taxes has been one of the more important changes brought about by the new Bankruptcy Law. The penalties, which could be very large, previously ranked together with mortgage claims, and thus often left the remaining creditors empty-handed and discouraged them from initiating the whole procedure.

While the liquidation is in process, the debtor and the creditors may still conclude a compromise agreement, restoring the debtor's solvency and terminating the whole proceeding. It is interesting to note that

---

[5] The moratorium may be extended by thirty days at the joint request of the debtor and creditors.

[6] The law requires unanimous consent of all of the creditors, which clearly raises the possibility of strategic behavior.

creditor unanimity is no longer required at this point, and a valid compromise agreement can be achieved if one-half of the creditors, holding at least two-thirds of the total claims, approve the compromise plan, which is then binding on the remaining creditors.

The effect of the change in the bankruptcy law has been immediately apparent. From 1986 through 1991, when the old bankruptcy law was in effect, only a handful of companies were liquidated, although the number of filings was much higher (1,000 companies, 50 of which were state enterprises). By contrast, at the end of April 1992, after only four months of the new law's operation, 381 Hungarian business organizations were under bankruptcy and 883 were under liquidation. The bankrupt companies had total income last year of Ft 119 bln, a fifth of which was derived from exports. The debt of those companies amounted to Ft 84 bln at the end of 1991, and their employment totaled 93,000 people.

But all this is still only a fraction of the Hungarian companies in the red. According to a report issued by the Industry Minister, 40–45 per cent of the industrial companies under direct state authority are facing bankruptcy. This prospect raises serious concerns about whether standard bankruptcy proceedings are the best way of resolving the problem of restructuring such a large fraction of the Hungarian economy.

The standard view, of course, is that bankruptcy should be an extraordinary event, with privatization remaining the most important tool of restructuring in Eastern Europe. In an interesting twist, however, the accounting firm of Price Waterhouse has been recently recommending bankruptcy to some Hungarian state firms as an alternative to the regular form of privatization, bypassing the process dominated by the State Property Agency (SPA) charged with the supervision of the transactions involving the sale of state assets. In this scenario selected assets of the state firms would be acquired by new entrepreneurs, dealing directly with the commercial banks as the main creditors and effective post-bankruptcy owners, rather than the SPA bureaucracy.

3B. Structure of ownership

Little data have been obtained on the distribution of companies and state enterprises by ownership category in Hungary. Information systems have not developed quickly enough to record the results of

Table 3B.1 Number of economic organizations

	1988 Dec	1989 Dec	1990 June	1990 Dec	1991 June	1991 Dec
State enterprises	2,377	2,399	2,408	2,363	2,362	2,267
Companies						
Joint-stock	116	307	520	646	868	1,005
Limited-liability	451	4,485	12,159	18,317	30,949	36,420
Partnerships and other entities	387	432	479	438	421	420
Cooperatives						
Agricultural	1,333	1,333	1,341	1,348	1,406	1,418
Other	2,439	2,510	2,569	2,629	2,694	2,705
Business unions and other organizations	0	0	66	65	63	0

Source: Monthly Statistical Bulletin no. 12/1991 and earlier issues, cited in *PlanEcon*

the rapid decentralization of economic control, having been designed to report almost exclusively on large state-owned units. A new statistical system is only now in the process of establishment, and the staff of the SPA concentrates on negotiating and regulating current transactions rather than on keeping statistics.

Nonetheless, certain data can provide evidence about the growth of the private sector. There has, for example, been enormous growth in the number of registered economic units; Table 3B.1 shows in particular the large increase in both joint-stock and limited-liability companies. Some of these are wholly-owned subsidiaries of state enterprises, some have mixed state and private ownership, and a large number are probably new private companies. Moreover, over 85 per cent of the new units were founded "without legal precedents," implying that there was no contribution of capital from a state enterprise, or, in other words, that in at least these cases there was no "partial transformation" resulting in full or partial state ownership of the new units.

Further circumstantial evidence on private sector growth appears in Table 3B.2, which provides the size distribution of registered economic units according to the number of employees. There is a high correlation between, on the one hand, the level and growth of the number of companies in the smallest group (employing less than twenty-one workers) and, on the other hand, the level and growth of the number

Table 3B.2 Number of companies (classified by employment)

Total number of companies	June 1990	Dec 1990	June 1991	Dec 1991	June 1992
Total number of companies employing:					
More than 300	2,560	2,599	2,376	2,395	1,935
51–300	4,199	4,469	5,030	5,372	5,589
21–50	3,435	4,129	5,303	6,169	6,521
Under 21	11,242	16,465	25,310	36,809	46,645
Under liquidation or unknown	1,821	1,808	1,936	2,011	1,604

Source: Central Statistical Office

of limited-liability companies already shown in Table 3B.1. Analysis of data on the size distribution according to legal form also reveals that nearly all limited-liability companies (about 92 per cent) have fewer than fifty employees and most (about three quarters) have fewer than twenty. It thus seems probable that most of these newly established companies are private companies, many perhaps of the "family business" type.[7]

In Hungary, however, it is also necessary to emphasize the importance of units with mixed ownership, created through the processes described below in Section 4 on privatization and Section 5 on corporatization. The State Property Agency, other enterprises, banks that are partially state-owned, other units of mixed ownership, as well as domestic private and foreign private and state investors may be joint owners of these mixed ownership cases. Although many individual cases can be cited, precise data about the magnitudes involved are unfortunately unavailable. The existence of cross-ownership and of ownership "chains," with various links belonging to

[7] This inference is further buttressed by the size of partial transformations: in the early period of spontaneous privatization, from 1987 to mid-1990, subsidiaries were created by state enterprises involving on average 10 per cent of the capital of the original enterprise. Given the huge size of most enterprises (only 3 per cent had fewer than twenty employees in June 1991 and about 58 per cent had over 300), and assuming that capital–labor ratios were not enormously different from those in the parent companies, and that each parent founded less than a large number of subsidiaries, most of the new units created in this fashion (i.e. that remained fully or partially state-owned) must have had far more than twenty employees.

state, private, and mixed units, render it next to impossible even conceptually to sort out who the real owner is and who is really in control.

According to the SPA's estimates, more than 10 per cent of former state assets are already controlled by the private sector. This figure represents the sum of (i) the non-state shares in companies which originated from partial or full transformation of state enterprises, but where the state still has a majority share; (ii) the property protection cases (sale of part of the assets to a non-state company or individual); and (iii) the *total* share capital of companies in which the share of the private sector exceeds 50 per cent. Further information on the extent of privatization can be found in the following subsection on foreign investment and at the end of Section 4B on privatization below.

Apart from the data (or lack thereof) on ownership of capital, some light on the size of the private sector may be shed also by employment data. An independent estimate,[8] based on data from the Central Statistical Office, suggests that at least 20 per cent of the active labor force was employed in the private sector in 1990. This figure is considered very conservative, and the proportion is certainly growing rapidly, but more recent figures are still unobtainable.

THE EXTENT OF DIRECT FOREIGN INVESTMENT AND JOINT VENTURES

Foreigners are a significant part of the ownership structure in Hungary; in fact, most privatization takes place through foreign investment. On the other hand, not all foreign investment involves the purchase of state assets: it may be "greenfield" investment, or it may involve private Hungarian assets. In a paradoxical twist, there may even be cases where foreign investment represents "reverse privatization," for instance when a bank owned by a foreign government or a former Comecon country state enterprise purchases a private Hungarian asset. Unfortunately, the data are insufficient for the relative size of these different categories to be distinguished. Nonetheless, it is clear that Hungary has attracted the most foreign investment of any of the countries of Eastern Europe.

According to the SPA, the amount of foreign investment in Hungary as of August 1992 totaled $4.1 bln.

The existing data allow no distinction to be drawn between direct foreign investment and joint ventures. Comparison of the totals in

---

[8] Unpublished information from the Research Institute for Labor.

Table 3B.3 Nationality of foreign investors, transactions* processed by the SPA (March 1990 to September 30, 1992)

Country	Number of companies	Total equity (Ft mln)	Foreign equity (Ft mln)
Austria	45	52,307	22,863
Germany	23	32,892	15,024
United Kingdom	20	16,241	8,464
France	10	16,911	5,790
Italy	7	5,294	2,713
The Netherlands	4	13,530	7,836
Switzerland	5	12,551	6,140
Sweden	4	5,464	4,766
USA	3	5,056	3,068
Russia	3	11,701	3,562
Other	3	854	328
Total	127	172,801	80,554

* Transformations, joint ventures, and sales of assets

Source: SPA

Table 3B.4 Nationality of foreign investors, all transactions as of August 1992

Country	Gross capital inflow ($ mln)
USA	900
Germany	500
Austria	400
UK	250
France	250
Other	1,000
Total	4,100

Source: Ministry of International Economic Relations

Tables 3B.3 and 3B.4 and 3B.5 shows that only about one per cent of the number and 25 per cent of the foreign capital in foreign investment transactions are processed by the SPA. This is due to the fact that foreign investors frequently set up new companies or participate in joint ventures involving relatively small amounts of capital, in which case they fall outside of the jurisdiction of the SPA.

Table 3B.5 Size distribution of companies involving foreign investors

Equity (Ft mln)	Number of companies		
	1990	1991	June 1992
0–1	2,019	3,406	4,785
1.1–10	2,453	3,839	4,394
10.1–50	696	1,009	1,081
50.1–100	178	320	348
More than 100	347	543	588
Total	5,693	9,117	11,196
Equity (Ft mln)	Total equity (in Ft bln)		
	1990	1991	June 1992
0–1	2.0	3.4	4.8
1.1–10	7.7	12.3	14.0
10.1–50	17.7	24.9	26.7
50.1–100	12.8	22.9	24.7
More than 100	233.9	412.1	443.8
Total	274.1	475.6	514.0

Source: Central Statistical Office
The CSO reports all foreign investment transactions, while the SPA figures in Tables 3B.3, 3B.4, 3B.6, and 3B.7 reflect only those which have received SPA approval.

Most major foreign investors are industrial companies from the same branch of industry as the purchased company. Institutional investors have so far shown little interest because of the rudimentary capital market. Large foreign banks may be interested in buying their Hungarian counterparts (i.e. the big commercial banks), but restrictions make it difficult, if not impossible. Of course, foreign investors can and do participate in the privatization of smaller banks, but these are not so attractive as they lack the nationwide branch chains. Smaller investors usually engage in trade or services.

Foreign investors frequently seek to gain a majority share in the companies either straightforwardly or through contracts which give

Table 3B.6 Sectoral breakdown of foreign investment, approved by SPA (March 1990 to September 30, 1992)

Sector	Number of companies with foreign equity	Total equity (Ft mln)	Foreign equity (Ft mln)
1. Agriculture	3	875	429
2. Food processing	23	54,515	27,397
3. Mining	2	1,150	778
4. Building material	10	7,586	4,198
5. Construction	19	10,216	6,123
6. Metallurgy	5	4,486	2,478
7. Machinery	22	37,239	24,469
8. Chemical industry	7	27,858	9,161
9. Trade	17	15,445	5,490
10. Other	4	4,101	3,020
Total	132	184,909	92,528

Source: SPA
The small discrepancies in the total and size of foreign investments in tables 3B.3, 3B.6, and 3B.7 seem to be due to incomplete reporting within the SPA

them an option to buy a majority share at a later date. But a remarkable feature of foreign investment in Hungary is the relatively high prevalence of minority stakes held by foreigners: the Hungarian managers often retain their positions of control. One interpretation of this somewhat unusual phenomenon is that deals have been struck between the managers and the foreign investors, perhaps an under-valuation of Hungarian assets in exchange for preservation of the managers' positions.

Foreign investors sometimes slash employment, but often provisions in the sale contract prevent this in the short term. Joint ventures are more commonly formed by buying through partial transformation, purchasing or receiving contributions of state assets, and it seems clear that the foreign investors would pick only the relatively well function-ing parts. This is the likely explanation for the fact that large closures have not been necessary among joint ventures to date (with the excep-tion of the Metallurgy Plant of Ozd).

Table 3B.7 Privatization with foreign participation (permits approved by SPA until September 30, 1992)

Mode*	Number	Total equity (Ft mln)	Foreign equity (Ft mln)
1. Transformation of SEs*	49	86,280	35,888
With foreign stake			
50 per cent or more	17	23,203	19,017
Less than 50 per cent	32	63,077	16,871
2. Joint ventures with SOE	64	63,116	27,666
With foreign stake			
50 per cent or more	29	20,244	11,348
Less than 50 per cent	35	42,872	16,318
3. Sale of assets	22	37,954	29,827
With foreign stake			
50 per cent or more	20	34,794	29,187
Less than 50 per cent	2	3,160	640
Total	135	187,350	93,381
With foreign stake			
50 per cent or more	66	78,241	59,552
Less than 50 per cent	69	109,109	33,829

* These cases include only those transformations in which foreigners participated.

Source: SPA

4. THE PRIVATIZATION PROCESS

Introduction

Unlike most other countries of the region, Hungary's economic system had undergone a significant amount of change even prior to the abandonment of communist rule in 1989. However, it was not until after the general election in early 1990, which resulted in the formation of the center-right government led by Jozsef Antall of the Hungarian Democratic Forum, that the task of drawing up a comprehensive program for the transition to a market economy began in earnest. The plans envisage simultaneous progress on privatization, macroeconomic stabilization, and economic reforms.

The government's declared objectives are, first, to reduce the share of state-owned assets in the "competitive sector," which excludes those large enterprises expected to remain under direct state control, to about 50 per cent by 1994 and, second, to facilitate simultaneously the emergence of the institutional framework of a working market economy. Achieving the 50 per cent target will necessitate both accelerating the privatization of state owned assets and encouraging the rapid development of the private sector. The significance of such a target depends of course on the definition of "private," particularly given the importance of mixed ownership in the Hungarian economy. The enormous difficulties in even measuring the state share, due to problems of valuation and the inadequacy of the data, also obscure the meaning of this target for the pace of privatization.

Compared to the other communist countries, Hungary was relatively open to free market concepts and to foreign investment even prior to 1989, and thus attracted the liveliest initial foreign interest in privatization. The early activity, however, consisted to a great extent of sales in those areas of the economy where the need for restructuring was least acute, the problems of debt were least intractable, and the issues of ownership were least problematic. Typically these were manufacturing units in consumer industries, where foreign investors could identify attractive opportunities and gain access to new markets. Other sectors of the economy were less straightforward to privatize, however, and the prospect remained that substantial numbers of state enterprises requiring major restructuring would attract no buyers.

These looming difficulties meant that the process of privatization risked losing rather than gaining impetus. Moreover, while support for the broad objective of creating a free market economy was initially widespread, the process received increasing criticism from several different angles. Many Hungarians came to see privatization sales as mainly benefitting foreign companies acquiring the most attractive businesses. Suspicion also grew that much of the "spontaneous privatization" either excessively favored managers or practically allowed them to appropriate state assets outright. These criticisms led to attempts to improve the monitoring and control of the process as well as to centralize and accelerate it through the establishment of the State Property Agency (SPA) in March 1990. Adverse reactions then developed against the growing extent of bureaucratic control exercised by the SPA and its perceived failures in accelerating and adequately controlling the process. Some elements of decentralization have been subsequently introduced.

4A. Organizational structure of state regulation of privatization

The process of large-scale privatization in Hungary is remarkably decentralized, relying predominantly on enterprise managers to initiate and carry out both corporatization[9] and privatization. This characteristic feature of Hungarian privatization, further described in Section 4B below, is important to bear in mind when considering the role of state regulation of privatization.

State regulation of privatization

Privatization is regulated by the State Property Agency (SPA), established by Law No. VII in March 1990. Although Hungary has no privatization ministry, the SPA is supervised by the government, and a minister without portfolio is assigned the responsibility for privatization (currently Tamas Szabo).

The SPA Managing Director (currently Lajos Csepi) and the eleven members of its Board of Directors are appointed to five-year terms and may be dismissed by the Prime Minister. The composition of the Board is not specified in the law; it currently includes seven members of governmental organizations and ministries (Industry and Trade, Agriculture, and Finance). The Board has the final responsibility to make decisions on transformations, privatizations and sales; however, it delegates this authority to the Managing Director for transformations (full or partial) involving less than Ft 500 mln and 1,000 employees, and for sales involving less than Ft 300 mln of assets from state enterprises to non-state companies.

The Annual Report of the SPA must be submitted to the parliament. Parliament is also responsible for setting the annual Property Policy Guidelines, which the SPA must observe in making its decisions. These guidelines are supposed to be revised each year to reflect the rapidly changing circumstances in which privatization must be carried out. In practice, however, the guidelines have been extended several times but never revised, and recently they have not even been renewed but simply allowed to expire, seemingly under the rationale that a new privatization law that will certainly change the basic legal

---

[9] Section 5 below contains a detailed description of corporatization (usually referred to as "transformation" in Hungary). Corporatization and privatization processes tend to be thoroughly intertwined in Hungary, so much so that the reader may benefit from reading Section 5 first.

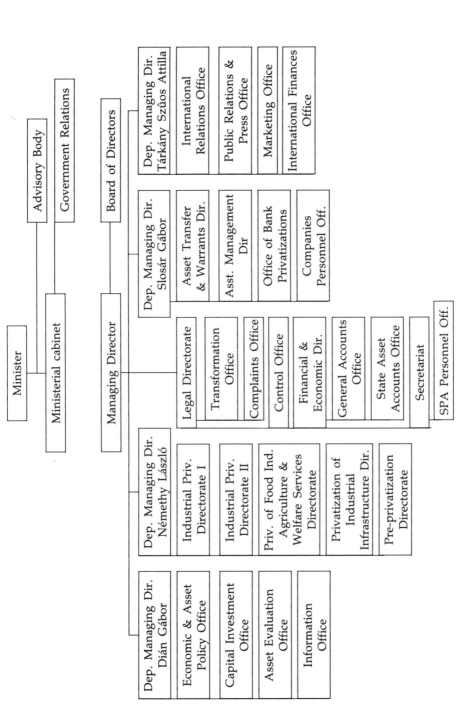

Chart 4A.1 Organizational structure of the SPA

framework is anticipated soon. The parliament has thus failed to wield even the formal influence it might have exercised over the actions of the SPA.[10] Aside from governmental supervision and these parliamentary controls, the SPA is independent, and its decisions cannot be appealed.

Principles of SPA policy

The main principles of the Property Policy Guidelines are competition, transparency and objective valuation. The guidelines require the SPA to promote transformation and privatization transactions that support economic competition, reduce the number of economic units in monopoly positions, create new jobs, and help develop efficient management skills that adopt new technology and attract foreign working capital. The promotion of competition and decentralization seems to receive little weight in practice.

Regarding foreign buyers, the SPA is supposed to favor sales to investors whose business plans envisage further investment of both money and expertise and avoid those that would negatively affect the hard currency balance, such as, for instance, a foreign acquisition of a company with monopoly power in the domestic market but little income from hard currency exports. The SPA is also apparently expected to protect the country's special natural endowments and characteristically Hungarian products with internationally known trademarks.

The guidelines thus represent a statement of what is desirable, rather than precisely specifying policies that must be followed: it is therefore impossible to determine whether the SPA is properly observing them. Moreover, incentives of the staff of the SPA are such that their most important concern may rather be to gain the highest price in the privatization sale, since the Agency's compensation system rewards them with bonuses tied to the revenue from the privatization sales they have accomplished.

The legal basis of SPA action – the tasks of the SPA

In accordance with the law establishing the SPA, state property in

---

[10] See Laszlo Urban, "The Role of the Parliament in Hungary's Privatization," forthcoming in Earle, Frydman and Rapaczynski, *Privatization in the Transition to a Market Economy*, Pinter Publishers and St. Martin's Press, 1992.

corporations (limited-liability and joint-stock companies) is held by the SPA. The volume of this property is expected to grow with an increase in transformations, but then be reduced as a result of privatization. The authority and tasks of the SPA are determined by several laws:

- the modified Law No. XIII of 1989 on the Transformation of State Enterprises (the "Transformation Law");
- the modified Law No. VII of 1990 on the State Property Agency and on the Management of State Property in State Enterprises;
- the modified Law No. VIII of 1990 on Protection of State Property Entrusted to State Enterprises;
- Property Policy Guidelines (annual);
- Law No. LXXIV of 1990 on Privatization of Properties of the State in the Retail Trade, Catering, and Consumption Services (the "Preprivatization Law").

According to these laws, the State Property Agency has five different tasks. The first is the protection of state property during transformation: to examine the intentions of state enterprises with regard to self-initiated transformation, corporatization and asset sales ("property protection cases"), to assist in the valuation of property, to screen out transactions that damage the state's ownership interests, and to monitor the implementation of approved plans. The second task is managing state-owned property after transformation and that of enterprises taken under state administration. Third, the SPA is sometimes supposed to initiate and prepare privatization programs determined by the government and directly supervise the implementation of the process. Fourth, the SPA is responsible for gathering and distributing information on the privatization process. Fifth, the Department of Preprivatization of the SPA organizes the registration, evaluation, and sale of the retail trade, catering and consumer services units in the Preprivatization Program.

Some attempts have been made or are under consideration to reduce the heavy responsibilities of the SPA in the area of property management. The "Property Supervisory Portfolio Packets" are essentially auctions of contracts to manage groups of enterprises and are supposed to improve and decentralize the exercise of ownership rights over state-owned shares. They have been launched twice: in the first package, seven companies were included with a total share capital of Ft 2,987.9 mln; in the second portfolio package, the number of companies was five, with total capital of Ft 173.0 mln. But both have so far proved a failure. The SPA tried to secure very high returns with no risk, so nobody ventured to participate.

There is also currently a plan under discussion that would found a new state organ, the State Ownership Company, to manage "long-term state holdings." The SPA would continue managing the privatization and asset management of "short-term state holdings."

4B. Overview of privatization programs

A distinguishing feature of the Hungarian transition process is its almost complete reliance on a case-by-case approach to the privatization of property. In the early period of so-called "spontaneous privatization," this individual approach was a result of the fact that the initiative to transform and privatize belonged entirely to enterprise councils, in practice the enterprise managers,[11] with essentially no control from any state organization. After public outcry over questionable transactions in late 1989 and early 1990, the state began to monitor and regulate this behavior; the chief actions were the Law on the Protection of State Property and the establishment and later strengthening of the State Property Agency. Nonetheless, the predominant pattern has remained the treatment of each transaction on its own terms rather than adoption of a set of strict rules applied to all of them. Although formally the SPA as well as enterprise councils now has the right to initiate,[12] managers have in practice continued to predominate in initiating and determining the process, albeit with the necessity to bargain with the SPA over the outcome. The failure of the SPA's attempts to centralize and accelerate the process through the so-called "active privatization" has further reinforced the power of the managers.

---

[11] Managers in Hungary had gradually acquired many ownership rights starting with reforms in 1968. See Laszlo Szakadat, "Property Rights in a Socialist Economy: The Case of Hungary," and Eva Voszka, "Spontaneous Privatization in Hungary," forthcoming in J. Earle, R. Frydman, and A. Rapaczynski (eds.), *Privatization in the Transition to a Market Economy*, Pinter Publishers and St. Martin's Press, 1992.

[12] In the case of enterprises under state supervision, only the SPA has the legal authority to initiate, but the managers may also propose a change of form or ownership. According to Maria Mora, "Changes in the structure and ownership form of state enterprises (1987–1990)" in *Economic Papers*, 1990, Economic Research Institute, and Eva Voszka in J. Earle, R. Frydman, and A. Rapaczynski, this distinction has made little difference in practice: in both the self-managed and state-supervised cases, the initiative has largely belonged to the managers.

It is certainly not the case that there are no rules and no policies for the privatization process in Hungary, but these rules and policies must be understood as functioning only as a framework within which bargaining among individual actors takes place. Laws describe possibilities without placing many rigid constraints on outcomes, which depend more importantly on the circumstances and the relative bargaining power of the actors in particular cases. This characteristic feature of Hungarian privatization renders generalizing about the process extremely difficult. The following sections are therefore only a brief introduction to the broad pattern of developments in Hungary thus far. Future CEU Privatization Project Reports will describe specific aspects of Hungarian privatization in greater detail.

Initiating the privatization of an enterprise

A precondition for privatizing a state enterprise is corporatization ("full transformation" into company form under the Transformation Law, 1989). A part of an enterprise may also be corporatized prior to privatization through the creation of a subsidiary ("partial transformation" under the Company Law, 1988), or it may be sold as an asset. Corporatization, further discussed in Section 5 below, has been encouraged by government policy since at least 1988 and is now mandatory for all enterprises by the end of 1992. However, it is generally not seen as an end in itself. Rather, the purpose is often to make it possible for domestic or foreign investors to acquire ownership stakes. The process of corporatization and the process of privatization are thus frequently linked in practice.

Motivations for corporatizing and for finding new owners may also be intertwined. The enterprise managers may benefit from partial transformation by securing greater independence from outside interference, but full transformation coupled with finding new owners can accomplish the same goal. Some accounts claim that widespread cross-holding relationships among supplier firms remove the property from state control and thereby accomplish this goal. Partial transformation also carries the benefit of leaving the responsibility for old debts with the parent enterprise. The latter creates easier access to new loans, as does full transformation on the argument that goodwill with commercial banks would be created. But sales of shares to outside investors or bringing in new owners through capital increases can also increase credit availability. This can be a crucial factor given that most state enterprises are struggling with the insolvency of their partners and therefore with their own liquidity problems.

Other important motivations for the company managers to initiate privatization include modernization, direct technical transfer, and widening of the market. If an enterprise manages to attract foreign investors, it also benefits from significant tax allowances. The hope of preserving employment and the possibility of receiving shares in the company may be attractions for employees more generally. However, privatization of a company can of course also lead to layoffs and partial or total liquidation, so in many cases insiders have been reluctant to launch a process fraught with such uncertainty.

Taxonomy of Hungarian privatization

SPONTANEOUS PRIVATIZATION
The term "spontaneous privatization" is used in two broad senses in Hungary. The first is the largely uncontrolled process of the "partial transformation" of enterprises, usually but not necessarily associated with acquiring new owners, in the period from 1987 to early 1990. In typical partial transformations, a state enterprise either establishes a wholly-owned subsidiary from which shares may be sold, or the enterprise may contribute some of its assets in kind, which are pooled together with other capital from domestic or foreign (almost exclusively the latter) investors in a joint venture. In either case, new companies are created that are partly owned by the state enterprise. According to unpublished data of the Ministry of Trade and Industry, 40 per cent of state enterprises in industry, trade, and construction had founded several hundred such companies with an average of ten per cent of their assets as of mid-1990.[13] The previous section describes motivations for managers to undertake these actions, and Section 5 below describes the corporatization process more fully.

Until just before the founding of the SPA, this process was largely unmonitored and unregulated, hence the term "spontaneous."[14] On the other hand, it must be emphasized that the result was in many

---

[13] Cited in Eva Voszka (in J. Earle, R. Frydman and A. Rapaczynski, 1992, op. cit.).
[14] But to the degree that it was encouraged and influenced by the state it was not entirely spontaneous. Among the most important influences was the provision that all new economic units, including those founded with assets from state enterprises, between 1988 and 1991 received a 50 per cent reduction in their profit tax. This preference has been discontinued since the beginning of 1992. See Eva Voszka (op. cit.) for further discussion of the role of the state.

cases strictly speaking not "privatization," because even in those cases where there were new owners, they were often state owned banks or other enterprises, for instance in supplier relationships. Broadly, these developments may also be considered privatization, as part of the "process of decomposition and denationalization of the traditional state enterprises."[15] The extent of actual privatization in the narrow sense of transferring property rights to new private owners can be better gauged by the quantity of foreign investment, discussed further below.

A still wider sense in which "spontaneous privatization" is sometimes used is to refer to any enterprise-initiated transformation or privatization transaction. As shown in Table 4B.1, even after the founding of the SPA relatively few approved transformations were initiated by it. Managers still initiate most transactions, often after negotiating contracts with outside investors, and then bargain with the SPA over their approval. Furthermore, although the SPA monitors and regulates transactions, it is not clear that it has had a large effect on the process, outside of perhaps screening out some particularly egregious abuses. In this sense, spontaneous privatization has been the predominant means of privatization in Hungary to date.

ACTIVE PRIVATIZATION
Besides attempting to control better the transactions initiated by managers, the State Property Agency has introduced two "active" programs designed to attract the widest possible interest in the restructuring of the economy, facilitate the acceleration of privatization, attract new investors into Hungary, and establish better coordination of state and company interests.

The First Active Privatization Program   Announced in September 1990, this program comprised twenty of the larger and generally better-performing state enterprises representing a wide cross-section of the national economy. To valuate and sell these enterprises, the SPA sought international consultants with substantial privatization-related experience. The conditions of an open competition were published, and about 300 offers were received. The consultants selected by the SPA included auditing firms and investment banks from England, France, Japan, and Hungary.

---

15 Laszlo Urban (in J. Earle, R. Frydman and A. Rapaczynski, 1992, op. cit.).

The twenty companies operate in a wide range of activities, including tourism, drugs and chemicals, glass-making, wholesale and retail trade, hotel and catering, machinery production, porcelain ware production, exhibition organization, foreign trade, transportation, book printing, housing, scrap processing, plastic production, and building material production. The size of the enterprises also varies greatly: the range of book values is Ft 61 mln to Ft 8.3 bln.

The companies were thought to be in good condition at the time they were first selected. The SPA anticipated that their sale would be completed quickly, that the public would be pleased, and that investors would be encouraged by this experience to take part in further privatization programs. In the event, however, the program has been a nearly complete failure for several reasons.

First, it is believed that the SPA has attempted to obtain unrealistically high prices, higher that any investor would be willing to pay. This may have been due to fears of the accusation that valuable assets had been sold to foreigners at giveaway prices or to the incentive pay received by SPA staff tied to sales revenue, as described above. Second, many of the enterprises have significantly lost value due either to the collapse of Comecon trade or to the worsening of the Hungarian recession. Third, the consultants were slow in valuing the enterprises and learning about the Hungarian economy.

Consequently, by the end of October 1991 only four of the twenty planned transformations were completed. Although by the end of January 1992 the number of completed transformations had jumped to eighteen, there has been only transformation and essentially no privatization, with only a few shares sold to private investors. By contrast, the company-initiated transformations were almost always followed by the successful sales of stakes to non-state investors.

In response to these problems, the SPA has subsequently concentrated on the enterprise-initiated and investor-initiated methods of privatization and refrained from planning any more privatizations under this type of "active" program.

The Second Active Privatization Program This program was designed to deal with the special problems of the so-called "shell enterprises," state enterprises that had transferred a significant part (defined as at least 51 per cent) of their assets to other companies, either subsidiaries or joint ventures. In the extreme case where nearly all assets have been transferred, the head office of the original enterprise has lost all its previous functions and retained only the role of holding entity. The shells have numerous organizational, financial, and legal problems.

One important danger is the loss of state property. The assets of highest value are most likely to have been transferred, leaving the shell with only debts and liabilities. Although the state enterprise can earn dividends from the new companies, this income is unlikely to be in proportion to the value of the enterprise's (usually undervalued) contribution to the company, and most of it goes to service debts incurred before transformation. Not only may the property be lost, but the situation may inhibit the privatization and re-organization of the remaining state assets.

The first phase involves twelve "holding" or "empty" state enterprises owning together more than 115 companies. The SPA does not intend to treat them all in the same way: some of them will probably be split up, while others will be transformed into regular holding companies.

SELF-PRIVATIZATION

In a return to greater decentralization and an attempt to accelerate the process of privatization, the Self-Privatization Program makes possible the transformation and sale of enterprises without direct involvement of the SPA. Enterprises choosing this path of privatization must employ independent consulting and property evaluating companies from a list compiled by the SPA. These consulting companies then arrange the sale, for which they are compensated with a percentage of the price plus bonuses tied to the speed with which the transaction is processed. The SPA must accept the resulting sales, but will impose sanctions on, or exclude from the list, those consulting firms whose procedure is found to have violated legal regulations.

The invitation for consulting firms to participate in this process was published at the beginning of June 1991. Applicant companies are required to have a minimal capital of Ft 10 mln and some previous experience in asset valuation.

As the method was new and untested, in the first stage only 400 small enterprises, with fewer than 300 persons and annual turnover and gross property value less than Ft 300 mln were eligible for the self-privatization program. So far 200 enterprises have contracts with the independent consulting and property evaluating companies. Because the first stage is generally viewed as successful, a second stage of self-privatization is planned in which the gross property value limit will be raised to Ft 1 bln implying that 600 more enterprises could be involved.

Self-privatization is of course a special case of spontaneous or enterprise-initiated privatization. Its special feature is that the role of the SPA is played by the consulting company; while apart from this, the process is just the same as in the case of an SPA regulated trans- actions, the privatization of the privatization process itself raises the possibility of a much less bureaucratic, more market-oriented transfor- mation.

PREPRIVATIZATION

The Preprivatization Program, enacted under Law LXXIV of 1990, concerns small shops in the retail, catering, and consumer service industries. The program began to be implemented by the end of 1990, and initiation of the process for all units was supposed to start no later than September 1992. The method used in over 80 per cent of the sales is an open auction, where the starting price is set by an consulting firm chosen by the SPA.

As in the small privatization programs of other countries, the real estate itself is often (about 70 per cent of the cases) not sold: instead the sale concerns the business, the equipment, the lease of the premises for a ten-year period, and the brand name. Many of the business premises are in fact already rented by private entrepreneurs, dating back to the reforms of "goulash communism." Municipalities are the owner of 80 per cent of these premises, but state enterprises own the businesses. Besides creating competition to operate these businesses and possibly changing the business owner, the chief effect of preprivatization is therefore to eliminate this "middleman" state enterprise, as the property itself usually remains with the municipality.

The state enterprises concerned have of course no interest in cooperating with this program. If they sell all their shops and restaurants, there is no need to have a central "coordinating" unit. A second problem has been that, in response to popular concern that it was selling state property at too low prices, the SPA sometimes set the starting price at auction so high that nobody was interested in buying. Nearly half the auctions are unsuccessful.

Nonetheless, the process of preprivatization accelerated in late 1991, and more than 3,000 out of a total of 10,000 shops had been sold by the end of April, 1992. Many of the remaining shops are ready for sale in the sense that the asset valuation is finished, but about 3,000 cannot be sold because of legal problems, for instance because the activity takes place in the real estate of some other entity.

INVESTOR–INITIATED PRIVATIZATION

The SPA announced a new, investor-initiated privatization method in February 1991 that is supposed to speed up privatization and extend the range of participants. Offers for the purchase of state enterprises or state-owned stocks can be made directly to the SPA. In the first few months after the announcement of investor-initiated privatization nearly 250 offers were made, covering a range of property from fractions of stocks or assets up to the purchase of entire companies. The offers came predominantly from foreign investors. After receiving the offer, the SPA usually calls an open or closed tender to see whether it is competitive. Of course, these tenders are not necessarily won by the investor making the original offer. As of the end of 1991, there were twenty completed cases and seventy to eighty still under way.

DISTRIBUTION OF SHARES TO LOCAL GOVERNMENT

Local governments receive ownership of the shares of a transformed state enterprise to the extent of the value of the enterprise's land that lies within the administrative borders of the given municipality.

CONTRIBUTION OF ASSETS TO STATE SECURITY FUND

There are plans to allocate part of the state's assets to the Social Security Fund, some Ft 300 bln by about 1995. However, the Social Security Investment Fund of the Social Security must first be created.

WORKERS' SHARES AND EMPLOYEE PREFERENCES

In the case of self-managing enterprises, 80 per cent of the proceeds of the sale of state property goes to the state, and 20 per cent is retained by the company,[16] to cover the issue of "workers' shares." These shares can be issued to the extent of 10 per cent of the total capital and can only be traded amongst the workers and pensioners of the company.

The workers and the management of a company can also buy shares preferentially. Preferences depend on the company and are not specified by law. The practice of the SPA is that the workers can buy workers' shares at 90 per cent discount and normal shares for 50 per cent of the price. The sum of the discount on both sales cannot exceed 10 per cent (in some exceptional cases 15 per cent) of the share capital

---

[16] When enterprises under state administration are sold, 100 per cent of the revenue goes to the state.

of the given company or the wage level in the previous year of the particular employee.

COMPENSATION

According to the Law on Compensation, bonds will be issued to former proprietors or their heirs to compensate them for losses due to the confiscation of physical assets (land, shops, houses, livestock, machinery, etc.) under the former regime. This compensation should be distinguished from reprivatization (restitution in kind); instead the bonds bear 17 per cent annual interest and can be used to acquire state property. The owners must report their losses to the Compensation Offices, whereupon compensation bonds are issued on a regressive basis (i.e., the higher the amount of the loss, the lower the percentage of it which will be compensated). A maximum of Ft 5 mln can be received by any individual.

The compensation bonds can be used to buy property (shares) from the SPA, land from the cooperatives, or houses from the local councils, or they may be exchanged with the Social Security Fund for a fixed pension or sold to interested investors. In the first four cases, compensation bonds must be accepted at face value. When the bonds are used to buy shares directly from the SPA, they cease to exist. However, when they pass to a local council, a cooperative or the Social Security Found, these bodies are supposed to use them to buy state property from the SPA (for example, it is suggested that a cooperative could purchase shares in a food-processing company). The amount of compensation bills to be issued is estimated by the Ministry of Finance at about Ft 60 mln.

The extent of privatization to date

In 1991 the total proceeds of the SPA from privatization amounted to Ft 39.18 bln. Hungarian private investors represented about Ft 7 bln, most of which came from the preprivatization program.

Table 4B.1 shows the number of the various categories of transformations and privatizations since the establishment of the SPA. This evidence points to the largely decentralized nature of enterprise transformations in Hungary. Most transformations are initiated by the enterprises or investors, rather than by the SPA.

Table 4B.1 Privatization transactions since the establishment of the SPA, March 1, 1990 to June 30, 1992

	Dec. 31, 1991	May 31, 1992	June 30, 1992
Transformations			
Total approved	218	343	373
Book value (Ft bln)	345.07	560.40	572.46
Transaction value (Ft bln)	465.20	1,274.40	1,295.50
Out of this:			
Self-privatization	20	85	97
Book value (Ft bln)	1.15	6.60	9.44
Transaction value (Ft bln)	1.56	8.10	11.41
Initiated by state enterprises or investors	180	214	232
Book value (Ft bln)	193.49	194.76	203.98
Transaction value (Ft bln)	281.48	345.15	362.94
State-initiated	18	44	44
Book value (Ft bln)	150.43	359.04	359.04
Transaction value (Ft bln)	182.16	921.15	921.15
Total rejected	11	11	13
Book value (Ft bln)	5.04	5.04	5.74
In progress	636	615	576
Book value (Ft bln)	304.47	282.18	276.22
Out of this:			
Self-privatization	353	368	336
Book value (Ft bln)	18.58	27.60	24.60
Initiated by state enterprises or investors	176	152	147
Book value (Ft bln)	129.70	120.82	116.10
State-initiated	107	95	93
Book value (Ft bln)	156.19	133.76	135.36
Joint ventures*			
Total approved	126	141	141
Book value (Ft bln)	21.34	12.97	12.97
Transaction value (Ft bln)	37.30	41.43	41.43
Out of this:			
With domestic partner	70	76	76
Book value (Ft bln)	3.73	4.09	4.09
Transaction value (Ft bln)	9.10	10.60	10.60

Table 4B.1   contd

	Dec. 31, 1991	May 31, 1992	June 30, 1992
With foreign partner	56	65	65
Book value (Ft bln)	17.61	17.88	17.88
Transaction value (Ft bln)	28.20	30.83	30.83
Total rejected	15	16	16
Book value (Ft bln)	0.71	0.86	0.86
Property protection cases**			
Total approved	207	276	282
Book value (FT bln)	8.59	10.28	10.37
Transaction value (Ft bln)	17.11	20.87	21.03
Total rejected	16	16	16
Book value (FT bln)	1.86	1.86	1.86
Total rejected	15	1.85	

* Joint ventures are transactions between the state enterprises and an external ("outer" according to the SPA terminology) investor, private, or a state company (enterprise).
** Property protection cases involve sales of parts of socialized enterprises.
Source: SPA

5. CORPORATIZATION

Corporatization, more often referred to in Hungary as "transformation,"[17] is a conversion of socialized enterprises into Western-style (joint-stock or limited-liability) companies, in most cases wholly owned by the state. While corporatization is thus often merely a change of legal form, it is supposed to clarify the legal property relations with respect to the converted enterprises and make them suitable for future privatization. Moreover, it is often expected that corporatization itself might influence the incentives of the existing management and employees, even prior to ultimate privatization, since the change in the legal form may eliminate or alter the various inchoate entitlements

---

17 "Commercialization" is the term used in Poland.

that particular actors may have claimed under the previous conditions of confused property rights. Thus, for example, the rights of the workers as participants in the Enterprise Councils of the so-called self-managed Hungarian firms are explicitly revoked in the transition to the more conventional governance structure of a joint-stock company, and the position of the management is usually significantly strengthened.

In Hungary, unlike other East European countries, the process of corporatization began in the last years of the communist regime, and it is more often than elsewhere accompanied by an immediate partial privatization of the transformed enterprise. This is usually accomplished through a sale of shares to insiders or to an outside investor, or by a new issue increasing the capital of the newly transformed company. Moreover, the impetus for privatization is also often quite different, in that it is initially provided not by the state, trying to reassert its powers as the owner, but by the managers, trying to shield the assets of their enterprises from the state.

The beginnings of corporatization in Hungary go back to 1987, when a number of enterprising SE managers discovered that some precommunist laws on commercial companies, dating back to the 19th century, had in fact never been revoked, and that the resulting legal loophole allowed the creation of subsidiaries capitalized with a portion of the assets of state enterprises. By that time the ideological grip of the state was loosening, and the new device offered interesting possibilities for managers interested in diverting a portion of state assets to their own control, and often at least partial ownership. An additional incentive was provided by the fact that the liabilities of the old SE were not transferred with the assets to the new "commercial company," thus opening new credit possibilities, and every new economic unit received a 50 per cent profit-tax reduction for three years.[18]

The practice begun in this way gained a firm legal basis in the Company Law of 1988, which formally gave the Enterprise Council of a self-managed enterprise the right to create a new corporate entity and exchange a portion of the enterprise's assets for the shares of the newly created joint-stock or limited-liability company. An important feature of the Company Law was that the registration of the new companies was made independent from the government (i.e., the

---

[18] This tax preference has been discontinued since the beginning of 1992.

owner of transferred assets), and was left to a special court, which could decline the application only if specific provisions of the Company Law were infringed. Through a widespread use of this mechanism, many socialized enterprises were transformed into mere shells, owning the shares of new companies created out of their assets. Significantly, these shells were still subject to the Law on Enterprise Councils, but were often left with no employees to speak of, thus leaving the management firmly in control of the decisions concerning the voting of the stock of the downstream companies.

The next legal act underlying the corporatization process was the Transformation Law of 1989, which allowed the conversion to a corporate form (joint-stock or limited-liability company) of whole socialized enterprises (rather than of a portion of their assets), with the state becoming the owner of the shares not otherwise disposed of through sales to insiders or other investors (often other state companies). Thus, unlike in the case of the partial transformations under the Company Law, a socialized enterprise converted under the Transformation Law goes out of existence altogether, to be replaced by a new entity in a corporate form. The successor company also takes all the liabilities of the old enterprise together with its assets, so that some of the abuses possible under the Company Law are eliminated. At the same time, however, the Transformation Law allowed the enterprise insiders to acquire 20 per cent of the shares of the new company at a discount of up to 90 per cent, and this provided a powerful incentive for the conversion process, especially in the period before corporatization was subject to any effective supervision. Not unexpectedly, the assets of many transformed enterprises were undervalued, and the payment for the insiders' shares is said to have often been made out of a special bonus voted for the insiders by the (insider-dominated) enterprise council immediately before the transformation.

The abuses of the early corporatization process provoked a public outcry and prompted the government to take some legal steps to assert its ownership rights over the remaining socialized property, although no genuine enforcement occurred until the first postcommunist coalition came to power. The most important of these steps was the creation of the SPA (in March 1990), charged with supervising the ownership transformation process. Shares which, at the point of transformation, are not sold to "outside investors," remain in the hands of the SPA, which acts as the holder for the state, and it is hoped that most of them will be sold later, except for the enterprises chosen to remain as long-term state holdings. In the meantime, the SPA is entitled to exercise the normal ownership rights associated with its shareholdings, including the appointment of the members of the board of directors. Although, as a result of the SPA's insistence on negotiated solutions and the existence of some gaps in its jurisdiction,[19] its supervision is not very stringent, the very presence of the SPA introduced a new element into the Hungarian corporatization process. (For more information on the creation and role of the SPA, see subsections on the SPA in Section 4A.)

The controlled corporatization process, freed from the abuses associated with the early phases of spontaneous privatization, is strongly supported by the SPA as a prelude to privatization. Eventually all socialized enterprises are supposed be transformed or liquidated, with the transformation of each enterprise begun by the end of 1992.

Procedures for deciding on transformation of state enterprises

Most transformations of state enterprises into a corporate form now are subject to approval and supervision of the SPA,[20] and the SPA decisions in these matters are final. There exist two separate procedures for the initiation and execution of the corporatization process, one applicable to state enterprises under state supervision and the other to the self-managing enterprises created under the Law on Enterprise Councils. (See subsection on legal forms in Section 3A.)

Transformations of enterprises under state supervision (the first category under the Law on Enterprise Councils) may be initiated and decided upon by the SPA, which is required to consult the affected enterprise, but is not required to follow the enterprise's recommendations. The enterprise may also petition the SPA to initiate the transformation process, but the SPA is not bound by the enterprise's proposals. In some cases the SPA may also allow a breakup of an existing enterprise, if the enterprise's subunits express their preference

---

[19] In the case of new transformations under the Company Law of 1988, the SPA supervises only the larger transactions, involving amounts in excess of $400,000, and the existing limits can often be avoided if a number of smaller partial conversions are linked together, as long as the combined assets spun off do not exceed 50 per cent of the assets of the original parent enterprise.

[20] See the preceding footnote for the exceptions to the SPA's jurisdiction.

for independence and the divestiture is both viable from a business point of view and capable of increasing competition.

The right of decision concerning the transformation of a self-managed enterprise belongs, at least in theory, to the Enterprise Council. Nevertheless, the decisions of the Enterprise Council are subject to the SPA's approval and possible veto. In practice, while the SPA actually blocks the transformation in some instances (see the cases in Table 4B.1 under the heading "Total rejected"), it has for some time adopted the policy of bargaining with the enterprises rather than simply vetoing their proposals. The enterprise can, of course, decide not to transform under the conditions laid down by the SPA, but the SPA also can, and sometimes does, take reluctant self-governing enterprises under direct state supervision (which means the abolition of the Enterprise Council and an effectively transfer of the enterprise to the first category – the non-self-managing enterprises – listed in the Law on Enterprise Councils). Thus, in reality the powers of the SPA are quite considerable, even if they are not used very often.

The Enterprise Council must make its decision concerning (full or partial) transformation by a two-thirds majority. The enterprise must then inform the SPA about the proposed changes, and provide it with details concerning the economic purpose of the transformation, the planned founding capital of the new company, the estimates of profitability, and the expected effects of the transformation on export figures, market development, employment, investment, etc. The enterprise is also required to inform the SPA about potential outside investors, whether foreign or domestic, and about any preliminary negotiations with such investors. The enterprise must also open its books to the SPA.

In response to the actions of an enterprise, the SPA may, in addition to approving or disapproving the transformation, propose its own conditions, such as a different method of sale or different conditions of tender, and it may request a new valuation, if the submitted one seems unrealistic or outdated. The time limit for the SPA to make its determination is thirty days, but the limit is suspended during negotiations, giving the Agency greater flexibility. As a matter of fact, in all the more significant cases, several rounds of bargaining and negotiations among the SPA, the enterprise, and outside investors are the rule before the final approval is issued.

The extent of corporatization to date

Prior to the founding of the SPA (in March 1991), there were no reliable data on the extent of the conversion of state enterprises into corporate forms, but some data (from the Ministry of Industry and Trade) suggest that 40 per cent of state enterprises put around 10 per cent of their combined assets into various subsidiaries before mid-1990. Other data show that, by the end of 1988, when the total book value of the 2,000 state enterprises was Ft 1,767 bln, Ft 109 bln (6.2 per cent) was already in the form of commercial companies. By the end of 1989, the figures are Ft 1,878 bln and Ft 172 bln (9.8 per cent) respectively.

Since the creation of the SPA, more than 300 enterprises have been corporatized or transformed (see Table 4B.1 in Section 4B above). The organizational structures of these companies differ; some operate as holding companies, and some are split up into independent units. Sectoral breakdown is presented in Table 5.1.

Table 5.1 Sectoral breakdown of transformed companies (based on a sample of 103, per cent of total)

Mining	2.91
Metallurgy	11.65
Machinery	14.56
Construction:	
materials	3.88
industry	6.80
Chemicals	2.91
Light industry	4.85
Food processing	21.35
Domestic trade	25.24
Services and other*	5.82

* This category includes the following activities, each with a share of less than 1 per cent: forestry, water management, business services, financial services, cultural services, and other services.

Source: SPA

As mentioned before, all remaining state enterprises are to begin undergoing transformation by the end of 1992.

POLAND

CONTENTS

1. INTRODUCTION

Brief history of reforms

During the early 1970s, the Polish government resorted to massive foreign borrowing in order to finance an unsustainable level of growth in both consumption and investment. By the end of the decade, foreign lenders' unwillingness to extend further loans led to the deepest downturn in the Polish economy since the Second World War. This situation significantly weakened the power of the Polish state authorities, who could not block the emergence of Solidarity, and agreed, in September 1981, to the workers' formal participation in the management of enterprises.

During the 1980s the government progressively relaxed its control over enterprises. At the same time, enterprises continued to press their demands for government subsidies and other forms of support. Unable to finance increasing levels of expenditures from tax revenues, the authorities were forced to rely increasingly on monetary expansion. As a result, the Solidarity-led government which assumed office in September 1989 faced an enormous budget deficit and rapidly accelerating inflation.

This first postcommunist government decided on a two-phase strategy of economic reform. During phase I, implemented in the fall of 1989, the government sought to regain a degree of control over the budget and correct some price distortions. It also created an unemployment compensation system, and elaborated the legal basis for bankruptcy procedures. The "big bang" phase II of the program began on January 1, 1990.

Main points of the reform program

The main policy measures and goals of the big bang reform program, launched in January 1990, were as follows:

- reduction of the governmental budget deficit from 7 per cent of GDP in 1989 to 1 per cent in 1990;
- beginning of a reform of the tax system;
- implementation of a restrictive monetary policy, including credit ceilings, and a switch from sharply negative to positive real interest rates;
- overnight liberalization of most prices;
- devaluation and internal convertibility of the domestic currency, the zloty, at a fixed exchange rate;
- drastic reduction in the rate of wage indexation, accompanied by a punitive tax on excess increases of an enterprise wage bill.

2. ECONOMIC ENVIRONMENT

The structure of output

In 1991, Poland's gross national product (GNP), in current prices, was Zl 823,800 bln ($77.9 bln).[1]

Table 2.1 The structure of GDP (per cent of total)

	1988	1991
Industry	44	33
Agriculture	13	15
Services	14	17
Other	29	35

Source: PlanEcon

Table 2.1's presentation of the structure of GDP in 1988 and 1991 shows the shift from industry to services and other sectors. This shift is evidently associated with the decline of the overgrown enterprises in the state sector.

Despite a deep recession in 1990, the state sector of the economy in 1991 continued to be dominated by large enterprises, which employed a significant proportion of the labor force. However, private sector employment has grown 25 per cent in 1991, relative to 1990.

Table 2.2 State enterprises in 1991

Number of employees	Number of enterprises
less than 50	459
51–100	232
101–200	1,367
201–500	1,870
501–1,000	991
1,001–2,000	532
2,001–5,000	232
more than 5,000	87

Source: Central Statistical Office

[1] The zloty–dollar exchange rate used here is the average rate for the year as calculated by *PlanEcon Review* and *Outlook for Poland* (June 1992). For the period covered by this report, these rates were as follows: 1989, Zl 1,439; 1990, Zl 9,500; 1991, Zl 10,576; 1992, Zl 13,871 (estimated).

Output

In 1990, GDP declined by 11.6 per cent, led by a dramatic drop of 22 per cent in industrial output. All other sectors also registered output decreases, ranging from 14.5 per cent and 12.6 per cent for construction and transport, respectively, to 0.4 per cent in services.

In January 1990 alone, output of the state industrial sector fell by 10 per cent, relative to December 1989 (21 per cent, relative to January 1989). During the same period, sales of machine tools, precision tools, and transport equipment declined by 25 per cent (12 per cent), 34 per cent (13 per cent), and 34 per cent (25 per cent), respectively. However, most other branches of heavy industry experienced little or no decline in output. Output in the manufacturing and mining sectors declined by 11 per cent (22 per cent) and 1 per cent (7 per cent), respectively, while sales of metallurgical products were higher in January 1990 than in December 1989.

After the initial fall, aggregate output continued to decline, albeit at a lower pace; by July 1990 it stabilized, and in August it slightly increased. As time progressed, the recession began to effect heavy industry. By June 1990, most branches of heavy industry experienced a 25–30 per cent decline in output, relative to June 1989. Interestingly, this is about the same percentage drop as experienced by light industry in January. By January 1991, overall industrial production was still 26 per cent below its average level in 1989.

In 1991, GDP fell by an additional 7.4 per cent, with industry and transport again suffering substantial declines of 15 per cent and 13.2 per cent, respectively. The decreases in other sectors were smaller in 1991 than they had been in 1990, with the trade sector showing a modest growth of 1.3 per cent. By February 1992, the industrial production index had fallen by a total of 41 per cent, relative to its average value in 1989.

The economy started to show some signs of improvement in 1992. The January–May average of the industrial production index was 8 per cent above the average for the last quarter of 1991.

Table 2.3 Industrial production (seasonally adjusted; 1989 monthly average = 100)

	Jan	Feb	Mar	Apr	May	June	July	Aug	Sept	Oct	Nov	Dec
1991	73.6	69.8	67.9	66.3	61.3	62.7	65.1	62.3	59.4	60.1	58.2	58.0
1992	62.3	63.4	65.3	67.5	62.8							

Source: PlanEcon

INVESTMENT

Following a 10 per cent drop in 1990, gross fixed investment declined by 6 per cent in 1991. Cuts in investment were brought on by the high cost of long-term borrowing, declining profitability on falling sales, liquidity problems caused by difficulties of collecting receivables from other enterprises, and heightened uncertainty concerning the future structure of enterprise ownership. These factors caused even relatively successful state enterprises to cut back on investment.

The smaller volume investment expenditure in 1991 was also redirected away from investment in plant and structures, which fell by 10 per cent, toward machinery and equipment, which declined by only 4 per cent. Notably, the share of investment goods in total imports increased from 15 per cent in 1990 to 17 per cent in 1991.

Household savings

The estimated level of Polish households' domestic and foreign currency savings increased from about $9.4 bln in December 1990 to $14.2 bln in June 1991.

Price liberalization

As of January 1, 1990, about 90 per cent of prices were freed from government control. Controls still existed on the prices of electricity, coal, gas, central heating, transport, and gasoline, but these prices were substantially raised from prior levels. The price of coal increased by 500 per cent, and that of electricity and transport each by 200 per cent. Periodic increases of government controlled prices have continued to be put into effect since 1990.

Inflation

In January 1990 the retail price index rose by almost 80 per cent. The price jump was steepest at the very beginning of the month. During the first three weeks price increases were above 20 per cent per week. The rate of inflation declined at the end of January, but prices continued to rise during the subsequent months. The overall Polish GDP deflator increased by 538 per cent in 1990.

Inflationary pressures re-emerged in early 1991, but increases in retail prices moderated later in the year, despite a rising budget deficit. The overall GDP deflator increased by 48 per cent in 1991.

Table 2.4   Retail Price Index (month-to-month per cent changes)

	Jan	Feb	Mar	Apr	May	June	July	Aug	Sept	Oct	Nov	Dec
1991	12.7	6.7	4.5	2.7	2.7	4.9	0.1	0.6	4.3	3.2	3.2	3.1
1992	7.5	1.8	2.0	3.7	4.0	2.5						

Source: PlanEcon

In January 1992, sharp increases of controlled prices of housing rents and utilities resulted in a 7.5 per cent increase in the retail price index. However, by June, monthly inflation had fallen below 3 per cent.

Behavior of wages

One of the key components of the January 1990 economic reform package was the policy designed to restrain wage increases. The degree of indexation was set at 30 per cent in January, and 20 per cent in February through April. In addition, a tax of 200 per cent was imposed on cumulative increases in the enterprise wage bill which exceeded the cumulative norm by not more than 3 per cent, and a 500 per cent rate applied for more "excessive" increases. The indexation rate was subsequently increased in April 1990, and the excess wage tax system was revised at the beginning of 1991.

Apparently due to highly restrictive credit policy, the average nominal wage bill consistently rose less than permitted by indexation during the first half of 1990. As real interest rates declined in July and August, monthly increases in the wage bill exceeded the norms specified by the indexation scheme. However, the cumulative level of the wage bill remained below the cumulative norm for most enterprises. Average net nominal wages increased by 398 per cent in 1990, yet failed to keep pace with inflation, resulting in a 22 per cent drop in real wages.

Average real wages levels did not recover in 1991, rising only 1 per cent per annum. In contrast, real wages in the six key sectors of industry increased 8 per cent between January and December 1991. However, they fell back by 19 per cent in January 1992. The average monthly industrial wage in Poland, in current US dollars, averaged $173 between January 1991 and May 1992.

Table 2.5 Real wage in industry (six key sectors; January 1990 = 100)

	Jan	Feb	Mar	Apr	May	June	July	Aug	Sept	Oct	Nov	Dec
1991	109.9	115.9	115.1	110.7	105.6	102.8	107.6	106.6	105.2	111.0	112.8	119.0
1992	100.4	99.7	106.9	106.5	95.9							

Source: PlanEcon

Table 2.6 Average monthly industrial wage (in current US dollars)

	Jan	Feb	Mar	Apr	May	June	July	Aug	Sept	Oct	Nov	Dec
1991	157.3	177.0	183.7	181.5	164.1	151.4	157.8	159.6	166.2	180.9	190.6	207.9
1992	185.6	178.6	171.8	175.1	166.3							

Source: PlanEcon

Unemployment

Following a sharp rise in unemployment during 1990, the number of unemployed continued to rise by approximately 90,000 a month between January and December 1991. The rate of growth of unemployment has since slowed, but by the end of March 1992, the number of officially registered unemployed reached 2.3 mln, around 12.2 per cent of the labor force. The regional distribution of unemployment is uneven. Industrialized and urban areas have much lower unemployment rates than less developed, rural regions. For example, at the end of March 1992, unemployment in the area around Warsaw did not exceed 5 per cent, while in north-eastern Poland it reached 21 per cent.

Table 2.7 Unemployment rate (as per cent of labor force)

	Jan	Feb	Mar	Apr	May	June	July	Aug	Sept	Oct	Nov	Dec
1991	6.8	7.0	7.3	7.5	7.9	8.6	9.6	10.1	10.7	11.1	11.4	11.8
1992	12.2	12.5	12.2	12.2								

Source: PlanEcon

State budget

Despite attempts to adhere to a strict fiscal policy, the state budget ended 1991 with a huge deficit. Following a small surplus in 1990, the original state budget for 1991, as accepted by the IMF, envisioned a small deficit of Zl 4,300 bln ($406.6 mln). However, due to the poor performance of most enterprises, corporate tax revenues and "dividends" from state enterprises fell short of targets. In addition, the proceeds from the sale of state enterprises turned out to be only a fraction of those expected. For the whole year, the budget deficit reached Zl 31,000 bln ($3 bln) – over seven times the initial target.

Failure to meet its 1991 fiscal targets cost Poland the support of the IMF, which suspended disbursement of a conditional adjustment loan. Securing parliamentary approval of the 1992 budget became the major challenge for the weak coalition government. Poland had only a provisional budget for the first quarter of 1992, and the final budget for the year was passed only in early June 1992.

The struggle to contain the budget deficit has continued in 1992. At the end of the first quarter of 1992, the deficit amounted to Zl 10,400 bln ($749.8 mln), as revenues fell short of expectations and expenditures exceeded planned levels. By the end of June 1992, the budget deficit reached Zl 25,700 bln ($1.9 bln). The budget deficit has been primarily financed through sales of Treasury bills to the banks.

TAXATION
Corporate tax is imposed at a flat rate of 40 per cent. Dividends paid to foreign investors are subject to a withholding tax of 30 per cent, unless they are exempt under a double taxation treaty. Employers are required to contribute 43 per cent of total employee wages to social security and 2 per cent to an unemployment fund.

A goods and services tax, similar to a value added tax, was introduced in April 1992. There is also a turnover tax, with rates ranging between 5 to 20 per cent.

Monetary policy

MONEY SUPPLY
The monetary and credit targets underpinning the big bang program were predicated on a smaller January 1990 price rise than that which actually occurred. Consequently, the resulting credit squeeze was

particularly severe. Between the end of December 1989 and the end of January 1990, M1 declined 18 per cent, and a similar drop occurred in M2. However, the drastic decline in inflation from February on, and some easing of monetary policy in the latter part of 1990, resulted in an overall annual decreases in real M1 and M2 of 40 and 50 per cent, respectively. Each of the measures of real money stock grew by more than 10 per cent in 1991.

INTEREST RATES

In December 1989, retail prices were rising at 17 per cent per month, and the National Bank of Poland set the discount rate at 13 per cent. On January 1, 1990, the Bank raised the discount rate to 36 per cent per month. This rate was expected to exceed the average January–February inflation rate, but prices rose faster than was foreseen, and the *ex post* January real interest rate was strongly negative. These new rates applied to existing as well as to new debt. As a result the rate increase imposed a major burden on the heavily indebted sectors of the economy, especially agriculture and construction, and these were granted special relief from interest payments.

Inflation subsided in February, and though the nominal discount rate was reduced to 20 per cent, the *ex post* real rate was now positive. In the following months, in anticipation of further decline in the rate of inflation, the discount rate was gradually reduced. For the first six months of the year the real *ex post* discount rate remained positive. In July, however, it became once again negative and remained so, on average at about 3 per cent, for the rest of 1990.

The cost of credit increased in real terms in 1991. According to the Central Statistical Office, the average real discount rate for the year was about 6 per cent.

Debt

Poland had $48.4 bln in gross hard currency debt at the end of 1991. This total was nearly the same as that in 1990. However, there were offsetting influences on the value of gross debt in 1991, which included the capitalization of unpaid interest, the strengthening of the dollar against European currencies, and some debt write-offs based on Poland's agreement with the Paris Club. At the end of February 1992, Poland's gross hard currency debt stood at $46.3 bln, with the decline largely due to the decrease in the dollar value of Polish debt denominated in other currencies.

The debt reduction agreement with the Paris Club – concluded in June 1991 – has been ratified through bilateral negotiations with almost all the countries participating in the Club. If successfully implemented, this unprecedented settlement will reduce the present value of the Polish official debt by at least 50 per cent.

However, Poland needs to meet a number of conditions in order to qualify for the entire reduction. First, it must adhere to an IMF-approved economic adjustment program. Having failed to meet its fiscal targets, Poland has had no access to funds from the IMF adjustment program since the summer of 1991. Poland must also remain current on its servicing payments on all remaining official debt owed to Paris Club countries. Failure to do so with regard to any single member country would invalidate the whole "master" debt reduction agreement.

According to the terms of the Paris Club accord, Poland is also supposed to complete an agreement on debt relief with the London Club of commercial bank creditors. These talks have been stalled, however, because the commercial banks continue to maintain that they cannot match the write-offs granted by governments on official debt.

Foreign trade

The value of Poland's convertible currency exports continued to rise in 1991. Following an impressive 41 per cent increase, to $12 bln in 1990, convertible currency exports rose by an additional 25 per cent in 1991. Convertible currency imports increased from $8.3 bln in 1990 to $15.5 bln in 1991.

When converted to US dollar equivalent value, exports to the former Comecon countries totaled $7.8 bln in 1990. Out of this total, the value of exports in convertible currencies was only $1.5 bln. Following the breakdown of Comecon trading arrangements, Polish exports to this group of countries dropped sharply by 65 per cent in 1991. However, the value of convertible currency exports to the former Comecon countries actually increased to $2.8 bln. In addition, exports to developed market economies increased from $9 bln in 1990 to $11 bln in 1991. This exceeded a $300 mln fall in exports to developing countries.

Convertible currency imports from the former Comecon countries increased from about $1.3 bln in 1990 to $3.2 bln in 1991. The rest of the 1991 increase in convertible currency imports consisted of $4.2 bln and $1.1 bln increases in imports from developed and developing countries, respectively.

During the first three months of 1992, receipts for exports increased 17 per cent and payments for imports declined 5 per cent compared to the same period of 1991. These developments generated a $385 mln trade surplus, a significant improvement from early 1991 when payments for imports exceeded export receipts by $258 mln.

Despite fairly high inflation rates and the recession, Poland has been able to maintain internal convertibility of the zloty since January 1990. Initially, the stable exchange rate of Zl 9,500 to the US dollar was one of the "anchors" of the stabilization program. In 1991, two important changes in exchange rate policy occurred. First, the zloty was devalued in May by about 17 per cent. At the same time the basis for calculating the rate was changed. The zloty was pegged to a basket of five western currencies instead of just to the dollar. Second, in mid-October 1991, the zloty exchange rate was switched to a crawling peg system that allows for a gradual and flexible devaluation of the currency in response to domestic inflation and changes in the relative exchange rates of currencies included in the basket. In late February 1992, the zloty was devalued by an additional 12 per cent.

3. PRESENT FORMS OF OWNERSHIP

3A. Legal framework of economic activity

Existing and planned legislation concerning property rights

The following are the most significant laws and regulations concerning property rights, forms of business of organization, and privatization in Poland:

— Arrangement Proceedings Act (1934);
— Bankruptcy Act (1934), as amended by the Insolvency Act (1990);
— Law on State Enterprises (1981);
— Law on Self-Management of State-Owned Enterprises (1981);
— Law on Cooperatives (1982);
— Law on Foundations (1984);
— Law on Economic Activity (1988);
— Joint Ventures Act (1988);
— Law Governing Changes in the Organization and Activities of Cooperatives (1990);

— Law on Land Administration and Real Estate Expropriation (1990 as amended);
— Law on Privatization of State-Owned Enterprises (1990) (Privatization Law);
— Special Regulation of the Ministry of Finance, No. 43, Item 334 (November 10, 1990) (on interest payments on leases under lease and sale arrangements);
— Law on Foreign Investment (1991) (Joint Venture Act);
— Act on Treasury-Owned Agricultural Property (1991);
— Polish Civil Code;
— Polish Commercial Code.

Recognized forms of business organizations

STATE ENTERPRISES

The 1990 Law on Privatization of State-Owned Enterprises (Privatization Law) provides for the transformation of state enterprises into state-owned joint-stock companies and limited-liability companies, as well as for their liquidation and the sale of their assets. It is not, however, now contemplated that all or even most of the state enterprises will be transformed or liquidated in the near future. Therefore the existing legal regime governing state enterprises, established by the Law on State Enterprises of 1981 and amended several times afterwards, together with the 1981 Law on Self-Management of State-Owned Enterprises, still controls a very substantial part of the Polish economy.[2]

The most characteristic feature of the Polish enterprise governance system is the dominant role of the workers. The historical background of this state of affairs goes back to September 1981, when the Polish government agreed to a Solidarity demand for legal guarantees of worker participation in the management of state enterprises. Despite the subsequent imposition of martial law and a temporary reassertion of state power through the military, the repeated attempts at a decentralizing economic reform in the 1980s marked a further shift of power from the state administration to the employees. In the characteristic Eastern European confusion of managerial and ownership rights, the demise of communism and the dismantling of the economic planning apparatus has further reduced the state's control over the enterprises,

[2] The Law on State Enterprises does not apply to the State Railroads, the Airports Authority, Polish Airlines (LOT), banks, and other minor exceptions.

leaving workers' councils[3] and general workers' assemblies as the dominant stakeholders and supervisors of enterprise activities.

The Law on State Enterprises gives enterprises the status of independent, self-governing, and self-financing economic units with their own legal personality. All enterprises are created by their "founding organs," which may be branches of the state administration (usually ministries), the National Bank, or local governmental units.

The law recognizes two types of state enterprises: ordinary enterprises and public utilities. With respect to public utilities, which are subject to special regulations of the Council of Ministers, the founding organs have pervasive authority over management (including the right to appoint and dismiss the director), and are obligated to subsidize operations if they are unprofitable but necessary to meet public needs. In the case of ordinary enterprises, however, the role of the founding organ is much more limited: it provides the initial assets of the enterprise, defines the initial scope of the enterprise's activities, and has a significant role in deciding upon the liquidation of the enterprise (see the subsection on bankruptcy and liquidation in Section 3A below). Otherwise, the founding organ can do relatively little without the consent of the employee council and the other actors inside the enterprise, although it is involved in such matters as plans to split up the enterprise and the general oversight on behalf of the state.

The assets entrusted to the enterprise by the founding organ remain formally the property of the state. They cannot be taken away, however, and the enterprise manages them without any outside interference; it even has the authority, when not constrained by particular statutory prohibitions (above all, the Privatization Law), to sell them at a public auction and keep any proceeds that exceed their book value.

The governing organs of a state enterprise are the Employee General Assembly, the employee council, and the director. The Employee General Assembly has the right to adopt the enterprise statutes, approve long-term business plans, and determine the ways in which the share of the profits earmarked for the workers is to be used. The employee councils, composed of fifteen members elected by the employees, approve the annual plans of the enterprise and its accounts for the past year and adopt the work rules, as well as pass

---

[3] The term "workers' council" (which is popularly used) will be used in this report interchangeably with "employee council" (which is the term used by the Law on State Enterprises).

on proposals for mergers and transformations of the enterprise. Most importantly, the councils essentially have the power to hire and fire the director, although they must follow a prescribed competitive hiring procedure.

Recent amendments to the Law on State Enterprises also introduced new procedures for the liquidation of state enterprises and for disciplining them in the case of poor economic performance. These procedures are discussed below, in the subsection on bankruptcy and liquidation. At this point, however, it should be mentioned that during the so-called "curative proceedings," which may be initiated when the enterprise fails to pay the "dividend" (in reality a tax on the assets contributed by the state), self-management of the enterprise is significantly curtailed, and all the powers of the employee council are transferred to a "curative commission," on which the employee representatives are in a minority.

COOPERATIVES
There are approximately 17,000 cooperatives in Poland, with several million members. They are concentrated in such sectors as services, housing, handicrafts, and food processing (where they account for over 90 per cent of production). There is also an extensive network of cooperative banks. Somewhat unique among the former communist countries, Poland did not have a large cooperative sector in agriculture.

While the parliament has been discussing drafts of new cooperative laws for some time, individual cooperatives in Poland continue to be regulated by the 1982 Law on Cooperatives. The only major legislative act in this area passed in the wake of the demise of the communist system was the 1990 Law Governing Changes in the Organization and Activities of Cooperatives, which focused on demonopolization and the abolition of the "cooperative unions" into which individual cooperatives had been forced under the communist regime. Many of these unions, including a huge press conglomerate controlling most of the Polish newspapers and periodicals, as well as printing facilities and the distribution network, served as a special economic fiefdom of the Communist Party, providing it with an independent source of income. The 1990 law dissolved the cooperative unions and mandated the appointment of special liquidators, charged with transferring most of the unions' assets to the individual cooperatives (usually without payment or at a very reduced rate), and selling the remainder to the public. The law also mandated new elections in all the existing cooperatives as well as their division into several new cooperatives if the members so desired. What the law did not provide for, in part because the assets of the cooperatives had often been originally contributed by the state, was the possibility of a transformation of the existing cooperatives into other types of business entities, such as joint-stock or limited-liability companies.

As already mentioned, the remaining cooperatives are still governed by the 1982 Law on Cooperatives which is quite ill-suited to the new conditions and clearly requires replacement. In the name of internal democracy, the law gives each member an equal vote, regardless of his capital contribution, as well as favoring the retention of earnings in special funds to be used for the common purposes of all members, and does not contain any clear statement that the distribution of profits among the members should be in proportion to their capital contributions. The law also precludes foreign persons from joining cooperatives, but permits membership by a joint venture with foreign participation.

FOUNDATIONS
The Polish law on foundations is quite liberal. It should be mentioned in the list of permissible business organizations, because the 1984 Law on Foundations permits foundations to undertake commercial activities in order to support their non-profit activities, and exempts the profits from such commercial activities from taxation. Foreign foundations are also allowed to open branch offices and conduct business activities.

BUSINESS ENTITIES OPERATING UNDER THE COMMERCIAL CODE
The formal break with the communist restrictions on private entrepreneurship occurred in Poland before the actual fall of the old regime. The 1988 Law on Economic Activity (effective as of 1989) granted every person the right to conduct independent economic activity, which was defined very broadly to include manufacturing, building, trading, and services. Individuals or associations of individuals in the form of commercial companies[4] or partnerships

---

[4] Note that, unlike in a number of other Central European countries, the term "commercial company" is used in the Polish Commercial Code to refer exclusively to joint-stock and limited-liability companies, and not to partnership and other business organizations.

were permitted to engage an unlimited number of employees. Commercial enterprises were simultaneously granted the right to perform any operation not forbidden by law, although certain limited activities (such as arms manufacture and the production of alcohol and tobacco products) were still subject to licensing.

Most business activities of private parties, as well as some of those of the state, are regulated by the Commercial Code, except for ordinary partnerships, which are governed by the provisions of the Civil Code. In addition to the ordinary partnership, the Commercial Code, adopted in 1934, and amended a number of times since, permits commercial entities to take one of following four forms: 1) registered partnership; 2) limited partnership; 3) limited-liability company; and 4) joint-stock company. All of the entities governed by the Commercial Code must be entered in the Commercial Register, and the registration procedure requires a ruling by a court. Notarial fees and stamp duties may be substantial, especially for smaller firms (up to 5 per cent of capital).

Ordinary partnership An unregistered partnership, governed by the provisions of the Civil Code, is a written agreement among individuals to pursue common economic objectives. Unless otherwise specified in the agreement, it is presumed that the partnership contributions are of equal value. Another presumption is that profits and losses are shared equally regardless of the value of each partner's contribution, although the partnership agreement may provide otherwise.

Partners bear joint and several liability for the obligations of the partnership, and each partner is entitled, indeed required, to take part in the management of the partnership's affairs. All other governance arrangements are left to the parties.

Registered partnership A registered partnership is formed by a judicial registration in the Commercial Register of an ordinary partnership operating a "larger" business.[5] Unlike in the case of unregistered ordinary partnerships, however, the rules of the Civil Code no longer apply, and registered partnerships are governed by the Commercial Code. Among other differences, the Commercial Code is more specific with respect to the partners' rights and obligations.

---

[5] The provisions of the Code defining the term "larger" were repealed in 1964, and thus the meaning of the term is left to judicial interpretation.

Partners of a registered partnership continue to be jointly and severally liable for the obligations of the partnership. They are viewed as active members, and a registered partnership cannot be managed by third parties to the exclusion of the partners, nor can a partner be involuntarily excluded from management, except by a court order issued for "important reasons." Unless the partnership agreement provides otherwise, no remuneration is due for a managing partner's personal services, but such services can be considered as the partner's contribution to the partnership. In the absence of contrary provisions in the partnership agreement, partners share equally in the profits, regardless of their contributions, but they can demand the payment of interest on their contributions at the stipulated rate of 4 per cent.

Limited partnership Limited partnerships were restored to the Commercial Code in 1991, after having been abolished in 1964. They are formed by a written notarized agreement, and must be registered in the Commercial Register. As usual, limited partnerships have two types of members: general partners who take an active role in management and have unlimited liability for the obligations of the partnership, and limited partners, who are essentially passive investors and whose liability is limited to the value of their contribution. The names of the general partners must, and the name of a limited partner cannot, be included in the name of the partnership. A general partner's contribution may take the form of his services. Foreign subjects may not form limited partnerships, but legal entities with foreign participation can become partners.

Unless the partnership agreement provides otherwise, limited partners are not entitled to manage the enterprise, but they have a right to take part in, and indeed must be consulted about, decisions involving changes in the partnership agreement or other matters which are outside the competence of ordinary management. The limited parners can also represent the partnership when authorized to do so.

Limited-liability company The limited-liability company (LLC) is a familiar Central European form of business organization, and Polish law is rather flexible, leaving many arrangements to the parties' discretion. As usual, the liability of a shareholder of an LLC is limited to his contribution, while the company's obligations extend to the limit of its assets. An LLC can be formed by one or more legal or natural persons (but an LLC with only one shareholder cannot wholly own another LLC). An LLC must have a minimum capitalization of Zl 40 mln (appr.

$2,900), and each share must represent a minimum of Zl 500,000 (appr. $36), with no limitations on non-cash contributions. All the share capital of the company must be fully paid in by the time of registration, and the company charter may require shareholders to make new contributions to the company, termed "supplementary payments," in order to increase its capitalization.

The shares of an LLC do not have to be of the same value, but they must be registered and cannot be offered to the public. Transferability of the shares is presumed to be unrestricted, but the company bylaws may provide that the consent of the other shareholders is required.

The highest organ of a limited-liability company is the Shareholders' Meeting, which approves amendments to the bylaws, the annual accounts, sales or leases of the company's assets, purchases of goods priced at more than 20 per cent of the company's original capital, reimbursement of loans made to the company, and mergers and liquidations. There are no mandatory quorum requirements.

The Management Board is made up of one or more individuals elected by the Shareholders' Meeting, and is charged with running the company's day-to-day operations. In addition, an LLC with more than fifty shareholders or capital exceeding Zl 250 mln (appr. $18,000) is required to have a Supervisory Board, with at least three members elected by the Shareholders' Meeting (unless the company bylaws provide otherwise), whose duty is to inspect the financial reports and oversee the running of the company. Shareholders holding at least 10 per cent of an LLC's capital can request the court of registration to appoint an expert auditor to review the company books and records.

Joint-stock company   A joint-stock company (JSC), the shares in which may be publicly traded, is formed by a minimum of three founders on the basis of a notarized agreement (special provisions are made for wholly state-owned JSCs), and must have a minimum capitalization of Zl 1 bln (ca. $72,000), with each share nominally valued at at least Zl 500,000 (ca. $36). Contributions in kind are permitted, but must be subject to expert valuation. The founders are required to open a bank account with 5 per cent of the initial authorized capital in order to satisfy any claims which might arise.

A JSC can issue bearer or registered shares. Different classes of shares are also permitted, including shares with special voting, dividend, or liquidation-priority rights, as long as their existence is noted in the company charter. It is also permitted to limit the number of votes any one shareholder can cast.

Shares in the JSC are subscribed on the basis of a prospectus signed by the founders, which must be published in the case of a public offer. The period of subscription cannot exceed three months, and the 1991 Law on Trading in Securities and Trust Funds, based in part on American models, regulates public trading. It requires, among other things, that shareholders increasing their holdings must notify the Securities Commission and the company concerned as soon as their holdings cross particular thresholds (10, 20, 33, 50, 66 or 75 per cent). The law also requires that any person intending to purchase a stake amounting to more than 33 per cent of the total issued share capital in a given company must make a public offer, informing the Stock Exchange and the Securities Commission of the proposed purchase, the intended date of the offer, and the offer price. Shares paid for through in-kind payments cannot be traded during the first two years of the company's operation.

The governance structure of a JSC is very similar to that of a limited-liability company, with a Supervisory Board of five or more members mandatory for any company with capital in excess of Zl 5 mln (ca. $360). The Supervisory Board may have the power to suspend and replace the Directors.

A JSC may have an auditing board at its own discretion. It must publish its annual tax return and an annual report.

MUTUAL FUNDS
There are special rules applicable to mutual funds, which are supervised by the Securities Commission. All mutual funds operating in Poland must be located in Poland. They are organized as joint-stock companies, and their shares must be registered (bearer shares are not permitted for mutual funds). A mutual fund's debt cannot exceed 10 per cent of its entire capital. No single founder can own more than 10 per cent of the shares. At least 90 per cent of the assets must be invested in publicly traded securities, Polish Treasury bills or the securities of the National Bank of Poland. The remaining 10 per cent of shares must be invested in securities that are capable of being priced frequently enough to estimate the fund's net capital stock. No more than 5 per cent of all funds can be invested in securities of any one issuer.

Regulations governing foreign ownership

Foreign investment in Poland is regulated by the Law on Foreign

Investment (also known as the Joint Ventures Act) of June 1991, which replaced the Joint Ventures Act of December 1988. Companies with foreign participation established under the 1988 Act are regarded as joint ventures within the meaning of the new law, but have been allowed to retain the tax concessions, import duty exemptions, and all other previously granted benefits.

The Law on Foreign Investment limits foreign persons to certain forms of investment, primarily joint-stock or limited-liability companies, although a foreign party may also establish a presence in Poland through setting up a site management office (to manage a particular project), a technical information office, a representative office (which may import goods for sale, provided invoices are issued by the parent company), or an agency (which may deal in the goods and services of a foreign company).

Establishment of a foreign business in Poland does not usually require any special permits, except when the business is involved in the operation of sea and air ports, the brokerage of real-estate transactions, the manufacture of defense material, the provision of legal services, or the wholesale trade of imported consumer goods. A permit is also required for the establishment of a joint venture with a state enterprise if the state enterprise is to be assigned shares in the joint venture in exchange for an in-kind contribution of real estate or a production plant (including a long-term lease). (This provision is clearly designed to retain governmental control over *de facto* privatizations which could provide dangerous temptations to insiders within state enterprises.) In order to prevent evasion of the permit requirements through the use of a domestic front-company, the law also treats as foreign parties all domestic entities in which foreign parties exercise managerial or ownership control.

The required permits are issued (within two months) by the Ministry of Ownership Transformations. In considering the application for a permit, the Ministry may reject requests which imperil the economic interests of the state or national security (without the obligation to give reasons for its actions), or may define requirements for the proportionate contributions of foreign and domestic parties or the proportions of votes for each party.

Companies with foreign participation are required to report the extent of that participation to the appropriate court for inclusion into the Commercial Register.

While the automatic tax holidays granted by the previous Joint Ventures Law are no longer available, the Ministry of Finance may exempt companies with foreign participation from the payment of corporate income tax if the contribution of the foreign party has a value in excess of Ecu 2 mln, if the company operates in an area of the country with high unemployment, if it transfers new technology to Poland, or if at least 20 per cent of the company's sales are for export. Foreign investors must establish their participation prior to January 1, 1994, for their company to be eligible for the tax exemption.

The law guarantees foreign investors full repatriation of after-tax profits (with no foreign exchange permits required), and allows foreign persons employed by joint vetures to exchange and repatriate their wages. (A 20 per cent tax is levied on the salaries of such foreign persons, unless international agreements require otherwise.) Foreign parties are also guaranteed to be indemnified for losses due to confiscatory actions of the government, and special investment protection agreements have been signed with Austria, Belgium, Denmark, Finland, France, Germany, Great Britain, Japan, the Netherlands, Norway, Spain, Sweden, and the United States.

Under the Law on Land Administration and Real Estate Expropriation (last amended in December 1990), foreign natural and legal persons are permitted to acquire land in Poland, but must first obtain a permit from the Minister of Internal Affairs (who must approve or reject the application within two months). The permits are often not very difficult to obtain, and the recently created Agricultural Property Agency intends to sell a significant proportion of state-held land to foreign investors.

Bankruptcy and liquidation

Bankruptcy in Poland is regulated by the Bankruptcy Act of 1934, updated and amended by the Insolvency Act of February 1990. Debtors seeking to avoid bankruptcy can also attempt to restructure their debts in accordance with the Arrangement Proceedings Act of 1934. Finally, the Law on State Enterprises contains a number of provisions relating to the bankruptcy and liquidation of state enterprises.

LIQUIDATION UNDER THE LAW ON STATE ENTERPRISES
Liquidations under the Law on State Enterprises are not, strictly speaking, bankruptcies, since the only ''unpaid creditor'' is most often the state which also happens to own the enterprises in question. Moreover, such liquidations are often only a covert form of ownership transformation, with the assets of the ''bankrupt'' sold at an auction,

most often to enterprise insiders who support the process.[6] Nevertheless, this form of winding up is the most common consequence of insolvency, and its effect, despite the differences with respect to traditional bankruptcy, is the closest Poland now has to a disciplining force hardening somewhat the notoriously "soft" budget constraint of the state enterprises.[7]

The reason why state enterprises do not go bankrupt in the more traditional way (through the process mandated by Bankruptcy Act) is that most of their creditors are state banks and other state enterprises, which themselves continue to be solvent only by rescheduling the bad debts and carrying them as assets on their books. In a familiar Eastern European syndrome, a creditor-induced bankruptcy would threaten nearly the entire state sector, and is therefore "unthinkable." Liquidations under the Law on State Enterprises are thus the only mechanism of winding up firms that the owner-state itself recognizes should no longer exist or that can be relatively easily transformed into more viable private businesses. Not surprisingly, these liquidations do not involve the very large state enterprises, where the resulting social problems would be more difficult for the state to handle, but are limited to smaller firms, usually those with fewer than 200 employees.[8]

What makes the somewhat disciplining effect of the liquidations under the Law on State Enterprises possible is the fact that, unlike most other important decisions concerning state enterprises, they do not have to be approved by the workers' councils (although the councils must be consulted). (See the subsection on state enterprises in Section 3A above.) Instead, the founding organ of the state enterprise is empowered to liquidate the enterprise, provided the Minister of Finance does not object to the liquidation within two weeks. The event that formally triggers the liquidation is that the enterprise is

---

[6] This is not to say that many of the insiders do not suffer from this form of liquidation. Indeed, according to information from the Ministry of Ownership Transformation, much of the unemployment caused by layoffs is related to this process.

[7] Liquidations under the Law on State Enterprises must be distinguished from liquidations under the Privatization Law, which are not insolvency-related and are in fact asset-sale forms of privatization. For more on this difference, see the subsection on privatization through liquidation below.

[8] The available data on the number of liquidations are summarized below, in the subsection on privatization through liquidation in Section 4B.

unable to pay the so-called "dividend," i.e. an asset tax on the capital contributed by the state.[9]

Faced with the enterprise's failure to pay the dividend, the founding organ may proceed directly toward liquidation or it may appoint a so-called "curative commission." The curative commission is composed of two representatives chosen by the employee council, two representatives from the Ministry of Finance, one representative from the bank creditors of the enterprise, and two representatives from the parent agency (the founding organ). The most important and immediate effect of the appointment of the curative commission is that it takes over powers of the employee council and temporarily recalls or suspends the firm's director. It then names a new temporary director, who is in charge of implementing the approved "curative" program of restructuring. If at the end of the proceedings the enterprise remains unable to pay all past and current dividends, the founding organ, after consultation with the Ministry of Finance, is required to liquidate the enterprise. The assets of the liquidated enterprise must be sold or contributed by the state to a successor company (a joint venture or a similar arrangement). For a further description of the procedures governing such sales, see subsection on the the sale of assets in Section 4B below.

PROCEEDINGS UNDER THE BANKRUPTCY ACT

These are the traditional bankruptcy proceedings. As a result of the amendments contained in the Insolvency Act of 1990, they can be brought by or against a state enterprise, as well as a private business, but not by or against individuals in their non-commercial capacity. As noted, however, the Act is not generally used to liquidate a state enterprise.

Both debtors and creditors can petition their local district court for a declaration of bankruptcy. Bankruptcy itself is very generally defined as the cessation of the payment of debts by an "economic subject" (as defined in the 1988 Law on Economic Activity). Debtors who do not petition the court to declare bankruptcy within fourteen days of failing to pay their debts face personal liability for damages caused to creditors by their inaction. A "short-term" (not defined by the Act) suspension of debt payments "due to temporary difficulties" is not,

---

[9] An enterprise may also be liquidated when its activities are no longer possible for legal reasons or when more than one-half of the the enterprise's assets either has the form of interests in other business entities or has been leased to other persons.

however, a ground for the declaration of bankruptcy. Business enterprises with legal personality are also declared bankrupt when their assets are not sufficient to satisfy their debts.[10] Several state enterprises (railways, airlines, airports, etc.), public utilities, forestry companies, local government units, institutions founded by acts of parliament, and state-run organizations whose obligations are secured by the Treasury cannot legally be declared bankrupt.

The petition for bankruptcy is examined by a three-member administrative court made up of professional judges. Prior to ruling on the petition, the court attempts to hear from the debtor, creditors, and, in the case of a state-owned enterprise, from the workers' council. The decision declaring a party bankrupt is subject to appeal.

Upon the declaration of bankruptcy, the debtor losses its power to manage and dispose of its assets. All debts become immediately due, and all non-cash debts are converted into cash obligations. All commissions and orders issued by the bankrupt are terminated, but rents or leases of the debtor's property continue in force. Employment contracts negotiated with the debtor as employer are not suspended by the declaration of bankruptcy, but may be abrogated by the court-appointed trustee. Within a month of the declaration, employees may terminate their employment with one week's notice. Payment of interest on the bankrupt's debts is suspended by the declaration, which may be quite advantageous to the bankrupt, especially in the inflationary environment of Eastern Europe. The declaration of bankruptcy also serves as a stay on any on-going proceeding against the bankrupt for the payment of debts.

The liquidation proceedings are administered by an official receiver under the supervision of a judge-commissioner. The receiver is responsible for compiling an inventory of the bankrupt's estate and arranging a public auction or unrestricted sale of the bankrupt's assets. The receiver must attempt, whenever possible, to sell an economic enterprise in its entirety, and he must solicit the opinions of the worker's council, the founding organs, and the organs authorized to represent the State Treasury prior to selling off a state enterprise.

Before the sale of its assets, the bankrupt may enter into an agreement with unsecured creditors for the satisfaction of their claims, provided the arrangement is approved by a majority of the creditors

---

[10] The question that is left open is how long uncollected debts from other enterprises may be held on the asset side of the ledger of a state enterprise.

holding at least two-thirds of the unsecured debt and the claims of the preferred creditors are guaranteed to be be satisfied. The court can refuse to approve the arrangement if proper procedures are not followed or if the arrangement conflicts with decency or public order. The arrangement is binding on all creditors, regardless of whether or not they submitted claims during the bankruptcy proceeding.

If the bankrupt's estate is liquidated, the proceeds left after the satisfaction of secured creditors' claims are distributed in the following order of priority: 1) court costs and support for the bankrupt and his family; 2) costs incurred in administration and liquidation of the bankrupt; 3) back taxes for the past two years; 4) payments to the social insurance fund due for the last year; 5) medical or funeral expenses of the bankrupt; 6) normal creditors; 7) interest payments (in the same order as the capital); 8) fines and penalties; 9) donations and bequests. All debts classified in one of these tiers are fully satisfied before any portion of the debts in a subsequent tier. While the priority of ordinary creditors over the satisfaction of fines and penalties is to be noted, the long list of preferential claims may well leave the ordinary creditor empty-handed (thus decreasing his incentive to petition for bankruptcy).

ALTERNATIVE TO BANKRUPTCY UNDER THE ARRANGEMENT PROCEEDINGS ACT

A debtor can seek to avoid bankruptcy proceedings through the debt restructuring alternative available under the Arrangement Proceedings Act of 1934 (the Arrangement Act). A petition for protection under the Arrangement Act can be brought to the local district court by an "economic subject" who has ceased to pay its debts or foresees the imminent cessation of payments. The advantage of the arrangement proceeding is that that it staves off the declaration of bankruptcy, which cannot be made prior to the final disposition of the petition, and leaves the petitioner in partial control of its assets.

The debtor's petition must include a list of assets along with a list of creditors and the value of the outstanding obligations. The debtor also submits a proposal for the rescheduling of its obligations, which can include deferment, installment payments, and debt reduction. Proposals submitted by state enterprises may also include a partial or complete transformation of the enterprise into a commercial entity. The proposal cannot discriminate among creditors without their express agreement to the less favorable terms.

Prior to acting on a petition submitted by a state enterprise, the court

must solicit the opinion of the founding organ or an organ representing the State Treasury. The court can also request the opinions of
other institutions concerning the usefulness of the enterprise from the
"national, economic, and social point of view."

A decision to reject (but not to grant) the arrangement petition is
subject to appeal. If the petition is granted, the court appoints a judge-
commissioner and an executive supervisor to oversee the proceedings
and the debtor's enterprise. After the announcement of the opening of
the proceedings the debtor cannot dispose of its assets or enter into
new obligations without the permission of the executive supervisor.
The announcement also serves to stay the payment of all debts,
including the execution of previous court judgments, and to suspend
the accrual of interest on all debts (which, again, may be very advantageous to the debtor).

As the next step, the judge-commissioner assembles at least one-half
of the listed creditors and presents to them the restructuring proposal
submitted by the debtor. Both the debtor and the creditors may
suggest amendments, and the proposal is adopted if it receives the
support of a majority of the voting creditors holding a minimum of
two-thirds of the debt. If the proposal reduces the debtor's obligations
by over 40 per cent, it must gain the approval of creditors holding at
least four-fifths of the debt. The court must refuse to approve the
arrangement if proper procedures have not been followed, if the agreement offends public decency or public order, and if the agreement
pertains to a state enterprise and the founding organ or the representative of the Treasury objects to it. The court can also reject a proposal
if it is excessively prejudicial to the creditors who voted against it. The
court's decision to approve or reject an arrangement is subject to
appeal.

Upon becoming final, the arrangement is binding on all creditors,
except those whom the debtor had deliberately not revealed and who
have not attended the proceedings. The approval of the arrangement
restores full control over its estate to the debtor.

3B. Structure of ownership

The size of the private sector

The private sector's share of the Polish economy was always
significantly higher than that in other communist countries, because a

large proportion of land remained in private hands. Excluding agriculture, however, the state sector (including cooperatives) accounted for 90 per cent of production and 85 per cent of investment in 1989.

The growth of the private sector in the last two years has been quite impressive. Recent estimates put the contribution of the non-agricultural private sector at 24 per cent of GNP in 1991, with its share in construction equal to 55 per cent, and the volume of private sector retail trade as high as 80 per cent of the total already at the end of 1990.[11] In terms of employment, the private sector (again excluding agriculture) is reported to account for 38 per cent of the economy's total number of jobs.

Most of the growth of the private sector has been in the form of small and medium size firms and, above all, individual entrepreneurship. At the end of 1991, there were nearly 1.5 mln private businesses in Poland, over 45,000 of which were joint-stock and limited-liability companies established under the provisions of the Commercial Code. There were also 17,300 cooperatives and almost 4,800 joint ventures (the number of the latter having grown three-fold during the year). It must also be kept in mind that official data probably significantly underestimate the actual numbers, since many businesses do not register, or under-report their revenues for tax purposes. This may be one of the reasons why the profitability of the private sector appears to be significantly smaller than that of the badly ailing state sector (see Table 3B.1).[12]

Table 3B.1 Average profitability of companies in each ownership category (as per cent of costs) (Jan–Sept, 1991)

State	7.6
Municipal	7.0
Cooperative	1.1
Foreign	5.1
Private	0.5
Mixed	4.8

---

[11] This figure, taken from a Ministry of Privatization publication, is somewhat high in the light of information from other sources discussed in the subsection on small privatization below, Section 4B.

[12] Another reason may be due to the artificiality of the state-sector accounts, in which many uncollectable debts appear as assets on the books.

Table 3B.2 Numbers of units and revenues for each ownership category (as per cent of total, Jan–Sept, 1992)[1]

Category	Number of units	Per cent of revenues
State	8,727	72.4
Municipal	673	1.2
Cooperative	17,381	14.4
Foreign	825	0.9
Private	44,226	3.7
Mixed	4,455	7.1
Other	175	0.3

[1] Only joint-stock and limited-liability companies are counted in the private sector.

There is a very heavy concentration of private businesses in the service and trade sectors, and change has certainly been much slower in manufacturing and other capital intensive areas of the economy. Of the much larger number of private businesses, only 340,000 units (as of the end of 1991) were in industry, and the overwhelming majority of these were very small. More significantly, the share of revenues of the nearly 45,000 private-sector commercial companies as a percentage of total revenues is still quite small (see Table 3B.2). (It may be interesting to note that between June and September the share of the private sector grew by 0.7 per cent of the total, and that of the mixed by 1 per cent.)

In terms of employment, while private companies are still quite small (only 2,100 private and 946 mixed firms had over fifty employees in September 1991), their size is clearly growing (there were only 1,769 and 836 such firms respectively in June of the same year). But there were still 319 state enterprises with over 2,000 employees, and only three private and eleven mixed companies in the same category.

FOREIGN INVESTMENT
There are no reliable figures on the total amount of foreign investment in Poland, since statistical information is not required from foreign participants. However, aggregate foreign investment as of July 1992 is estimated at around $800 mln, $670 mln of which is estimated to have been brought in since 1989. Among the investor countries, the largest share is held by Germany (30 per cent of companies, and 23 per cent of capital), followed by the United States.

There exist more accurate figures on the number of companies with foreign participation: there were 5,147 such companies in November

1991, and their number has grown by 810 since September of the same year (the total of firms with foreign participation was only 949 in 1989). The proportion of joint ventures to wholly-owned foreign companies has been steadily rising, reaching 66 per cent by the end of 1990, and 84 per cent by November 1991. In most of the bigger joint ventures, the foreign partner holds a majority stake or a minority ownership stake with a majority of the voting power.

Most of the foreign investment is in rather small firms: in September 1991, only 402 firms with foreign participation employed more than fifty people, and only one (Wedel) was quoted on the Warsaw stock exchange. The total revenue of companies with foreign participation and over fifty employees was Zl 9,418 bln ($680 mln) in the first nine months of 1991, and profits in that period for the same companies totaled Zl 392 bln ($28.3 mln).

4. THE PRIVATIZATION PROCESS

Introduction

The privatization process in Poland is characterized by a tension between the centralist schemes of the postcommunist governments and the pressure of enterprise insiders to decentralize control over ownership changes at the enterprise level. The tension has been further exacerbated by the parliamentary weakness of the successive governments, and the political paralysis resulting from the absence of a stable parliamentary majority.

The government formulated its initial privatization plans in an atmosphere of considerable optimism. Despite the fact that the first postcommunist government in Poland consisted of a coalition appealing to the Solidarity tradition, its economic leaders were more influenced by the liberal point of view, and many of them believed that the main goal of the postcommunist structural reforms was to establish a traditional capitalist system of corporate governance that would put an end to the spontaneous (as well as often illegal) appropriation of state property by the local *nomenklatura* and limit the extraordinary powers of the workers' councils at the enterprise level. This was supposed to have been accomplished, first, by a speedy process of corporatization (known in Poland as "commercialization"[13]),

---

[13] Because of the conversion of state enterprise into a commercial-type company governed by the Commercial Code.

which would impose a new legal regime on the state sector and recentralize the decisions concerning future ownership transformation, and second, by rapid privatization through the type of sales pioneered in Great Britain. On both counts, the government's optimism was somewhat premature: the interests of the insiders turned out to be much more difficult to override than originally expected, and British-style methods of privatization were shown to be of little use in the largely *sui generis* situation of a postcommunist economy.

The Privatization Law, enacted after several months of intense discussions in the summer of 1990, already reflected a series of compromises. It created a centralized organ in charge of all privatization efforts – the Ministry of Ownership Transformations (referred to here as "Ministry of Privatization") – but also gave the employees a virtual veto power over the corporatization decision. (For more details, see Section 5.) As an inducement for the insiders to cooperate with the government's desire to establish a centrally set framework of privatization programs, the law also provided that up to 20 per cent of the shares of each company could be purchased by workers and management at a 50 per cent discount off the issue price, with the total value of the discount limited to the total wages paid to the company employees during the previous year.

The actual experience of privatization has forced further compromises and a number of delays. The range of the privatization techniques actually adopted has been designed to allow the government to formulate general privatization plans, but also to give insiders a large degree of choice with respect to the type of the program in which their enterprise would be included. The unstable political situation and the conflicts among the government, the parliament, and the president have also led to an increasing politicization of the privatization process. The government has been unable to muster a parliamentary majority behind its "mass" privatization program, which includes a program of free share distribution to the population, while President Walesa contributed to increasing popular expectations with respect to such giveaways by making unrealistic promises in his election campaign and subsequent messages to the parliament. Only in the area of so-called "small privatization," involving stores, workshops, and other small units have the ownership changes proceeded apace.

The political problems of privatization have rather deep roots in Poland. Public opinion polls have been showing a steady decline of support for privatization, with 58 per cent of the population, in October 1991, believing that large industry should be exclusively state-owned, 57 per cent believing that the state should own a part of shops and retail outlets, and 22 per cent believing that banks should be owned only by the state. Thirty-three per cent of the population (as compared with only 12 per cent a year earlier) thought that privatization was proceeding too fast, and 34 per cent (as opposed to 44 per cent a year earlier) thought it was proceeding too slowly.[14]

4A. Organizational structure of state regulation of privatization

The Ministry of Ownership Transformations

Immediately upon taking office, the Mazowiecki government moved to establish a governmental office devoted to overseeing the privatization process. The first such office was that of the Government Plenipotentiary for Ownership Transformations, who was an undersecretary of state in the Ministry of Finance. Among the most important tasks of the office of the plenipotentiary were to stop the unauthorized spontaneous privatization of state property and reassert state control over the privatization process, to prepare the new Privatization Law, the securities law and other acts required for the opening of the stock exchange in Warsaw, as well as to formulate the new government's overall privatization program.

The tasks of the plenipotentiary were eventually taken over by the new Ministry of Ownership Transformation, which was authorized in April 1990 and created in September. The ministry is responsible for basically all aspects of the privatization process, from proposing new programs, preparing necessary legislation, converting state enterprises into commercial companies, and exercising the state's ownership rights in the converted companies, to selling state companies and assets and training professionals in the field of corporate governance and securities markets.

The organizational structure of the Ministry is given in Chart 4A.1. The chart is largely self-explanatory, especially once the reader becomes familiar with the Ministry's programs, but a few clarifications may be in order.

The Department of Selection helps choose enterprises for particular

---

[14] Public opinions poll conducted between October 2 and 9, 1991, by the Center for Public Opinion Research, Warsaw.

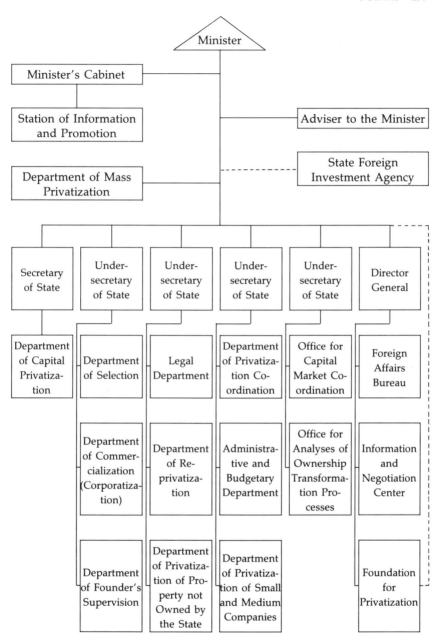

Chart 4A.1   Organizational structure of Poland's Privatization Ministry
Source: Privatization Information Center

programs and responds to their requests for permission to follow a particular path toward privatization. It also provides enterprises with information concerning the most appropriate form of privatization. The Department of Founders Supervision oversees state property held in the (corporatized or "commercialized") form of joint-stock and limited-liability companies. (In fulfilling this task, the department takes over the role played by the "founders" – usually the sectoral ministries – with respect to state enterprises prior to their corporatization.) The Department of Privatization of Property not Owned by the State deals with the privatization of municipal and cooperative properties. The Department of Privatization Coordination has thirteen local offices and maintains communications between the ministry and local enterprises and authorities.

Other state organs

The parliament's Commission of Ownership Transformation deals with legislative matters concerning privatization. The Prime Minister can order the corporatization of an enterprise despite the opposition of the workers' council – an important, if not often used, weapon in the hands of the Ministry of Privatization in its negotiations with enterprise insiders. The Ministry of Finance controls the program of debt forgiveness for the privatized enterprises – the significance of this already important function is bound to increase with time, together with the growth of inter-enterprise debts and the privatization of the banking sector. The Ministry of Finance must also agree to any installment sales used in the many privatizations through liquidation.

In addition to the Ministry of Privatization, the most important bodies involved in the privatization process are the "founding organs" of state enterprises, most commonly the Ministry of Industry (as heir to the various sectoral ministries) or the local authorities (in the case of municipal property). The founding organs must be consulted in connection with the corporatization of state enterprises (see Section 5 below), and they play an important role in the liquidation of state enterprises, which have been the most common occasion of their privatization (see the subections on bankruptcies (Section 3A) above, and privatization through liquidation (Section 4B) below).

The Agricultural Property Agency, created in the spring of 1992 on the basis of 1991 Act on Treasury-Owned Agricultural Property, will play a significant role in the privatization of state farms. It takes over existing state farms and appoints interim managers who are charged with preparing a restructuring plan leading to eventual sale or leasing to private parties.

4B. Overview of privatization programs

Poland's approach to privatization provides for a range of different programs and techniques, and the relative emphasis of the Polish authorities with respect to these programs has changed significantly over time. The first objective of the government was to end the uncontrolled appropriation of state property by insiders (so-called "spontaneous privatization").

Simultaneously, the authorities intended to speed up the creation of a substantial private ownership stake in the overwhelmingly state-owned industrial sector through the means of so-called "capital privatization." This traditional method involved attempts at selling the shares of previously corporatized enterprises through public offerings, trade sales, management and employee buy-outs, or a combination of these methods. This program met with only very limited success – as of June 1992, only thirty-two companies were more than 51 per cent privatized through all of these forms of capital privatization, bringing in only $159.5 mln in revenue – and the emphasis slowly shifted to other methods.

The most important of these was so-called "privatization by liquidation." This name is somewhat misleading, since it implies the sale of failing enterprises; it in fact consists of sales or leases of the assets of state enterprises (which are often in relatively good condition), without the enterprises' prior conversion into commercial companies. The enterprises then go out of existence – hence the name "liquidation" – to be replaced by whatever business entities the new owners of the assets decide to register.

To bolster its sales program for larger state enterprises, the Ministry of Privatization initiated, in the summer of 1991, another approach, known as "sectoral privatization." Strictly speaking, sectoral privatization was merely a preparatory program, in which an overall privatization policy was to be developed with respect to a number of state enterprises grouped together because of their related activities.

In the last days of the Mazowiecki government (October 1990), and during the next administration (with Janusz Lewandowski at the head of the Ministry of Privatization), a new program of so-called "mass privatization" was launched, based on the free distribution of shares and the creation of active privatization intermediaries. Although this program ran into protracted parliamentary and political difficulties, disappointment with capital privatization has kept it alive, and the return of Mr. Lewandowski to the Ministry of Privatization raises the prospect of its being pursued with renewed vigor.

The difficulties and delays encountered in the privatization process also led to demands for some interim measures, which would be short of the state's total disengagement. In particular, an increasing number of critics argued that privatization was impractical, given the deteriorating situation of the state sector, and that more emphasis should be placed on "preprivatization restructuring." As a result, the Ministry of Privatization responded with a program of its own, proposing long-term management contracts in lieu of immediate privatization.

Small and medium enterprises, and the services and distribution sectors have been targeted by specially designed programs. The most successful of these has been the so-called "small privatization" of retail outlets and small businesses, rapidly leading to a predominant position of the private sector in this area. For somewhat larger enterprises (those with up to 500 employees), the Privatization Ministry also designed a program known as "quick privatization," leaving room for greater involvement of governmental ministries.

The successive Polish governments in power since 1989 have shied away from a general return of confiscated property to its former owners, mainly because of the administrative and legal difficulties which the opening up of restitution claims could entail, and the resulting threat of even further delays in the whole privatization process. As a result, Poland is somewhat of an exception among the Eastern European countries, in that it still does not have a reprivatization law, although several drafts have been proposed and debated by the parliament; the most recent in August 1992. Some reprivatization program is expected, however, and the very possibility of such a program, together with the the problem of unclear titles, has effectively blocked the privatization of housing and delayed changes in agriculture. The only reprivatizations that have taken place so far were those that returned to previous owners the nationalized property which was taken illegally at the time of the original nationalization.

What follows is a more detailed explanation of the more important Polish privatization programs.

Spontaneous privatization

"Spontaneous" or "nomenklatura" privatization, is the name given in Poland to a process of unsupervised and uncontrolled conversion of state property into private ownership by the members of the communist elite, most of which occurred prior to the advent of the first Solidarity government. The most common forms of such conversion were not clearly illegal, although they obviously involved abuses of political power. In a typical transaction, a state enterprise (often nominally bankrupt) would be transformed into a commercial company (on the basis of the Law on State Enterprises), with insiders ending up with a large portion of the shares through the means of a manipulated offering at an unrealistically low price. Alternatively, the members of the *nomenklatura* and their families created private companies (sometimes with the participation of foreign investors) which then entered into sweetheart deals with state enterprises and siphoned off their resources. Transactions of this kind often involved exporting goods produced at subsidized prices, leasing equipment belonging to state enterprises at artificially low prices, and mediating in the dealings between state enterprises and the private sector.

The actual extent of spontaneous privatization is not known, and despite much public outcry and anecdotal evidence of huge fortunes made through the process, no study of this phenomenon contains even remotely reliable data. However, spontaneous privatization played an important role in shaping the rest of the Polish privatization programs, and can be seen as a principal reason behind the Polish programs' heavy reliance on central governmental control.

Capital privatization

PUBLIC OFFERINGS

A public offering (initial public offering or IPO) of the securities of a corporatized state enterprise is, from the point of view of administration, the most complex and time-consuming method of privatization. In practice, it can be applied to only a small number of companies, each of which must have a good reputation and reliable products. The response of the Polish public to the IPOs was very restrained, and the government has just about given up its hopes of privatizing a large section of the economy through this method. Employees of the targeted companies also showed a marked lack enthusiasm for capital privatization, which, given the need for the workers' councils' consent to initial corporatization (see Section 5 below), necessitated a great deal of time-consuming public relations work.[15]

Public offerings of the securities of privatized state enterprises initially held great attraction for the Polish authorities. The process had been tried with considerable success in other countries, both developed and developing, and the authorities could rely on the expertise of foreign investment banks and accounting firms that had participated in apparently similar transactions in the West and expressed great interest in expanding their activities into Poland. Above all, it promised an immediate move into the prestigious world of quintessentially capitalist finance: the introduction of stock exchanges, a myriad of financing instruments, banking institutions, mutual and pension funds, etc. The government's confident intention in 1990 was to begin by selling twenty "good" firms through IPOs. Foreign firms were hired to prepare the issues by analyzing and valuing each company, with Polish consulting firms serving as trainees. Legislation was adopted to open the stock exchange in Warsaw (based on the French model of the Lyons bourse), symbolically located in the building formerly housing the Central Committee of the Communist Party. Groups of targeted buyers included foreign investors, domestic private investors, institutional investors, and employees of the enterprises to be privatized.

Among other pitfalls, the effort proved to be based on a serious underestimation of the difficulty of setting accurate offering prices for companies in the rapidly changing economic environment of a postcommunist economy. Even though the companies selected were supposed to be those best suited for immediate privatization, they had for the most part no track record of functioning in a market economy. Their mix of assets was mostly the function of a clamoring for scarce investment resources in a central allotment system rather than a result of genuine business decisions. Their book values and accounts were not only calculated according to the unsuitable communist accounting system, but also contained figures corresponding to centrally set prices of inputs and outputs that bore little relation to market values. Finally, the valuators, in order to arrive at a realistic picture of the company's condition, needed the cooperation of the insiders, who often felt threatened by the process, and were interested in keeping the initial

---

[15] An enterprise targeted for an IPO must first be converted into a joint-stock company, since limited-liability companies cannot be publicly traded.

price as low as possible, since their right to buy the company shares at a discount had a cap equal to their salaries for the past year. In this situation, traditional valuation methods familiar to western accountants were of little use, the ultimate figures were necessarily quite arbitrary, and the public had little confidence in the outcome.

An additional problem with the original IPOs, which also contributed to the lack of public confidence in the success of the program, was the absence of a "core" or "strategic" investor in the first wave of the companies put up for sale, i.e. someone who would be willing to acquire a substantial block of shares, bring in more capital and expertise, and monitor the insiders' performance.

As a result, only five companies[16] were privatized by IPOs in 1990, raising some Zl 300 bln ($21.6 mln at the time) in revenue, of which nearly a quarter was spent on administrative costs. The final receipts were lower than the initial asset valuation of Zl 500 bln and some of the shares were reportedly purchased by state banks. In addition, despite very significant inflation during the 1990–92 period, (see Section 2), all but one of the companies involved were still trading significantly below their issuing price in 1992. Perhaps significantly, the only exception to this was a company (Exbud) in which the management had purchased a significant block of shares.

Table 4B.1 Distribution of shares of the companies privatized in the first IPOs

Company	Number of shares (in thousands)				
	Total	IPO	Workers	Mngmnt	State
Tonsil	1,500	750	300	0	450
Prochnik	1,500	1,200	300	0	0
Krosno	2,200	1,100	440	0	660
Exbud	1,000	450	200	175	0
Kable	1,000	830	170	0	0

---

[16] Exbud, Tonsil, Krosno, Prochnik, Slaska Fabryka Kabli.

Table 4B.2 Share prices of the companies privatized in the first IPOs

Company	Share price (in thousands of zloty)				
	Nominal	Issue	Market*	Ratio 1#	Ratio 2+
Tonsil	40	80	32.6	1.31	.21
Prochnik	20	50	36.5	8.18	.46
Krosno	50	65	28.2	73.6	.15
Exbud	50	120	415	3.03	1.2
Kable	50	70	41.8	12.78	.24

* Average for 10 weeks before April 14, 1992
# Price to earnings
+ Price to book value

Six more companies "went public" in 1991, with hopes for a larger number in 1992. One of the lessons drawn from the experience was that IPOs should be combined with another method designed to bring in a significant strategic investor.

TRADE SALES

A trade sale is the name applied in Poland to sales of large blocks of shares outside the financial markets, usually through a public invitation to tender, a public auction, or a negotiated private placement. A public offering may, but need not, be linked to a trade sale. The prospective investor often initiates this type of privatization, but sometimes the management also puts in an offer. The investor is usually a foreign company, with its own investment goals, often ready to take over the management of the company. The active investor normally acquires the majority of the shares; in some cases, such as the Wedel chocolate company, it holds a minority stake but a special class of shares entitling it to a majority of the vote.

In most trade sales, following the initial negotiations with an interested buyer, the ministry hires an adviser to handle the sale and announces a public invitation to tender. In selecting the winning tender, the ministry weighs a number of factors in addition to price, such as the investor's readiness to bring in additional capital and expertise, and the potential for maintaining employment. Altogether, until the end of February 1992, public invitations to tender have been issued for seventeen ultimately privatized firms, with the total assets of Zl 2,138 bln[17], of which Zl 1,208 bln was sold through the tenders. In addition, significant stakes (worth Zl 104 bln) in three companies (with assets of Zl 153 bln) were sold at an auction.

MANAGEMENT/EMPLOYEE BUY-OUTS

Management and employee buy-outs have been primarily used in the privatization of small and medium size companies, and they always take the form of leveraged buy-outs, with the state serving as the creditor. The loan is raised on the security of the company's assets and is supposed to be paid off from the profits.

Despite initial expectations that insider buy-outs would be a popular form of privatization, only a very small number of companies have been privatized in this way. The Ministry of Privatization lists only two companies (with combined assets of Zl 93 bln) as having been partially privatized (through a sale of Zl 78 bln worth of shares) through employee buy-outs as of the end of February 1992. In a small number of other cases, management has been a significant investor. Apparently, a much more popular route of insider privatization has been found in the method of privatization through liquidation.

Privatization through liquidation

If the number of companies and the size of the assets involved is taken as the measure of success, privatization through liquidation has been the most successful Polish privatization program outside the field of very small units (retail stores etc.). However, since very little information is available on the performance of the privatized companies in the wake of the state's withdrawal from the position of ownership, it is difficult to judge the program's success in terms of its effect on the restructuring of the sold or leased enterprises. Nearly all of the companies involved face very high levels of indebtedness, in terms of funds needed to cover both operating expenses and lease payments to the state. In a deeply recessionary environment, many of the firms have been experiencing shrinking markets and may be facing bankruptcy. However, given the general state of the Polish economy, any other result would be quite surprising.

The popularity of privatization through liquidation is due to the

---

[17] Given the fluctuations of the zloty over time, it is difficult to give a dollar equivalent of this sum; it stood at $194 mln.

potential advantages it offers to the insiders of the privatized enterprises, and their ability to control and manipulate the process to their benefit. Although this type of privatization is certainly much more controlled than the "wild" privatization of the last days of the communist regime, it is also clearly the outlet for the continuing pressure for a decentralized and "spontaneous" form of ownership transformation.

Rather than proceeding through corporatization of the state enterprise involved and the subsequent sale of the shares of the new company (as in the capital privatization), privatization through liquidation begins with a decision to liquidate the state enterprise. This technique has been widely used for both viable and bankrupt operations, but the two cases must be clearly distinguished. In the case of bankrupt enterprises, the proceedings are governed by the 1981 Law on State Enterprises, and the assets of the liquidated enterprise must be sold or contributed by the state to a successor company (such as a joint venture or a similar arrangement). (See the subsection on bankruptcy and liquidation in Section 3A above.) In contrast to these "insolvency liquidations," viable state enterprises may be liquidated on the basis of Article 37 of the Privatization Law, and it is only these cases that will be referred to here as "privatization through liquidation." In these cases, the state enterprise nearly always has a successor (which often takes the assets with the liabilities), and the assets of the enterprise, in addition to being sold or contributed to another company, may also be *leased* to a new company specially created for this purpose by the employees of the liquidated state enterprise. In fact, this form of leasing has been the most common path of privatization through liquidation.

Leasing arrangements

Generally speaking, all privatizations through liquidation can be initiated by the "founding organ" (usually a sectoral ministry or a local authority) or the workers' council of the enterprise involved. The decision is up to the founding organ, with the consent of the Ministry of Privatization (the Ministry has twelve days to issue its decision). In cases in which the assets of the liquidated enterprise are to be leased, however, the agreement of the workers' council is required, and the lease must be made to a (joint-stock or limited-liability) company of which the majority of the employees of the liquidated state enterprise must become shareholders.[18] The new company must be capitalized at the level of at least 20 per cent of the liquidated state enterprise prior to the lease. The actual lease is then signed by the founding organ of the liquidated enterprise.

The process leading up to the lease usually involves a coalition between management, workers' council, and the unions, and bargaining with the founding organ over the value of the assets to be leased. One of the inherent moral hazards involved is that the insiders, who have both the best access to information and actual control over the company's operations, are clearly interested in coming up with a low valuation prior to the leasing contract. The arrangement creates an incentive for the insiders to reduce the enterprise's cash flow, since valuation has traditionally been based on the firm's discounted future cash flows. As a solution to this problem, valuation procedures are to be modified.

The usual term of the contract is five to ten years and there are three types of these contracts:

- lease and sale;
- tenancy with an option to purchase;
- tenancy without the option to purchase.

The *lease and sale arrangement* (or closed-end lease) involves a number of separate steps under the Polish law. At the time the original contract is signed, the new company (lessee) acquires only a leasehold (which under Polish law is a contractual right, and not a proprietary interest) on the assets of the liquidated state enterprise. At the same time, however, the parties also sign a contract obligating the founding organ of the state enterprise (lessor) to convey title to the lessee at the end of the lease, if the lessee has made all the payments and satisfied the other conditions of the lease. This second contract also determines the price at which the assets are are to be conveyed, and the payments on the lease are so calculated that the assets are fully paid for at the end of the lease (see below). Finally, when the lease is terminated, a separate notarial act is necessary to convey title from the lessor to the lessee.

---

[18] If the employees do not purchase their shares in the new company within two months from the workers' council's decision, the lease can be made without the employee majority requirement.

The yearly payments on the lease, governed by a special regulation of the Minister of Finance of November 10, 1990 (No. 43, item 334), are calculated as follows: the value of the leased assets divided by the length of the contract term, plus an additional payment equal to the still unpaid portion of the value of company multiplied by three-quarters of the refinancing rate used by the National Bank of Poland (or 30 per cent, whichever is lower). Effectively, then, the lessee pays the agreed upon price of the assets in installments, with an interest rate that is capped at a level that, given inflation in Poland, has been significantly negative in real terms. In addition, in the first year, the lessee can make only one-third of the interest payments due, and only one-half of those due during the second year, with the remainder due at the end of the third year of the contract.

The *tenancy with an option to purchase* is a similar arrangement to lease and sale, except that instead of paying the principal (equal to the agreed upon value of the assets), the lessee makes a smaller yearly payment for the option to buy the assets at the end of the lease. If the lessee, at the end of his contract, chooses to buy the property, it can acquire it at the then prevailing market price, with the amount paid for the option deducted from the purchase price.

Finally, the *tenancy without the option to purchase* is an arrangement in which the lessee pays only the amount equal to the "additional" or interest payments on the lease and sale, and must pay the full market value of the assets if it decides to purchase them at the termination of its contract.

In practice, all actual leasing arrangements are of the first type, since the lessees are unwilling to take the risk of the rise in the purchase price during the term of the lease. Typically, following the signing of the leasing agreement, the only monitoring of the arrangement done by the founding organ or the Ministry of Privatization regards the collection of the payments, unless there are complaints from the employees of the new company, in which case the founding organ may make some inquiries.

Sale of assets

Another method of privatization through liquidation, which is also used with respect to "insolvency liquidations" under the Law on State Enterprises, is to sell the assets of the liquidated company to private natural or legal persons. The decision to proceed with the liquidation theoretically belongs to the founding organ and the Ministry of

Privatization, but the Ministry routinely requires that the workers' council and the director of the enterprise be consulted.[19] In practice, in the cases governed by the Privatization Law, the insiders are usually the ones who initiate the procedure, and they are the prime bidders for the assets of the liquidated enterprise.

Liquidation sales must always be public in nature and must be advertised in the local and national press (radio and TV have also been occasionally used). Individuals or companies wishing to participate receive information brochures prior to the sales, and are given the opportunity to inspect the enterprise's records and operations.

The sale is organized by the founding organ. To establish a minimum selling price and to help in the evaluation of the offers, the founding organs use expert advisers and consulting companies. The winning bid need not be the highest in monetary terms; issues such as credibility of the buyer are also taken into account, and a bid received from the employees of the liquidated company receives special consideration.

The Ministry of Privatization, in cooperation with the Ministry of Finance, offers the following terms of payment to assist buyers during the current shortage of domestic capital:

- The purchase price of an enterprise is payable partly in cash (no less than 40 per cent of the total) with the rest payable in 16 equal installments payable quarterly over four years, with the possibility of a one-year grace period;
- The sums payable in cash are counted to have a value 1.25 times greater than the sums payable in installments;
- The same interest terms as those made available in the case of leasing arrangements (see above) are provided.

Contribution in kind

The assets of a liquidated state enterprise may also be contributed in kind by the state to a new company, usually a joint venture formed by the State Treasury with a domestic or foreign participant.[20] The

---

[19] Following the corresponding provisions of the Law on State Enterprises, the Privatization Law also gives the Council and the director a right to challenge the decision of the founding organ.

[20] In exceptional cases of insolvency liquidation, where there is no other prospective buyer, a liquidated enterprise's assets may be used as a contribution to the capital of an existing wholly state-owned company.

State Treasury's shares may then be made available for purchase by the employees, other individuals, or a corporate investor. It should be noted that in the present context, the new company does not necessarily take over the preexisting obligations of the liquidated enterprise, including its existing labor contracts. Also, since the liquidated state enterprise is not being transformed into a wholly state-owned commercial company, the employees are not entitled to preferential share purchase terms, as otherwise provided for the insiders by the Privatization Law.

The process described here is under the control of the founding organ, which negotiates on behalf of the state with the other parties and represents it on the Supervisory Board of the new company, but the agreement of the Ministry of Privatization must also be obtained.

The results

As of the beginning of March 1992, 1,055 state enterprises have been liquidated, of which 589 were closed down because of their poor financial condition, and 466 were liquidated under the Privatization Law. The process led to the creation of 545 new economic units, most often (in 384 cases) joint-stock or limited-liability companies formed by the employees and leasing the assets of the liquidated enterprises. In twenty-one other cases, the employee-owned companies entered into joint ventures with the founding organs of the liquidated enterprise, and in 140 cases a mixture of techniques has been used. Although the main employee participants are white-collar workers, blue-collar workers are reported to be quite active purchasers (buying between 20 and 60 per cent stakes in the new companies). Insiders also often seek out outside investors, who become partners in the new company and provide the entity created by the insiders with additional capital.

Although no good data concerning the size of the transactions involved are currently available, there were 155 liquidated enterprises (89 under the Privatization Law) with over 500 employees, 268 (149) with between 200 and 500 employees, and 632 (218) with under 200 employees. Although the enterprises liquidated because of poor performance were scattered throughout the sectoral spectrum, those liquidated under the Privatization Law were overwhelmingly in construction (206), trade (87) and industry (98). By far the most popular method of privatization through liquidation was the lease and sale, but the creation of joint ventures using liquidated enterprise assets as capital is becoming more frequent, especially in the case of small enterprises.

As can be seen from these figures, privatization through liquidation, with its room for initiative and the acquisition of property rights by insiders, has been the most common form of state property transformation in Poland. It is also likely to remain so, unless the mass privatization program (see below) is finally realized. At the same time, the shortage of domestic capital and the increasing inability of the employees to come up with the necessary contributions has placed a question mark over the future of privatization through liquidation. Although liquidation might still remain the favorite route of management, the employees' control of the workers' councils may effectively block the procedure, especially since such transformations threaten the workers' security and their effective control of a large number of enterprise decisions.

Quick privatization

At the beginning of July 1991 the Ministry of Privatization launched a program known as "quick privatization" or "quick sale" of small and medium sized enterprises. Under this program, which is formally a part of privatization through liquidation, the founding organ takes the initiative for privatization, and invites potential investors (corporate bodies and individuals, including employees) to enter into negotiations. The companies are put together in groups of approximately six units, and the sales are processed together. While this route of privatization is now used only for sales to domestic persons, there are plans to extend it to include foreign investors as well. The Ministry of Privatization, which must approve any sales negotiated by the founding organs, seeks to conclude sales on the basis of a minimum 40 per cent cash payment, with the balance payable in installments. Interest is calculated according to the Ministry of Finance procedure outlined above (see the subsection on privatization through liquidation).

Forty-six enterprises have been included in this program as of March 1992. Thirty-five of these had fewer than 200 employees. Fourteen enterprises were sold before that date, most of them in the early phases of the program. One of the sold units had over 500 employees, one over 200, and the rest fewer than 200 employees. Five of the sold enterprises were in agriculture, and four each in industry and construction.

Mass privatization with the use of intermediaries

The Polish mass privatization program is intended to privatize partially several hundred large commercialized enterprises through an indirect distribution of their shares at a low nominal price. The enterprises involved are being transformed into joint-stock companies, and 60 per cent of their shares will be distributed to specially created financial intermediaries. The intermediaries, called National Investment Funds, will then become the legal owners of the shares, and will be charged with monitoring the performance of the companies in their portfolio, and either restructuring or selling them, either in whole or in part. Shares in the funds themselves will then be distributed to Polish citizens.

The mass privatization program is currently in the enterprise selection stage; further progress awaits the passage of enabling legislation by the parliament. As in other types of Polish privatization, participation is largely decided by consensus among all interested parties: managers, workers, the founding organ, and the Ministry of Privatization. The eligibility criteria described below were first determined by the Ministry of Privatization, after which the Central Statistical Office searched its database for eligible enterprises, which were then sent "invitations" to participate.[21] Although the authorities initially exerted some pressure on the enterprises to speed up the process, inclusion in the program was ultimately voluntary, with the enterprises willing to participate having to secure approvals from their management, the workers' council, and the Anti-Monopoly Office.

The stated policy of the Ministry of Privatization is to exclude from the program all enterprises which can be realistically expected to be privatized through other methods, those that are potential or actual monopolists, and those in poor financial condition. A point system was used to rate enterprises on profitability, assets to liabilities ratio, and the ratio of revenues to payments due. Thus, while the Polish program excludes the enterprises that are the clearest winners (since a buyer for them can probably be found), it attempts to include only the "best" among the remaining ones. One of the problems, however, has been that, in the rapidly deteriorating economic conditions of the

---

[21] Throughout its work on the program, the Ministry has been assisted by the British investment bank, S.G. Warburg & Co. A Polish consulting agency was also employed to assist the Ministry in the enterprise selection. Other consulting groups worked on special tasks related to the distribution of shares among the population, public relations, etc.

state sector, a number of enterprises were becoming ineligible during the selection process itself. According to the ministry, the enterprises included in the program are also in principle larger than average.

As of the summer of 1992, 182 enterprises have been selected for the "first wave" of the program, while seven are partially accepted and nine are still being analyzed. These 200-odd enterprises have a total book value of about $2.7 bln, or about six per cent of the total book value of the approximately 8,000 state enterprises. Other data about the characteristics of the selected enterprises are not yet available.

The ministry is analyzing an additional 130 enterprises for a second wave (which according to sources inside the Ministry of Privatization is supposed to be "better" than the first), and further waves are under consideration. Thus, although the initial wave is relatively small, given the scale of the Polish economy, it is hoped that the program will grow significantly in the future. The relationship among these successive waves is not yet clear: it is not known, for example, whether the same funds would participate in each wave and whether there would be separate share or certificate distributions.

As for the distributees, all citizens eighteen years and older (some 27 million people) will be eligible to participate in the program for a price meant to cover its administrative costs, which are estimated at less than $20 per person, or about 10 per cent of the average monthly wage.

The shares of the commercialized enterprises will be divided into fixed proportions: for each company, one National Investment Fund (the "lead fund") will receive 33 per cent, with the other funds dividing equally the remaining 27 per cent. The state will retain 30 per cent (nonvoting while in state hands, except in the event of an "emergency"), and employees will receive up to 10 per cent free of charge. This last provision differs from the procedure specified in the Privatization Law, which allows the workers to buy up to 20 per cent of the shares of the privatized companies at a 50 per cent discount, with the subsidy limited to one year's salary. The change, which will require parliamentary approval, was designed to avoid the problems associated with the valuation of the shares to be distributed to the workers, but the question of the limit to be placed on the subsidy has not been clearly resolved: unless it is capped in some way, a free distribution of 10 per cent of the shares of some companies to the insiders may create an enormous windfall for the employees.

Three possible ways of disposing of the 30 per cent state holding are being considered at this time: to sell it and generate revenue for the budget, to capitalize the social security (pension) system, or to compensate victims of expropriation and persecution. One proposal is to divide the 30 per cent, with two-thirds going into the social security fund and one-third for compensation.

After the first year of the funds' operation, special "investment certificates" will be distributed to the population. The details are not yet fully worked out, but the certificates will constitute an entitlement to a fraction of a share in each fund; they will become tradable and exchangeable for the actual voting shares of the funds, but only when a certain degree of concentration of holdings takes place. The express rationale for the delay in the distribution of the investment certificates is to allow time to observe the financial performance of the companies in the funds' portfolios, but the practical difficulties in the distribution process have also played a role (with the ministry very eager to initiate the process of establishing the funds as soon as possible). One of the consequences of this is that citizens will have no choice of the fund of which they would like to become shareholders. The shares of the funds are expected to be traded on the Warsaw Stock Exchange.

The funds will be established and licensed by the Ministry of Privatization; no free entry into the mass privatization program will be permitted. The number of the funds is not yet determined, with figures between ten and twenty most often mentioned, depending on the size of the program and the quality of the applicants to run them. The National Investment Funds, which will be governed by special legislation, will not be allowed to issue new shares; they will be formed as closed-end joint-stock companies.

Although various bidding schemes have been considered to allocate the lead (33 per cent) blocks of shares of the privatized enterprises among the funds, including a proposal of an auction in which each fund would be given a fixed number of points with which to bid, these seem to have been rejected in favor of a plan establishing a random order of the funds and allowing each fund in turn to pick one enterprise at a time. Because the enterprises in the program vary enormously in size, there is no guarantee that all fund portfolios will be of a similar size. It is also not clear what will happen if no fund wants a particular enterprise. If the funds are required to "take the bad with the good," they may plead for subsidies or concessions later, on the grounds that they were forced to take nonviable companies into their portfolios.

It is intended that the funds have a significant component of foreign management, but members of the Supervisory Board will be mostly

Polish. These board members are expected to be selected by an eighty-person committee currently in the process of being constituted by the ministry. The fund managers will be selected from among international fund managers, investment bankers, and management and consulting firms through a tender process expected to be administered by the funds' Supervisory Boards in cooperation with the Ministry of Privatization. Among the selection criteria will be regional and international experience and reputation; the size of the management fee for which the applicant will be willing to settle may also play a role in the decision.

The fund managers' compensation will consist of a fixed and a variable component. The former is supposed to cover "only operating costs," but given the initially small size of the program, these may be very high relative to the value of the capital. Although various versions of the variable component have been informally proposed, the current idea appears to be that the management would receive 1.5 per cent of the shares of their fund annually. The current draft also sets a limit of 15 per cent on the total of the fund shares that can be owned by the management, thus implicitly limiting the first period of fund operation to ten years. The initial contract will be for four years, with provisions for annual review.

The funds are intended to be active in the management and restructuring of the companies of which they own the "lead" share; fund managers will be members of the management boards of these companies and will be expected to monitor their management's performance. The funds will be able to buy and sell shares in all companies, but in order to assure the continued presence of a "core investor," they will be restricted in their ability to sell their lead shares: if the sale of their "lead" shares were to bring their holding to less than 20 per cent, they will be required to find another lead shareholder willing to hold more than 20 per cent of the shares.

Although the program has been approved by the Parliamentary Commission of Ownership Transformation and was submitted to the full parliament in April 1992, it had not been considered by the full house by the end of the summer.

Sectoral privatization

As mentioned before, sectoral privatization is not really privatization. Rather, it is a method of grouping together a number of enterprises for the purpose of a systematic analysis which may result in their subsequent privatization. The name "sectoral" may also be misleading, if it is understood to imply that all companies in a given branch of industry must be included. "Sectors" are rather loose groupings of between five and thirty firms in related areas.

In launching the sectoral privatization program, the ministry was attempting to achieve a number of objectives. To begin with, the failure of the capital privatization program and its very high cost, made the authorities look for a way of combining the analysis of a number of enterprises, in order to save costs and develop a more effective strategy for the future. Secondly, the ministry was under pressure from both insiders and outsiders to privatize certain sensitive areas, such as the tobacco industry, and may have felt unsure how to handle a complex situation. Sectoral privatization allowed it to postpone immediate privatization in some cases, while at the same time preparing an "industrial policy" of sorts that would allow it to proceed with more confidence and expertise at a later date.

The process of sectoral privatization began by grouping 143 companies into thirty-six very diverse sectors, such as aviation, shipping, automobile production, pharmaceuticals, tobacco, electronics, fruit processing, breweries, household chemicals, confectionery, construction, potato products, canneries, shoe production, meat and sugar industries, etc. Some of the units in the program were already transformed into commercial companies, others were still state enterprises.

Following the selection, terms of reference were prepared by the ministry and investment banking, consulting, and accounting firms were invited to submit proposals to become official "lead" or "sectoral" advisors to the ministry for particular sectors. All the sectoral advisors were either foreign firms (most often paid from various aid programs) or consortia of such firms and Polish consulting groups. Each lead advisor chose its own subcontractors, and conducted a detailed analysis of the sector, taking into account both the domestic and international situation, in order to determine a comprehensive privatization and development strategy for the whole sector. At the same time, the advisor was supposed to analyze the position of individual companies in its sector, investigate the possibilities of their sale or capitalization, and advise the ministry on the appropriate actions to be taken, which may include restructuring prior to privatization, liquidation, or privatization through one of the existing ministry programs. In the normal case, the sectoral adviser was expected to remain the ministry's official adviser with respect to subsequent transactions concerning individual companies in the sector.

While it may be too early to pass definitive judgment, sectoral privatization has not yet produced the expected results. The advisers have been producing extensive papers diagnosing the conditions of Polish industry, but few actual privatizations have followed from their reports. To be sure, the informational benefits to the ministry may be considerable and the future may still show their value. But given its high costs and low immediate returns, the ministry is not planning an expansion of this program.

Preprivatization restructuring (management contracts)

One of the more recent programs of the Ministry of Privatization is deferred privatization, combined with issuing management contracts for an interim restructuring period. Since participation in this program is purely voluntary on the part of the enterprises, the program is mostly designed to motivate current insiders of firms that cannot be privatized at the present time, by giving them a direct interest in the company's performance and ultimate privatization. Sometimes a management contract may also be necessary for the sale of the firm to a passive investor, such as a creditor bank that decides to buy a stake in the company on the condition that a proper management structure is put in place.

For the prospective managerial group, whether composed of insiders or outsiders, the management contract designed for this program offers an opportunity to acquire significant equity stakes in the company at the time of its privatization in exchange for a relatively low down-payment and the managerial effort leading to restructuring and privatization.

The process under this program is initiated by the companies which want to be included. After an approval from the Ministry of Privatization is secured (good financial standings and peaceful labor relations are among the important selection criteria), the supervisory board of the corporatized state company publicizes an invitation to tender for the best restructuring plan. A crucial part of the offer is the valuation of the company offered by the prospective management group, the so-called "tender value." This valuation not only provides the most important criterion for the selection of the winner, but also determines the amount of deposit to be paid in by the management group and constitutes the benchmark against which its remuneration will be measured.

Upon the selection of the winner by the supervisory board controlled by the ministry, the main incentive contracts are signed for a four-year period by the Ministry of Privatization. The supervisory board, on behalf of the company, will also conclude an additional contract with the winning group, fixing the management's salary and yearly bonuses. The task of the management is to restructure the company, increase its value, and sell it before the end of the contract period.

The management group that wins the tender is obliged to make a financial deposit which is set as a fraction of the management's valuation of the enterprise, as set forth in its initial tender. The deposit is equal to 5 per cent of the tender value of up to Zl 10 bln ($830,000); 2 per cent of the tender value above Zl 10 bln and below Zl 150 bln and 1 per cent of the value above Zl 150 bln. Management groups funded by foreign capital must make a financial deposit twice as large as the domestic management groups, with management groups funded jointly by foreign and domestic capital making double payment on the portion invested by the foreign party.

The deposit is in part a form of credit from the management to the company, and in part a security deposit in connection with the assets entrusted to the management group. It will be returned to the management group after the termination of the business contract as the percentage of the value of the company equal to the ratio of the initial deposit to the tender value of the company. Thus, for example, if the management group posts a deposit equal to 4 per cent of the price at which it initially valued the company in its tender, it is entitled to receive at the termination of the contract 4 per cent of the company's stock or 4 per cent of the cash brought in by the sale of the company's assets. The deposit is subject to forfeiture if the supervisory board, after arbitration procedures, shows that the management acted in bad faith and to the detriment of the company, or if the company goes into bankruptcy. (The Ministry of Privatization is also considering the possibility of accepting financial deposits in the form of material assets or debts. In the latter case, creditors might become involved in the restructuring process, and a secondary market for company debt might develop.)

The management fee for the interim period is 70 per cent of the increase in the company's value during the life of the contract. The balance of the increase in value is divided between the employees (20 per cent) and the supervisory board (10 per cent). The fee is paid in the form of shares of the company at the time of its sale. The management contract may be terminated as soon as 51 per cent of the shares of the company are sold to private investors, including the shares sold to employees at a discount in compliance with the Privatization Law and the shares awarded to the management group as a fee for its services. The management will not be entitled to its fee if the shares are not sold prior to the expiration of the main management contract.

Since the program has been launched only recently, no contracts had been signed as of May 1992. But forty-three firms at that time were interested in participating, and the ministry selected twenty-eight of them for inclusion. Based on incomplete calculations, the average book value of these firms was ca. $3 mln.

Small privatization

Small privatization concerns shops and other small units which are the property of the local, rather than central, authorities. The assets of these small units and are controlled by the Communal Commercial Activity Law, rather than the Law on State Enterprises, and the ordinary liquidation procedures do not apply. Indeed, there is no formal "program" of small privatization. Instead, local authorities are relatively free to decide about the future of the businesses under their control, and they most often lease or rent them to private parties.[22]

Because of the decentralized nature of small privatization, there is some confusion about the forms it takes and about the extent to which the small units under local control have been actually privatized.

In December 1989, there were about 151,000 shops in Poland. About 124,000 of them were operated within the state and cooperative sector. If the floor surface of the private shops is compared with that of the public sector, the share of the private stores is seen to have been even smaller than these numbers would indicate: it amounted to just 5 per cent of the total.

The main question concerning the procedure used in the process of small privatization was whether the communal property would be rented at market rates (determined by an auction open to all participants) or whether it would be allocated administratively (mostly to insiders) at bureaucratically-set prices. One study of these procedures shows that only 9.3 per cent of the over 10,000 municipally owned shops rented in the first half of 1990 were allocated by an

---

[22] Part of the reason for the preference for leasing over sale of shop space is that titles to real property in the hands of the communes and municipalities are often very unclear.

auction, despite the fact that prices set at auctions were often thirty to forty times higher than bureaucratically-set rents.[23] Even when auctions were conducted, bidding was often limited to insiders, or the insiders would get preferential treatment in the form of rental "givebacks." The pressure by insiders, often threatened with unemployment and supported by labor unions, was very intense, and the argument was commonly heard that high rents would result in higher retail prices and slow down the privatization process.

There seems also to be some confusion concerning the number of the shops and small service outlets actually privatized. As we have noted before, an official publication of the Ministry of Privatization claimed that 80 per cent of some 100,000 existing small and medium size retail stores had been privatized in 1990.[24] Other sources within the ministry stated that there were 40,000 state stores left at the end of 1990, and a total of 300,000 stores were private (this number clearly include new stores as well). Minister Lewandowski, for his part, stated in September 1991 that three-quarters of retail trade were in private hands at that time. Sources outside of the ministry cite much smaller numbers of municipal and cooperative stores sold or leased to private parties in 1990 and 1992: these figures vary from 30,444 as of mid-1992 (Tamowicz) to 35,000 for 1990 (Central Planning Office).

Reprivatization

As explained before, Poland still does not have a reprivatization or restitution law, despite pressures from the office of the president and a number of legislative proposals, some endorsed by the government. Nevertheless, in anticipation of the reprivatization program, over 100,000 claims have been filed with various offices in Poland, including the Ministry of Privatization, where an Undersecretary of State has been charged with matters related to reprivatization. In the absence of appropriate legislation, only a very small fraction of these claims can be satisfied, notably those in which the property of the previous owners was taken by overzealous state officials acting without proper

---

[23] P. Tamowicz, "Small Privatization – An Inside View," in J. Earle, R. Frydman, and A. Rapaczynski (1992) (eds.), *Privatization in the Transition to a Market Economy* (Pinter Publishers and St. Martin's Press, 1992).

[24] Ch. Bandyk, *Privatization in Poland, Warsaw*, 1991. Both figures are contradicted by other sources.

legal basis under the nationalization laws. Some 195 such cases of restitution were noted prior to 1992, including some seventy hotels, forty-seven flour mills, twenty-three brick yards, and eleven bakeries. But it is estimated that in agriculture alone, some 1.2 mln hectares of land, valued at over $1 bln, were nationalized illegally in the years following the Second World War.

5. CORPORATIZATION

Corporatization, or "commercialization" as it is generally termed in Poland, is the transformation of state enterprises into wholly state-owned joint-stock or limited-liability companies governed by the rules of the Commercial Code (rather than the Law on State Enterprises). The new company takes over all the rights and liabilities of the former state enterprise, and its initial capital is equal to the value of the assets of the old enterprise. As a part of the transformation, the Ministry of Privatization, with the consent of the Ministry of Finance, can take over a part or all of the company's debt.

Corporatization was first made legally possible by the Law on State Enterprises, and a small number of state firms had been transformed into commercial companies before the advent of the first postcommunist government. Most of these transactions were in fact a part of the already described phenomenon of spontaneous privatization, and one of the purposes of the Privatization Law was to subject this type of transformation to state control, and to make it into a prelude to the new privatization process.

The crucial feature of the new corporatization was supposed to be a reorganization of corporate institutions and the replacement of the unclear and multiple authority structure of state enterprises (involving a combination of founding organs, workers' councils, trade unions, and management) with the standard hierarchical system of corporate governance familiar in the capitalist countries of Central Europe. The hope behind the idea of corporatization, as with much of the initial privatization effort in Poland, was not only to rationalize the governance structure of the enterprises, but also – perhaps above all – to reassert the state's ownership rights, and overcome the confusion between the decentralization of managerial authority and the obfuscation of property rights, characteristic of reformist thought under communism. Although corporatization was never viewed as a form of privatization, it was seen as an important step in that direction. It was to make the company formally ready for privatization by virtue of its new legal form, which was suitable for private ownership. More importantly, it was also supposed to introduce a more rational system of governance into the state sector, to change the incentive structure of corporate insiders, and to make the state companies more responsive to the forces of the market. In this sense, it was hoped that corporatization was more than just a formal transformation; it was also supposed to lay the material foundations of the new system of ownership. In the event, these more far-reaching expectations have not been fulfilled, and corporatization has played essentially the role of the first, purely formal stage on the way to ownership transformation.

Initiating the process of corporatization

The Privatization Law authorizes two paths leading to the corporatization of a state enterprise. The first, specified in Article 5, allows the Minster of Privatization to transform the enterprise upon the joint request of its managing director and workers' council, following a consultation with the general assembly of all employees and the founding organ, or upon the request of the founding organ, with the consent of the director and the workers' council, again following consultation with the general assembly of the employees. Thus, the management and the employees have an effective veto over all Article 5 transformations.

The second path to corporatization, specified in Article 6 of the Privatization Law and clearly conceived of as exceptional, allows the Prime Minister, upon the request of the Minister of Privatization, to transform a state enterprise without the consent of the insiders, although their opinion must be solicited by the Minister of Privatization.

Given that insiders were given an effective veto power over the normal course of corporatization, the authorities offered them several inducements to agree to the process, despite the fact that corporatization would inevitably lead to the diminution of the workers' control over the enterprise. As we have seen, capital privatization, for which corporatization is an indispensable first step, was "sweetened" by a promise of preferential sales of the shares of the new company to the insiders. Another inducement is the fact that corporatized entities may be exempted from an asset tax (misleadingly called "dividend") levied on a portion of the capital of state enterprises. Finally, insiders were offered a further incentive in the form of a 20 per cent reduction of the very restrictive excess wage tax (the so-called "popiwek"), levied on wage increases above allowable limits. (The wage tax is completely abolished once the majority of the company is privately owned.)

The criteria for approval of corporatization

The Privatization Law stipulates that the Minister of Privatization may deny, within three months from the date of submission, the request to corporatize a state enterprise "because of the enterprise's economic and financial conditions or an important national interest." The minister's refusal must be accompanied by a statement of reasons, and a list of conditions upon which the transformation will be permitted. The minister's decision is also subject to judicial review.

On the basis of these provisions, and with a view to the effective implementation of privatization after corporatization, the minister has established a number of criteria for the selection of enterprises scheduled for corporatization. These include: (a) the size of the enterprise in terms of its annual turnover, number of employees, and the absence of monopolistic position; (b) its historical and anticipated performance; (c) its legal situation, especially with respect to the ownership of land and buildings and the absence of an artificial multi-plant structure; (d) the likely interest of potential domestic and foreign investors; (e) good labor relations; (f) a clear development strategy; (g) ownership of a known and recognized trademark. Priority for corporatization is also given to enterprises which present the MOP with a specific privatization program.

Generally speaking, insofar as insider-requested corporatizations are concerned, the minister has refused to transform enterprises that do not raise the prospect of speedy privatization. This is in part due to recognition of the fact that corporatization makes sense only as the formal first step toward privatization, but also in part to the fact that the Ministry of Privatization does not want to take over the duties of the Ministry of Industry and other founding organs, thus becoming a wholesale caretaker of the rapidly deteriorating state sector. As a result, however, the majority of the Polish enterprises have been left in their old labor-dominated form.

In those cases in which there were realistic prospects of speedy privatization, the minister has been much more eager to corporatize, even if the enterprises themselves were sometimes reluctant. Thus, for example, when the ministry was preparing its mass privatization program (see above), which required a large number of enterprises for its success, the ministry actively identified suitable units and exerted some pressure on them to transform, raising, among other things, the prospect of a compulsory Article 6 corporatization. In line with the voluntary and consensual nature of the Polish privatization programs, however, even in the case of mass privatization, the enterprises were ultimately given the choice of opting out of the program if they wanted to follow other alternatives. (See the subsection on mass privatization, above.)

Corporate governance of the transformed enterprises

Corporatized companies are in practice under the control of the Ministry of Privatization, acting on behalf of the State Treasury.[25] Since the state holds all of the shares, the role of the shareholders' meeting in wholly state-owned companies is played by the ministry, except that one-third of the supervisory board is elected by the employees of the new company. As the shares held by the state are sold or otherwise disposed of, the new owners acquire all the rights attached to them. When over 50 per cent of the shares are in private hands (including the employees), the employees lose their right to elect one-third of the members of the supervisory board.

The supervisory board of a wholly state-owned company is usually composed of six members, with the ministry entitled to appoint two-thirds of the members. According to the ministry's policy, at least one of the board members is supposed to be a lawyer, one an economist, and one a marketing specialist. The ministry also maintains a special training facility, which trains about forty to sixty board candidates per month. They must complete a special course and pass an examination organized by the ministry. A single person often serves on several boards, and the remuneration of the members is quite lucrative.

Implementation

As of the end of February 1992, 407 state enterprises have been converted into wholly state-owned companies. One hundred and thirty-nine of them were transformed in preparation for the mass

---

[25] There have been a number of voices demanding the creation of a special office of State Treasury, distinct from the Ministry of Privatization and charged with the disposition of state shares in commercial companies. A law creating the office of State Treasury was prepared, but not passed, by the parliament.

privatization program; of the remainder 202 were converted into joint-stock companies, and sixty-six into limited-liability companies. The new companies constituted 5.3 per cent of the firms in the state sector, and were very heavily concentrated in industry and construction.

Only limited information is available on the actual governance practices and performance of the newly transformed enterprises. Because of the "sweeteners" introduced to induce the insiders to agree to corporatization, the process, contrary to the initial designs, may have been linked to a softening of budget constraint of the converted enterprises. The little systematic research that is available,[26] as well as anecdotal evidence, indicate that insiders have continued to dominate the new structures following corporatization. As a rule, there have been no significant changes in the key management positions in the new companies, and the power of management seems to have somewhat increased as a result of the transformation. The power of the workers, on the other hand, has been significantly diminished, both because of the dissolution of the workers' councils and because the workers' representatives on the supervisory boards tend to identify with the other ministry-appointed members. (Apparently, the training provided by the ministry to all board members, including the workers' representatives, plays a significant role in this respect.) Nevertheless, union activists, both on the boards and on the floor, reportedly continue to play an important role in enterprise decisions, especially with respect to employment policies.[27] Other informal reports indicate that the supervisory boards are either passive or simply ignored by the insiders.

---

[26] D. Chelminski and A. Czynczyk, *Spoleczne Bariery Prywatyzacji*, Warszawa, 1991.
[27] Apparently, the maintenance of employment has often been demanded by the workers' councils as a condition of their approval of the initial decision to corporatize.

ROMANIA

CONTENTS

1. INTRODUCTION

Brief history of reforms

Prior to December 1989, Romania's economy was rigidly controlled by a totalitarian government. There was no pre-reform period, and the revolution represented an abrupt break with the old system. Early in 1990, concerted repeal of the anachronistic laws of the former socialist regime began, and laws regulating many new economic activities were enacted. The new constitution enshrined protection for private property rights. Central planning was dismantled, prices and foreign trade were liberalized, and the national currency, the leu, became internally convertible. These developments coincided with the reform of the tax system, sharp reduction of state subsidies to enterprises, and the establishment of a social safety net.

Banking reorganization resulted in the creation of the two-tier system in late 1990. Central bank functions were given to the newly independent National Bank of Romania, which became responsible for the control of monetary and credit aggregates, and exchange rate policy.

The commercial transactions of the National Bank were transferred to the newly established Romanian Commercial Bank. The former specialized banks – Romanian Bank for Foreign Trade, Investment Bank, the Bank for Agriculture and Food Industry, and the Savings Bank – gained the status of commercial banks. Under the new banking law, commercial banks are permitted to operate as universal banks.

2. ECONOMIC ENVIRONMENT

The structure of output

In 1991, Romanian gross national product (GNP), in current prices, was Lei 2,452 bln ($32.1 bln).[1] The structure of GDP in 1988 and 1991 shows the shift from industry to services and agriculture (see Table 2.1).

---

[1] The leu exchange rate is the average for the year calculated by *PlanEcon*. The following Lei/dollar rates are used in this report: 1989, Lei 14.9; 1990, Lei 22.4; 1991, Lei 76.4; 1992, Lei 263.4 (estimated).

Table 2.1 The structure of GDP (per cent of the total)

	1988	1991
Industry	54	46
Agriculture	11	15
Services	15	19
Other	20	20

Source: *PlanEcon*

The current physical structure of the economy is characterized by large and highly concentrated heavy industry, with energy-intensive technologies, insufficiently developed agriculture and services. This peculiarly Eastern European economic structure is mainly the result of two factors: a super-centralized, dictatorial management system, and an artificial foreign trade system, Comecon, created among the former socialist countries.

Table 2.2 Industrial enterprises in 1990

Enterprises classified:	Number of enterprises
By value of fixed assets (thousands of Lei)	
less than 100	760
100–1,000	1,008
more than 1,000	334
By number of employees	
less than 200	141
200–3,000	1,620
over 3,000	341

Source: *Statistical Yearbook* 1990

Output

In 1990, GDP declined by 7.3 per cent, led by a 16.6 per cent drop in industry output. However, trade, agricultural, and service sectors grew 23 per cent, 11 per cent, and 4 per cent, respectively. In 1991, all sectors registered declines, with a 37 per cent drop in trade

Table 2.3 Industrial production (adjusted for time worked; 1989 monthly average = 100)

	Jan	Feb	Mar	Apr	May	June	July	Aug	Sept	Oct	Nov	Dec
1991	65.5	65.5	70.7	73.9	74.4	76.0	68.8	66.4	66.7	63.8	58.3	55.9
1992	58.0	64.0	60.0	57.0								

Source: *PlanEcon*

reversing the 1990 gain. Industrial output fell by another 19 per cent, and GDP plummeted 14 per cent.

Industry has not posted any gains in output, since the overthrow of the communist regime. Industrial production in the last quarter of 1991 was 41 per cent below the fourth quarter of 1989, when adjusted for actual time worked. During the January–April 1992 period, industrial production was 40 per cent below its level for the same period in 1989.

INVESTMENT

In 1990 and 1991, gross investment in fixed capital fell drastically by 38.3 per cent and 20 per cent, respectively. The resulting level of fixed investment in 1991 was about 50 per cent lower than the 1980 level. This drop in investment was much larger than the 2 per cent decline in GDP, over the same period. The share of gross fixed investment in GDP remained high, 25 per cent, in 1991.

Household savings

By the end of 1991, domestic savings deposits totaled Lei 244 bln ($3.19 bln). This represented a drop in both real and nominal terms relative to the value of deposits in 1990. However, these estimates do not include savings held outside the official domestic banking system.

Price liberalization

Before December 1989, prices were set and controlled in the context of a comprehensive central planning and management system. The government decided to liberalize prices gradually in order to spread over time the impact of higher prices. The first step was taken in early 1990. The purchase prices offered by state wholesalers of food products to small agricultural producers were gradually increased.

Food prices, except for twelve basic foodstuffs, were freed on April 1, 1991. At that time, prices of consumer goods were also liberalized. The retail price index jumped 26.5 per cent in April 1991.

Table 2.4   Retail Price Index (month-to-month per cent changes)

	Jan	Feb	Mar	Apr	May	June	July	Aug	Sept	Oct	Nov	Dec
1991	14.8	7.0	6.6	26.5	5.1	2.0	9.5	11.2	7.3	10.4	10.9	13.7
1992	19.5	12.5	10.0	4.7	25.0	7.5						

Source: *PlanEcon*

In October 1991, the government reverted to explicit control over prices set by state enterprises. They were compelled to declare any planned price increases, ninety days prior to the effective date of higher prices. The government does not control or regulate prices set by firms in the private sector.

Inflation

In 1990, the GDP deflator rose 14.1 per cent. This was followed by a dramatic increase of 237.7 per cent in 1991.

Successive phases of price liberalization were followed by significant price increases. After the first phase in 1990, the consumer price index level increased by 80.4 per cent between October 1990 and March 1991. The second phase of price liberalization, implemented in April 1991, was followed by another jump in prices. The third stage, implemented in July 1991, resulted, by the end of December 1991, in a cumulative, 244.5 per cent, increase in consumer prices.

Table 2.5   Consumer Price Index (October 1990 = 100)

		1992				
	Dec 1991	Jan	Feb	Mar	Apr	May
Consumer prices	444.5	531.2	597.4	657.3	688.0	771.3
Foodstuffs	490.5	596.7	670.8	723.8	768.6	893.7
Non-food products	418.7	500.9	571.3	638.7	661.2	724.9
Services	398.2	447.2	481.6	538.1	555.9	586.0

Source: National Commission for Statistics

Between October 1990 and December 1991 food prices increased by 390 per cent, prices of non-food products rose by 318 per cent, and prices of services were up 298 per cent.

Behavior of wages

Price liberalization was accompanied by some relaxation of wage setting. Rigid, centralized control over wages in the state sector was replaced by wage ceilings for six occupational categories, a tax on excess growth of enterprise wage funds, and an indexation scheme providing partial (50 per cent) compensation for inflation. Analogous to prices, wages are not controlled or regulated in the private sector.

Nominal wages increased 11 per cent in 1990 and 190 per cent in 1991. Following a 6 per cent increase in 1990, real wages fell precipitously, by 14 per cent, in 1991.

Table 2.6 Average nominal and real wages (October 1990 = 100)

		1992				
	Dec 1991	Jan	Feb	Mar	Apr	May
Net nominal wage	346.3	380.9	372.5	447.8	459.2	518.7
Net real wage	77.9	71.7	62.4	68.1	66.7	67.3

Source: National Commission for Statistics

However, the real wage index in industry increased 4 per cent between January and December 1991. It subsequently fell 14 per cent during the first four months of 1992. Nominal wages expressed in current US dollars dropped sharply from $115 per month in January to $77 in April 1992.

Employment and unemployment

Total employment in Romania has been about 11 mln during the period 1989–1991. The share of employment in the state sector increased from 68.7 per cent in 1989 to 72.9 per cent in 1990. Growth of employment in state agriculture, services, and other non-industrial sectors exceeded declines of employment in state industry and

Table 2.7 Nominal and real wages in industry (January 1990 = 100)

	1991											
	Jan	Feb	Mar	Apr	May	June	July	Aug	Sept	Oct	Nov	Dec
Nominal wage index	115.5	112.2	110.0	102.4	123.0	125.1	130.5	132.6	148.3	160.8	52.4	62.0
Real wage index		80.2	73.6	70.3	85.8	99.3	100.6	97.3	87.3	90.6	87.9	86.9	83.4

	1992											
	Jan	Feb	Mar	Apr	May	June	July	Aug	Sept	Oct	Nov	Dec
Nominal wage index	65.1	62.8	75.3	77.1								
Real wage index		76.7	66.7	72.9	71.4							

Source: *PlanEcon*

construction. In 1991, the movement of labor to the emerging private
sector resulted in a lower, 66.4 per cent, share of employment in the
state sector.

At the end of December 1991, about 2.5 per cent of the labor force
was officially registered as unemployed. The unemployment rate
continued to increase during the first quarter of 1992. It reached 4.8
per cent in April 1992.

Table 2.8 Unemployment rate (as per cent of labor force)

	Jan	Feb	Mar	Apr	May	June	July	Aug	Sept	Oct	Nov	Dec
1991	0.0	0.1	0.2	0.6	0.9	1.2	1.4	1.6	1.7	1.7	1.8	2.5
1992	2.9	3.4	4.6	4.8								

Source: *PlanEcon*

A special unemployment fund was created in February 1991. It was
financed by a 4 per cent payroll tax paid by enterprises in the state and
private sectors and a 1 per cent wage tax payable by employees.

Local unemployment offices of the Labor Ministry are responsible for
the administration of unemployment benefits and retraining schemes.

Unemployment benefits are payable for 270 days to all unemployed (including new entrants), except for members of agricultural cooperatives, as follows:

- persons with prior employment of one to five years: 50 per cent of the previous monthly wage, but not less than 75 per cent of the minimum wage;
- persons with prior employment of five to fifteen years: 55 per cent of the previous monthly wage, but not less than 80 per cent of the minimum wage;
- persons with prior employment exceeding fifteen years: 60 per cent of the previous monthly wage, but not less than 85 per cent of the minimum wage;
- college graduates and persons with prior employment of less than one year: 60 per cent of the minimum wage;
- university graduates with higher degrees: 70 per cent of the minimum wage.

State budget

After posting a surplus of Lei 60 bln, or 7.5 per cent of GDP, in 1989, the state budget registered a mild deficit in 1990: Lei 3.8 bln, or 0.4 per cent of the GDP. Current budget revenues increased from Lei 307 bln in 1990 to Lei 498 bln in 1991. However, growth of expenditures resulted in an increase of 1991 deficit to Lei 40.6 bln, or 1.7 per cent of GDP.

TAXATION
Profits up to Lei 1 mln ($3,800) per annum are taxed at 30 per cent. The tax rate increases to 45 per cent for profits above Lei 1 mln. Corporate income tax is supplemented by social security and unemployment premiums (25 and 4 per cent of enterprise payroll, respectively). All newly established private companies or joint ventures are exempt from corporate taxes on reinvested profits for up to two years, depending on the nature of their activity.

The system of turnover taxes was revised in November 1990. The prior tax levied only on sales revenues of final products was replaced by a tax charged on sales of final and intermediate goods. However, rates on intermediate goods are substantially below those on final goods. The introduction of value added tax, replacing turnover taxes, is planned for early 1993.

The next step in the ongoing tax reform will be the replacement of the current system of separate taxes on personal incomes derived from different sources by one tax on the total personal income.

Monetary policy

INTEREST RATES AND CREDIT
The instruments of monetary control used by the National Bank of Romania include direct credit controls, and cost of refinancing. Real value of aggregate credit fell sharply between January and November 1991. The nominal value of aggregate credit increased by about 46 per cent, between January and November of 1991. However, a twofold increase of the GDP deflator resulted in a sharp drop in the real value

Table 2.9 Interest rates (per cent per month)

	NBR refinancing credit			Commercial banks		
				credits		deposits
	short term	long term	credit lines	short term	long term	
1991						
Jan, 1–Mar, 31	8.0	8.0	–	11.0–11.5	6.0–10.0	6.0–10.0
Apr, 1–May, 31	9.5	9.0	–	10.0–14.0	11.0–14.0	6.0–10.0
June, 1–July, 31	12.0	10.25	–	12.0–14.0	12.5–14.0	6.0–10.0
Aug, 1–Sept, 14	14.5	12.5	–	11.0–16.5	12.5–14.0	6.0–10.0
Sept, 15–Sept, 30	18.0	15.0	–	11.0–16.5	10.25–15.0	6.0–10.0
Oct, 1–Oct, 31	–	–	18.0	12.25–22.0	10.25–15.0	6.0–10.0
Nov, 1–Nov, 30	–	–	18.0	13.0–33.0	13.0–19.0	6.0–12.0
Dec, 1–Dec, 31	–	–	18.0	28.0–36.0	13.0–19.0	17.0–28.0
1992						
Jan, 1–Jan, 31	–	–	28.0	28.0–36.0	27.0–38.0	17.0–28.0
Feb, 1–Feb, 29	–	–	28.0	27.0–38.0	27.0–38.0	17.0–28.0
Mar, 1–Mar, 31	–	–	28.0	28.0–36.0	27.0–38.0	17.0–28.0
Apr, 1–Apr, 30	–	–	28.0	60.0–80.0	27.0–38.0	18.0–23.0
May, 1–May, 24	–	–	65.0	60.0–80.0	65.0–80.0	20.0–55.0
May, 25–May, 31	–	–	80.0	68.0–85.0	65.0–80.0	20.0–60.0

Source: National Bank of Romania

of credit. This contraction was followed by a transitory, 37 per cent, increase in real credit in December 1991. Real credit continued to decline during the first four months of 1992.

The National Bank increased the refinancing rate from 3 per cent at the beginning of 1991 to 18 per cent for short-term, and 15 per cent for long-term credits in September 1991. On October 1, 1991, refinancing credits were replaced by credit lines, credit auctions, and fixed term credits.

The interest rate charged by the National Bank on refinancing credit lines was adjusted periodically. It increased from 18 per cent in October 1991 to 80 per cent in June 1992.

Debt

Communist rulers ruthlessly carried out the policy of foreign debt repayment, at the cost of drastic reductions of domestic consumption and investment. In consequence, Romanian gross convertible currency debt was only $100 mln in 1989. Despite relatively large increases in 1990 and 1991, the gross currency debt of $2.7 bln, at the end of 1991, represented only 8 per cent of GDP.

In 1991, Romania received about $900 mln from the IMF and the World Bank. The Group of 24 industrialized countries has agreed to supply Romania with up to $1 bln in aid, but no funds were available by the end of 1991. Out of a total of over $500 mln in economic aid committed to Eastern Europe under the PHARE program, only 3 per cent is designated for Romania.

Foreign trade

Foreign trade activities used to be carried out by about fifty specialized trade organizations. Since February 1990, state enterprises, and companies in the private sector have been permitted to carry out their own foreign trade transactions.

The licensing system was reviewed as part of the liberalization of foreign trade. Beginning in 1991, except for some special cases involving official, government funds or agreements, and goods in short supply, import and export licenses are issued automatically and are used solely for statistical purposes. However, in order to protect Romania's convertible currency reserves, the Trade and Tourism Ministry can establish, at the request of the National Bank, quantitative restrictions on imports.

A new customs tariff, based on the harmonized system of GATT, was adopted in September 1991. It became effective on January 1, 1992. It applies to all imported goods.

Since September 1990, the fraction of foreign currency earnings to be surrendered by exporters (at the official exchange rate) has been reduced from 100 per cent to 50 per cent. However, joint ventures and foreign companies were exempt from this requirement.

Internal convertibility of the leu was introduced in November 1991. The two previous exchange rates – the official exchange rate (Lei 60 to $1) and the inter-bank market rate (which at that date had reached Lei 300 to $1) – were unified. The unified exchange rate has been determined daily by the National Bank and authorized commercial banks. The inter-bank currency market was expanded.

According to *PlanEcon*, Romanian convertible currency exports, in current US dollars, dropped from $5.9 bln in 1990 to $4.1 bln in 1991, while convertible currency imports fell slightly from $5.6 bln in 1990 to $5.4 bln in 1991.

Following the breakdown of Comecon trading arrangements, Romanian exports to these group of countries plummeted by 40 per cent in 1991. Exports to the developed market economies, and developing countries also fell by 24 per cent and 21 per cent, respectively. Imports from the former Comecon countries dropped sharply by 60 per cent, while imports from the developed market economies, and developing countries fell by 30 per cent.

3. PRESENT FORMS OF OWNERSHIP

3A. Legal framework of economic activity

Existing and planned legislation concerning property rights

The following are the more important Romanian laws concerning property rights, business organizations, and privatization:

- Law No. 15/1990 Concerning the Reorganization of State-Owned Enterprises into Commercial Companies or *Regies Autonomes*;
- Law No. 31/1990 Concerning Business Organizations (the Company Law);
- Law No. 18/1991 (Land Law);

- Law No. 35/1991 Concerning Foreign Investments (Foreign Investment Law);
- Law No. 36/1991, Concerning the Establishment of Commercial Companies and Farming Associations in Agriculture;
- Law No. 58/1991 Commercial Companies Privatization Law;
- Law of July 1992 for the Amendment of Article 212 of Law No. 31/1990;
- Law No. 447/1991 Concerning the Assumption by the State and Commercial Banks of Losses Incurred by Economic Agents with State Capital and of Non-Performing Bank Credits in 1989–1990;
- Decree-Law 54/1990 On Organization and Conduct of Economic Activity Based on Free Initiative;
- Decree-Law No. 61/1990 Concerning the Sale of State-Owned Housing;
- Government Resolution No. 1228/1990 Concerning the Methodology for Concessioning, Leasing and Management Contracts;
- Government Resolution No. 88/1991 Concerning Measures for the Sale of State-Owned Housing;
- Government Resolution No. 562/1991 Concerning Downpayments and Instalment Payments for the Sale of State-Owned Housing;
- Government Resolution No. 634/1991 Concerning the Methodology for the Sale of Assets of Commercial Companies with State Capital;
- Government Resolution No. 758/1991 Concerning the Amendment of G.R. No. 634;
- Government Resolution No. 858/1991 Concerning the Establishment of the National Agency for Privatization and the Development of Small and Medium Sized Enterprises.

Recognized forms of business organizations

STATE ENTERPRISES AND STATE-OWNED COMMERCIAL COMPANIES

Under communist rule, the Romanian economy was probably the most centralized in Eastern Europe. The state enterprises were little more than administrative divisions of the state apparatus. An economic pyramid descending from the planning office and the sectoral ministries to the huge intermediate conglomerates (*centrale*) and the individual enterprises (often still containing a number of separate factories) gave very little autonomy to the basic production units.

Following the fall of the Ceausescu regime, the new government provided for a large-scale reorganization of state enterprises and a new governance system regulated by the 1990 Law Concerning the Reorganization of State-Owned Enterprises into Commercial Companies or *Regies Autonomes* (the Reorganization Law). This law divided the old state enterprises into two categories: those operating in strategic areas of the economy, such as the armament industry, the energy sector, mining and natural gas operations, the post office, or the railway service, which were to remain in state hands, and all the others, which would be subject to privatization. The first category of enterprises were to be reorganized into so-called '*regies autonomes*' (autonomous administrations); the second category was to be converted to a commercial company form, notably single-owner limited-liability companies or single-owner joint-stock companies, the shares of which were to be subsequently sold or distributed to private owners through the different privatization programs. All state enterprises were required to be reorganized within six months of the law's coming into effect, except for agricultural units, which were given an extra three months. They were to be organized by the national government or, if they were to serve local purpose, by the municipalities.

Regies autonomes *Regies autonomes* are legal persons and are said to operate on the basis of financial autonomy. They own their assets, but they need the approval of the competent ministry for a transfer of real estate or the settlement of disputes which involve over Lei 10 mln ($38,000).

A *regie autonome* is managed by a Council of Administration made up of seven to fifteen members selected for four-year terms by the competent ministry or by the chief of local administration, with the proviso that the Council must include a representative from the Ministry of Finance, and where appropriate, a representative from the Ministry of Resources and Industry, the Ministry of Trade and Tourism, and of the competent sectoral ministry. Members will serve four-year terms. The Council drafts the bylaws (which must be approved by the founding authority), and, with the advice of the competent officials, selects one of its members as the Director or General Director to manage the daily operations of the company.

A *regie autonome* is required to prepare an annual statement of accounts to be approved by the Ministry of Finance or the territorial directorate of finance in the area where the company is headquartered. The revenues of a *regie autonome* must exceed its expenses, unless operating losses are approved by the Ministry of the Economy, after consultation with the Ministry of Finance. The losses must be incurred for good reasons in the performance of public services. In order to support the development of the *regies autonomes*, the state may grant subsidies in the form of credits with preferential interest rates, state orders, cash, or tax reductions.

All *regies autonomes* are required to create reserve and development funds and are required to make payments to social security funds, but the law does not stipulate any minimum value of these funds. Five per cent of the remaining after-tax profits must be deposited in an employee profit-sharing fund. The remaining balance is paid to the state or local administration budget.

A *regie autonome* can make investments in order to fulfill its purpose, and it may obtain investment credits with the approval of the State Ministry for Economic Orientation. It may also take loans of up to 20 per cent of its gross revenues of the previous year to cover losses incurred in a single year.

State-owned (single-owner) commercial companies In accordance with the Reorganization Law, state enterprises other than those reorganized as *regies autonomes* have been converted into single-owner joint-stock or limited-liability companies, with the state becoming the owner of all the shares. Corporatization is dealt with more extensively in Section 5 below while the normal structure of commercial companies is discussed later in this section. At this point, however, the focus will be on the distinctive features of state-owned commercial companies. One of these is that the powers of the General Meeting of shareholders in a state-owned joint-stock or limited-liability company are exercised by a State Representatives' Council appointed by the relevant ministry or local authority. The members of the Council usually include the representatives of the branch ministry, the Ministries of Finance and the Economy, local authority, and professional specialists from inside or outside the commercial company. The State Representatives' Council appoints the Council of Administration, which plays the same role as in a regular commercial company. Apparently, the State Representatives' Councils have not been very effective in monitoring the behavior of their companies, but they undoubtedly give the state organs an effective capability of hiring and firing all the officers of the company and assure ultimate state control.

Until the full liberalization of economic exchanges and the elimination of the centralized allotment system, the Reorganization Law also obliged state-owned commercial companies, along with *regies autonomes*, to meet the supply tasks set up by the Ministry of

Resources. Also, unless there are at least three business agents marketing the same product in Romania, the government has the right to set the prices of any subsidized state company.

The Reorganization Law contains specific provisions concerning subsidies to commercial companies, prohibiting such grants for more than four years, and stipulating that the amount of the initial subsidies must be reduced annually by 20 per cent.

The Reorganization Law allows state-owned companies to associate with each other for joint activities of common interest. This has led to the creation of a number of holding companies, which are described further in Section 5 below. State-owned companies and companies with state participation may also form new commercial companies with Romanian or foreign legal or natural persons in order to further their commercial efforts.

COOPERATIVES

As in all communist countries, cooperatives were an important sector of the Romanian economy. Although they were in fact governed by the same strict centralized system as state enterprises, legally they were not a part of the state sector. The fact that the assets of the cooperatives did not belong to the state became significant in the wake of the fall of the Ceausescu government: cooperatives are not subject to the same regime of privatization.

The cooperatives were most active in three areas of the Romanian economy: agriculture, small industry, and consumer services. Each of these sectors had its own hierarchical regional and national organizations.

The most important sector was agriculture, where cooperatives owned 51.3 per cent of the land in 1990 and employed 22 per cent of all labor. The 1991 Land Law allowed the breakup of the agricultural cooperatives and returned up to 10 hectares per family of land to the previous owners or their heirs, as well as other classes of persons described further in Section 4B. A new law created a framework for new kinds of agricultural associations.

Outside of agriculture, however, the old cooperative system is still functioning, although without the strict centralized control. As of this time, no law has been passed to reform the governance structure of the nonagricultural cooperatives, and they fall outside the existing transformation and privatization programs.

COMMERCIAL COMPANIES

Two legal acts have regulated private business activity in Romania since the fall of the Ceausescu regime: the Decree-Law 54/1990 On Organization and Conduct of Economic Activity Based on Free Initiative (the Decree), and the 1990 Law Concerning Business Organizations (the Company Law). The decree was a transitional measure authorizing the creation of small, private entrepreneurial associations. It recognized the following entities:

- small enterprises of up to twenty wage-earners;
- associations with "lucrative scope" (associations of not more than ten persons set up as partnerships to pursue profitable activities);
- family associations (which could be formed only by members of the same household);
- activities carried out independently by natural persons.

Only citizens domiciled in Romania were permitted to form any of these entities. Small enterprises and legal persons organized on the basis of the decree were allowed to continue their activity for a limited period of time after the passage of the Company Law, but are obliged to reorganize themselves into one of the forms of business organizations recognized by the Commercial Law. Currently, therefore, private business entities in Romania, as well as the corporatized state enterprises, are comprehensively regulated by the Company Law.

Romanian business entities, collectively referred to in the Company Law as "commercial companies," can take one of the following five permissible forms: 1) partnerships; 2) limited partnerships; 3) limited partnerships with share capital; 4) limited-liability companies; and 5) joint-stock companies.

General partnership General partnerships are formed by contract among individuals, with each partner bearing joint and unlimited liability for the obligations of the company. The transfer of partnership interests is allowed if the partnership agreement so provides. The partnership is managed by one or more managers elected by majority vote from among the partners.

Limited partnership A limited partnership is formed contractually by one or more partners who bear joint and unlimited liability (the "general partners") and one or more other parties ("limited partners") who are liable for the obligations of the company only to the extent of their capital contribution. The transfer of both limited and general partners' interests is regulated by the partnership agreement.

Only a general partner, elected by the majority of all partners (presumably including the limited partners), is allowed to manage a limited partnership. The law does not require, however, the total passivity of limited partners, who, when expressly authorized, can conclude agreements on behalf of the partnership and take part in its internal administration.

Limited partnership with share capital   Limited partnership with share capital ("share partnership") is a limited partnership which issues shares to the public. It may be founded by at least five persons. Share partnerships have the same liability rules as limited partnerships, but they are otherwise primarily regulated by the rules governing joint-stock companies, including the rules for public subscriptions and share transferability.

The formation of a share partnership must be authorized by the appropriate court, which must seek the advice of the Chamber of Commerce concerning the usefulness of the partnership and the reputation of the founders.

Share partnerships must be managed by a general partner, but limited partners can be authorized to enter into transactions on behalf of the partnership.

Limited-liability company   A limited-liability company is a familiar Central European form of non-public business organization, with the liability of the shareholders limited to their capital contributions. A limited-liability company cannot have more than fifty shareholders or be capitalized at under Lei 100,000 ($380), with each share having nominal value of at least Lei 5,000 ($19). Contributions in kind can represent no more than 60 per cent of the capital, and no bonds may be issued.

The shares in a limited-liability company are not negotiable instruments. The transfer of shares among shareholders is unrestricted, but transfers to third parties must be approved by shareholders representing at least three-fourths of the registered capital.

The main organ of a limited-liability company is the General Meeting of shareholders. Somewhat unusually, the decisions at the meeting require an absolute majority of both the shares and the shareholders. The day-to-day management of the company is entrusted to one or more "administrators" elected at the General Meeting. If there are multiple administrators who are required to work together, all decisions must have their unanimous support, with disagreements settled by the majority of the shareholders. Auditors (selected by the shareholders) must be employed by companies with more than fifteen shareholders.

Joint-stock company While the Romanian joint-stock company (JSC) corresponds to the publicly traded business corporations in the other countries of the region, it has a number of noteworthy features according to the Company Law.

A JSC must have a minimum capitalization of Lei 1 mln ($3,800), and, except for state-owned companies, at least five shareholders. The liability of the shareholders is limited to the payment for their shares. The official authorization of a founding of a JSC is subject to the same procedure as in the case of limited partnerships with share capital (involving judicial hearings on the usefulness of the proposed company and consultations with the Chamber of Commerce), which may make it quite cumbersome. The court can also order an independent valuation of any in-kind contributions, even if they have been previously approved by the constitutive meeting of the company.

A JSC may issue bearer and registered shares (with a minimum nominal value of Lei 1,000 ($3.80)), but no provisions are made for the issuance of different classes of shares. A set of rules regulates public subscriptions and other sales of a JSC's shares to the public (apparently including sales by individual shareholders who advertise their sale). In all such cases, the prospectus containing specified information about the company must be approved by the competent court, and, in the case of secondary sales, must be published in the two most widely circulated newspapers in the town where the company's headquarters are located.

The constitutive meeting of a JSC requires the attendance of more than 50 per cent of the subscribers. Among other tasks, it determines the value of non-cash contributions and approves any benefits granted to the founders. Somewhat unusually, every subscriber has one vote at the constitutive meeting, regardless of the number of subscribed shares, with subscribers making non-cash contributions being prohibited from voting on resolutions concerning the valuation of such contributions. Proxies are limited to representing a maximum of five votes.

The supreme organ of a JSC is the General Meeting of the

shareholders, which must be attended by the holders of at least half of the share capital. Each share is entitled to one vote, but the bylaws and the foundation contract can limit the number of votes any one shareholder can cast. Proxy votes are permitted, but the administrators and employees of the company may not serve as proxies if their votes are necessary for the required majority.

The operations of a JSC are run by one or more "administrators" appointed at the General Meeting. If there are two or more administrators, they form a Council of Administration, which convenes at least once a month, and, unless the bylaws stipulate otherwise, is responsible for the hiring of employees. The head of the Council of Administration and at least one-half of its members must be Romanian citizens. The Council of Administration may delegate a part of its power to a Managing Committee composed of members of the Council. The Managing Committee must convene at least once a week. The execution of the operations of the company can be entrusted to one or more executive directors who cannot be members of the Council of Administration.

A JSC is also required to have an odd number of "auditors," elected by the General Meeting for three-year terms. The majority of the auditors must be Romanian citizens, at least one must be a legally certified or expert accountant, and the rest must be shareholders. In all companies in which the state holds at least 20 per cent of the shares, one of the auditors is named by the Ministry of Finance.

JSCs are required to maintain a reserve fund. At least five per cent of the company profits are to be set aside each year until the fund has a minimum value equal to one-fifth of the registered capital. Any premium captured from the sale of shares must also be deposited in the fund.

Changes in the capitalization of a JSC, as well as mergers, liquidation, the issuance of bonds, and any change in the bylaws, require a complicated approval procedure, involving potentially two extra-ordinary shareholders' meetings and a majority of at least one-third registered capital. Moreover, shareholders who do not agree with a decision to change the business location, the company's headquarters, or the corporate form have the right to withdraw from the company and obtain payment for their shares.

Regulations governing foreign ownership

Unless superseded by contrary provisions of an international agreement or convention to which Romania has acceded, foreign investment in Romania is regulated by the 1991 Law Concerning Foreign Investments (Foreign Investment Law).

A foreign natural or legal person may invest in new Romanian companies, either with wholly foreign-owned capital or in partnership with a Romanian legal or natural person, purchase shares or bonds of an existing company, or enter into a concession or lease contract with a state-owned company. Standard protection of foreign investment is offered, including full compensation for any nationalizations considered to be in the public interest.

Foreign investments have to be registered and approved by the Romanian Development Agency (RDA). The RDA examines the financial records of the investor, the area and legal form of the investment, and the amount of capital to be invested. The RDA may request information from central and local governments, and from state-owned companies operating in the same field. The application is deemed to be accepted if the RDA does not notify the investor that it has been rejected. The decision of the RDA on the application is not subject to appeal.

Foreign investment can be made in any sector of the Romanian economy provided that it does not affect Romania's national security and defense interests, or harm the public order, health, or good morals. This has been interpreted to exclude foreign investment in, among others, the armaments industry and the medical sector. Foreign investors may acquire ownership rights over chattels, factory buildings and other real estate, but cannot directly hold title to land or own residential buildings other than those "auxiliary to an investment." It is possible, however, for Romanian companies with majority foreign participation to own land, if the Romanian partners contribute it as their share for the duration of the joint venture.

Foreign investors have the right to take part in the management and administration of their investment, but a company with foreign participation may only hire foreign employees in management and expert job positions. Also, as noted previously, the majority of the members of the Council of Administration and auditors of a commercial company must be Romanian citizens.

Since the establishment of the uniform rate of exchange, all after-tax profits and capital gains may be repatriated, but an additional 10 per cent tax is levied on repatriated profits. Like all Romanian companies, the companies with foreign participation must carry out their activities in Romanian currency, and convert their export proceeds into lei.

Foreign investors receive substantial tax holidays and releases from custom duties on their in-kind capital contributions and imports of raw materials. Profit tax holidays for two to five years are granted, depending on the area of the company's activities, and further substantial tax reductions are available for investments which increase exports, create jobs, or develop new technologies.

Bankruptcy and liquidation

Romania has no bankruptcy law. Certain provisions of the Company Law regulate liquidation of commercial companies, but there are no provisions concerning either voluntary or forced bankruptcy declaration, and no provisions relating to the priority of creditors. The need for a bankruptcy law is acknowledged, but the legal void remains. In the absence of specific legislation, no formal bankruptcies have occurred.

Far from being able to institute a workable regime of bankruptcy, the government has been forced to bankroll much of the state sector in the last few years. Given the catastrophic financial conditions of many state-owned companies, the state decided to assume 90 per cent of their losses registered as of December 31, 1990 (Law No. 447/1991 Concerning the Assumption by the State and Commercial Banks of Losses Incurred by Economic Agents with State Capital and of Non-Performing Bank Credits in 1989–1990). State and commercial banks were also required to absorb 10 per cent of their bad loans to state enterprises.

In order to ensure that the state companies do not expect another bailout in the future, the law provided that any economic unit with state capital which incurred losses after 1990 would be subject to bankruptcy proceedings. But another financial crisis in the state sector led to another debt-clearing operation in the fall of 1991.

3B. Structure of ownership

Nearly all data on economic units (firms and enterprises) in Romania concern only state-owned commercial companies. Only limited data are available for the private sector and cooperatives, and there is

Table 3B.1 Employment in state and private sectors (end of 1991)

	Employment (thousands)	% (share)
State Sector	7,111.1	65.1
of which:		
Commercial companies[1]	4,242.0	38.8
Other state[2]	2,869.1	26.3
Private Sector	3,808.2	34.9
of which:		
Private companies[3]	751.7	6.9
Individual and cooperative farmers	2,529.0	23.1
Non-agricultural cooperatives[4]	535.0	4.9
Total	10,919.3	100.0

[1] The number of commercial companies is valid for the end of June 1992, but differs only negligibly from the end of 1992.
[2] Includes regies autonomes, public administration, and other state institutions.
[3] Estimate by the CEU Privatization Project from registration data (in Table 3B.2) calculated under the following assumptions: each operating family association had employment of 2 and each entrepreneur had employment of 1; the share of family associations in the total of family associations and entrepreneurs was the same at the end of 1991 as in June 1993 (when this breakdown is available); the size distribution by employment of commercial companies and the proportion of all companies actually operating was the same at the end of 1991 as in September 1991 (when this breakdown is available); and the average number of employees for companies in a given range of employment was equal to the lower endpoint of the range plus 40% of the different between the two endpoints (since the distribution is positively skewed), and companies with more than 100 employees had an average of 150 employees.
[4] Workers (members and employees) in the handicraft (small industry and consumer services) and consumer (mostly retail trade and catering) cooperatives.

Source: National Agency for Privatization and CEU Privatization Project estimates.

almost no information about the *regies autonomes* (the state enterprises expected to remain mostly in state hands). Data collection has fallen behind the changes in ownership and legal forms, partly due to the fact that the parliament has yet to approve new laws on accounting and statistics.

No figures for the ownership structure of the Romanian economy in terms of capital and output could be obtained, but some estimates are possible for employment. Table 3B.1 shows the division of total employment at the end of 1991 between the state sector, which includes state-owned commercial companies plus *regies autonomes* and public administration, and the private sector, which includes registered private companies plus both agricultural and non-agricultural cooperatives. The state is obviously still quite dominant, with a share of total employment equal to 65 per cent, about 60 per cent of which is accounted for by the state-owned commercial companies. Since these companies are scheduled for privatization over the next seven years, the implied target of the Romanian transition policy is a state sector of about a quarter of total employment, including both public administration and some state enterprises.

Although cooperatives were subject to the same central planning system as state enterprises before 1990, their property belongs to their members, rather than the state, and they are thus legally private. Agricultural cooperatives were a very important sector in the Romanian economy, accounting for 51.3 per cent of the arable land and 22 per cent of the national labor force. Their dissolution in 1991, and the redistribution of their land to members and to former land owners (described in Section 4B below), means that nearly 80 per cent of arable land is now privately operated. State farms ("State Agricultural Enterprises"), which were clearly owned by the state, were transformed into state-owned commercial companies. Other important cooperatives operate in small industry, consumer services, trade, and catering. Close to 10 per cent of industrial employment was in cooperatives representing 25 per cent of all industrial enterprises; these were mostly relatively small, at least by Romanian standards (200–500 workers), and in the field of small industry. Almost 50 per cent of the total number of retail trade and catering units in Romania are owned by cooperatives, although they are mostly small shops in villages and account for about 20 per cent of sectoral employment.

The figure in Table 3B.1 for the number employed in private companies, about 7 per cent of total employment, represents an estimate of new private sector growth rather than the result of privatization. Essentially no privatization had taken place in Romania at the end of 1991, a situation that has changed somewhat in 1992. This estimate, explained in the footnotes to Table 3B.1, is a rough calculation based on the data of Table 3B.2, which contains the division of private companies according to the category of legal form (family associations and entrepreneurs on the one hand, and commercial companies on the other) for September 1991, December 1991 and June 1992; and the number of units operating and the size distribution of the number of employees for commercial companies in September 1991.

Table 3B.2 Number of private companies

	September 30, 1991	December 31, 1991	June 30, 1992
Total private companies	223,947	230,880	327,967
of which:			
Family associations and individual			
entrepreneurs	153,336	154,472	180,861
operating	120,942		
Private commercial companies	70,611	76,408	147,106
operating	53,946		
of which:			
less than 5 employees	29,508		
5–20 employees	15,482		
21–50 employees	8,577		
51–100 employees	324		
over 100 employees	55		

Source: National Agency for Privatization

According to these data from the National Agency for Privatization, there were about 328,000 registered private firms in June 1992, of which nearly 147,000 were commercial companies, more than double the 71,000 at the end of 1991. As of the end of September 1991 (the last time for which this information is available), about three-quarters of the companies were operating, and the size distribution indicates that most of the private commercial companies were quite small: 73.4 per cent had fewer than twenty employees. The rapid growth in the number of companies implies that the private sector was rapidly expanding, and the estimate of total employment in private companies can be extrapolated to mid-1992. Using the data from Table 3B.2 and applying assumptions analogous to those described above for the end of 1991 estimate, private company employment was about 1.3 mln in June 1992, or 12 per cent of total employment.

These are the only data and estimates currently available for the private sector. Newly-established firms are legally required to register with the Commercial Register, but little information is available subsequently. Tax data are not useful for estimating the size of the private sector, since many private firms, especially in trade, are exempt from

Table 3B.3   Sectoral distribution of state-owned commercial companies[1] (as of June 1992)

Sector	Commercial companies		Registered capital		Employees	
	Number of units	% share	Value (Bln Lei)	% share	No. of persons	% share
Industry	1,425	24.0	731.5	52.6	2,294,953	54.1
Agriculture and food ind.	1,872	31.6	301.2	21.7	797,027	18.8
Domestic trade	621	10.5	66.5	4.8	237,393	5.6
Construction	463	7.8	61.8	4.4	366,033	8.6
Transportation	512	8.6	87.8	6.3	181,485	4.3
Tourism	202	3.4	29.2	2.1	78,402	1.9
Other	836	14.1	111.9	8.1	283,674	6.7
Total	5,931	100.0	1,389.9	100.0	4,238,867	100.0

[1] 1991 data were unavailable for 200 commercial companies.

Source: National Agency for Privatization

taxes for an initial period ranging from six months to two years. This may also introduce an upward bias into registration data, as companies are set up for periods just long enough to capture the tax benefits before being dissolved and reconstituted in another form.

Much more information is available with respect to state-owned commercial companies. Table 3B.3 shows the distribution of the number of units and their employment and book capital across branches of activity (sectors or industries); by all three indicators, this part of the state sector of the Romanian economy remains clearly dominated by industry and agriculture. Table 3B.4 contains information on the size distribution of the commercial companies according to employment and registered capital. By contrast with the private sector, state-owned commercial companies are still mostly very large: only 0.3 per cent of employees work for companies with fewer than fifty employees, 4.8 per cent for companies with fewer than 200, and 17.8 per cent for companies with fewer than 500. On the other end of the distribution, companies with more than 1,500 employees account for 53.7 per cent of total employment. Thus, this sector is still quite

Table 3B.4 Size distribution by employment and capital of state-owned commercial companies (as of June 1992)

Indicator	Number	% share
Number of employees		
less than 50	428	7.4
	(10,986)[1]	(0.3)[2]
51–200	1,484	25.8
	(189,513)	(4.5)
201–500	1,724	29.9
	(553,464)	(13.0)
501–1,000	1,023	17.8
	(723,271)	(17.1)
1,001–1,500	388	6.9
	(483,468)	(11.4)
1,501–2,000	254	4.4
	(441,773)	(10.4)
over 2,000	450	7.8
	(1,836,502)	(43.3)
Registered capital		
less than 100 mln Lei	3,537	59.6
100–500 mln Lei	1,926	32.5
over 500 mln Lei	468	7.9

[1] Numbers in brackets represent total number of employees working at firms with employment size of the given range.
[2] Numbers in brackets represent the share of the number of employees within each range in the total number of employees.
Source: National Agency for Privatization

concentrated, despite the splitting up of approximately 2,000 former state enterprises to form the approximate 6,000 commercial companies. Together, Tables 3B.3 and 3B.4 illustrate the hypercentralized and hyperdistorted character of the part of the Romanian state sector that is slated for privatization and likely to undergo drastic restructuring.

The only data available for the *regies autonomes* show that, at the end of 1991, 390 entities of this type were in operation, with a total capital of Lei 1,752.3 bln, accounting for about 53 per cent of the total capital in the state sector. The *regies* are thus on average relatively large enterprises. No further details are currently available on the distribution of the *regies autonomes* by sector or size.

Also relevant to inferring the size of the private sector is the extent of foreign investment.

FOREIGN INVESTMENT

As of the end of March 1992, 10,394 commercial companies with foreign capital had been established, with total registered foreign capital of $323.1 mln. The number of companies with foreign capital has been steadily increasing: starting from a total of 1,589 companies in 1990 (when the establishment of joint ventures was still regulated by a Decree adopted in 1972), there was an average increase of 1,608 companies for each quarter of 1991 (Law No. 35/1991 Concerning Foreign Investments, passed in April, set forth more favorable provisions for foreign investments), which accelerated to 2,372 in the first quarter of 1992.

Table 3B.5 Evolution of foreign investment in Romania

Period	Number of Joint Ventures	Capital[1] (mln. USD)	Average Capital (Thous. USD)
through 1990	1,589	112.4	70.74
1991 1st quarter	808	18.9	23.39
1991 2nd quarter	1,747	29.9	17.12
1991 3rd quarter	1,917	70.2	14.42
1991 4th quarter	1,961	37.0	18.87
1992 1st quarter	2,272	54.4	22.93
Total (cumulative)	10,394	323.1	32.17

[1] Foreign capital contribution.

Source: Romanian Development Agency

It is interesting to note that the average size of investments has fallen significantly: in 1990, it was $70.74 mln, but in 1991, it fell to $24.24 mln, and in 1992, to $22.93 mln. This can be explained by the fact that the first wave of foreign investment, in 1990 and the beginning of 1991, involved mainly joint ventures between state-owned companies and foreign investors, the latter hence being large foreign companies. Since mid-1991, investors have included smaller foreign firms and individuals, who started investing after it became permitted under the Foreign Investment Law.

Table 3B.6   Size distribution of foreign investments (as of March 31, 1992)

Investments (thous. US$)	Companies		Total foreign investment		Average investment
	Number	% share	mln US$	% share	thous. US$
over 1,000	42	0.40	184.8	57.21	4,400.0
500–1,000	32	0.31	20.6	6.38	643.8
100–500	209	2.01	42.1	13.03	201.4
50–100	281	2.70	18.3	5.67	65.1
less than 50	9,380	94.57	57.2	17.71	5.8
Total	10,394	100.0	323.0	100.0	31.1

Source: Romanian Development Agency

Thus, the figures in Table 3B.6 show that, as of March 31, 1992, there was a relatively large number of small-scale foreign investments, but also a few so large as to have notable effects on the economy as a whole. Over half of the total value of all foreign investment is attributed to only 0.4 per cent of the companies involved. Conversely, the large number of smaller investments, represented by 94.57 per cent of all commercial companies with foreign participation, account for only 17.71 per cent of foreign capital investment.

Data on the distribution of foreign investments by field of activity at the end of March 1992 are presented in Table 3B.7. Companies with foreign participation have often registered more than one field of activity, so the figures for the number of companies in each field cannot be added. It is nevertheless apparent that trade, tourism, transportation, and the food industry dominated, in declining order of importance. Unfortunately, no information is collected to classify the firms by book value of assets, revenues, profitability, exports, and employment.

The number of countries from which foreign investments have originated has also increased considerably. While sixty-nine countries had invested in Romania in 1990, this number grew to ninety-eight in 1991 and to 104 in the first quarter of 1992. Moreover, at the end of March 1992, there were twenty-three countries which had invested in 100 or more Romanian companies and twenty-nine countries whose

Table 3B.7   Foreign investment by field of activity (as of March 31, 1992)

Field of activity	Number of companies
Extractive	101
Construction	665
Electronics	1,128
Electrotechnics	1,058
Transportation	4,603
Communication	546
Light industry	2,427
Food industry	3,149
Agriculture	1,697
Infrastructure	2,082
Trade	9,848
Banking	408
Tourism	4,941
Other	9,185

Note: Most of the joint ventures declared more than one field of activity; consequently, the sum of the numbers is larger than the total number of joint ventures.

Source: Romanian Development Agency

Table 3B.8   Foreign investment in Romania: most important countries of origin (as of March 1992)

Country	Capital[1] (thous. USD)	Number
France	54,311.4	493
United Kingdom	50,431.8	170
USA	43,820.1	567
Germany	30,201.5	1,460
Italy	18,814.4	1,094
Holland	15,852.9	180
Turkey	15,308.0	1,054
Spain	11,878.0	43
Austria	8,427.3	289
Israel	8,273.2	385
Dominican Republic	7,552.5	2
Syria	7,539.0	941

[1] Foreign capital contribution.

Source: Romanian Development Agency

total investment in Romania had exceeded $1 mln. Table 3B.8 shows the twelve most important origin countries, with total capital invested and number of companies for each. Major companies which have made significant investments include Phoceene de Metallurgie and Bouygues, Asea Brown-Boveri, Coca-Cola, Colgate-Palmolive, Shell, Alcatel, and Ciments Francais.

4. THE PRIVATIZATION PROCESS

Introduction

Privatization is viewed as one of the key elements in Romania's transition to a market economy. The centerpiece of the government's policy is an ambitious mass privatization giveaway scheme designed to privatize all of the state-owned commercial companies within seven years, as set forth in Law No. 58 (Commercial Companies Privatization Law, or simply Privatization Law) of August 1991. The Privatization Law took as its point of departure the corporatization of state enterprises, under Law No. 15 of July 1990, whereby all of Romania's state-owned enterprises were transformed into either joint-stock or limited-liability companies ("commercial companies"), to be privatized subsequently, or into state-owned companies (*regies autonomes*), to remain under state control.[2] Law No. 15 also created the National Agency for Privatization (NAP) and outlined the "30 per cent transfer" or free distribution program.

While this "large privatization" program is being organized, the NAP has begun to implement programs to sell, lease, or contract out the management of enterprise assets, mainly small retail outlets,[3] and an "early privatization" program to sell shares in a small number of selected state-owned companies. In addition to the plans and

---

[2] The *regie autonomes* may, however, be transformed later in whole or in part into commercial companies, which would allow them to enter the privatization process at a later date. More information about these legal forms can be found in section 3A above, and about the corporatization process in Section 5 below. Assets of the *regies* may also be privatized separately: see the program for the "Sale of Assets" in Section 4B below.

[3] These programs essentially correspond to the concept of "small privatization" in some other East European economies. In some discussions of Romanian privatization, sales of assets are included in the early privatization program (sales of shares in companies privatized prior to the free distribution program), but in terms of selection, procedure, size, and timing, the two programs are quite distinct.

programs underway for the privatization of business units, the return of land to private ownership is provided for under the legal framework of the Land Law (Law No. 18/1991), applicable to about 75 per cent of Romania's agricultural land, over 8 mln hectares. State-owned apartments, aside from those involving complications in defining ownership rights over buildings that were taken over by the state under the communist regime, are being sold.

4A. Organizational structure of state regulation of privatization

The Privatization Law applies to all of the approximately 6,280 commercial companies organized pursuant to Law No. 15, and to those *regies autonomes* which may subsequently be transformed into commercial companies. The law provides for the creation of five so-called "Private Ownership Funds" (POFs) and one "State Ownership Fund" (SOF), which will divide the responsibilities amongst themselves for interim management of the commercial companies, and, together with the National Agency for Privatization (NAP), will share the responsibilities for privatization. At the level of state-created bodies, therefore, control of the process is spread over a number of new institutions.

However, insofar as inclusion in the program for particular enterprises is mandatory and methods of privatization will be determined by the three types of state-created institutions, little initiative and influence are left to the enterprise managers or workers; in this sense, the mass program is quite centralized. But there are also some elements of decentralization. In the process of corporatization, the management and employees often initiated splitting the former enterprise into smaller units. In the early privatization, the sale of shares in whole business entities is initiated by the enterprises themselves, and the sale of assets may be proposed by the enterprises as well as by an interested buyer, although the NAP has the ultimate decision-making authority in both cases. The Privatization Law allows the possibility that the SOF may contract out some of the privatization transactions to investment management companies. Finally, managers and workers may make proposals for employee buy-outs, particularly of the smaller enterprises.

The National Agency for Privatization (NAP)

The NAP, the full name of which is actually the "National Agency for Privatization and the Development of Small and Medium Sized Enterprises," is the government body formally responsible for the coordination, guidance, and control of the privatization process. It is charged not only with implementing the program of privatization of state-owned commercial companies, but also with encouraging the creation and development of private small and medium-sized enterprises. It is supposed to coordinate these programs with the government's overall restructuring strategy, with the foreign investment policy, and with technical assistance for privatization.

Although the NAP was created under Law No. 15/1990, it was only with the Privatization Law that its tasks were more fully specified. The tasks listed in this law can be categorized in four groups, the first pertaining to the early privatization program, the second to the sale of assets, the third to the free distribution program, and the fourth to sales of shares and to general activities:

1 a) to establish criteria for the selection of enterprises to participate in the early privatization;
 b) to select the participants;
2 a) to issue regulations for the procedure for sales of assets, approved by the government;
 b) to prepare lists of assets offered for sale;
3 a) to publish the methodology for the distribution of the Certificates of Ownership;
 b) to coordinate the distribution of Certificates of Ownership;
 c) to prepare draft statutes (bylaws) for the Private Ownership Funds and submit them to the government for approval;[4]
4 a) to submit draft methodologies concerning sales of shares;
 b) to approve, within thirty days, the sale of shares in a commercial company and its terms, in the event that the SOF loses its majority stake in the company through this sale;
 c) to assist companies involved in the privatization process;

---

[4] According to the law, the statutes are then supposed to be submitted to parliament for final approval. In fact, the draft statutes were submitted in Spring 1992 to parliament, which went into recess, however, without voting on them. The basic statutes were enacted by government decree in the interim.

d) to approve contracts of special assistance with foreign consulting firms;

e) to verify the legality of documents concluded under the law;

f) to publish periodically an Information Bulletin.

A fifth category of tasks pertaining to private sector development was inherited from a previous organization, the National Council for Small Enterprises, and a sixth category involves leasing, contracting out, and concession arrangements:

5 a) to develop guidelines and strategies for the development of new private enterprises;

b) to coordinate foreign assistance to these small and mid-sized enterprises.

6 to coordinate the leasing of business premises, the contracting out of the operation of business units, and the concessioning and subconcessioning of public services, production units, and land.

The NAP acquired new tasks and powers through Government Resolution No. 858/1991 Concerning the Establishment of the National Agency for Privatization and the Development of Small and Medium Sized Enterprises:

7 to supply a draft statute for the establishment and operation of the State Ownership Fund;

8 to conduct evaluations and feasibility studies, to undertake consulting and brokering, and to charge for these services.

According to the "Shareholder's Agreement," the annex to the statute setting up the Private Ownership Funds, the NAP acquires an additional responsibility:

9 through its local branches, to organize the privatization of small enterprises.

Other than this last privatization function, the NAP is supposed to be no longer directly involved in privatization once the SOF and POFs have been set up.

The organizational structure of the National Agency for Privatization is presented in Chart 4A.1.

The NAP is under the supervision of the government, and the Prime

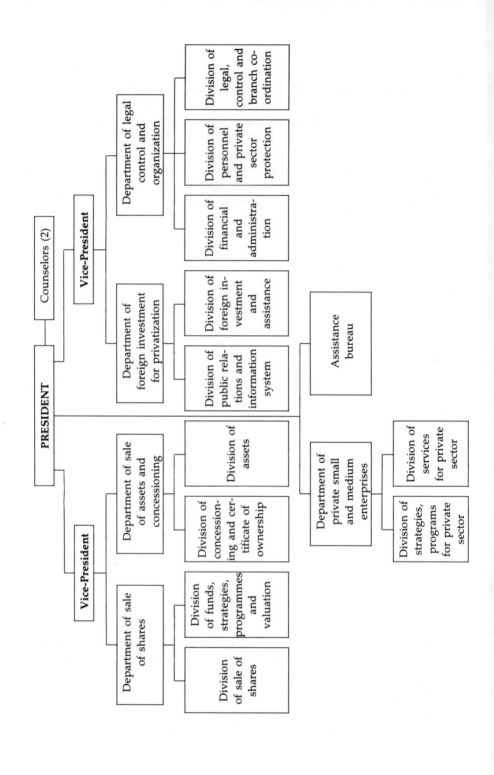

Minister appoints the President (sometimes called "Secretary of State") of the NAP. The Prime Minister's Council for Reform cooperates in outlining the strategies that the NAP is supposed to implement.

In order to carry out its tasks according to the law, the National Agency for Privatization is supposed to cooperate with the Ministry of Economy and Finance, branch ministries (which have their own departments of privatization and restructuring that set forth proposals), other central and local public administration bodies, financial and banking institutions, and other domestic and foreign organizations.

The State Ownership Fund (SOF)

The SOF, created under the Privatization Law, is a public institution charged with transferring to private ownership the shares in commercial companies under its administration, initially 70 per cent of the shares in each company. According to the law, its tasks are as follows:

a) to draw up and execute an annual program of privatization, such that 10 per cent of all shares are sold each year, thereby liquidating the state's holding by the end of a seven-year period;
b) to define minimum performance criteria for the commercial companies, including dividend policy;
c) to restructure or liquidate commercial companies;
d) to cooperate with the Private Ownership Funds in accelerating the privatization process;
e) to exercise normal rights as shareholders.

However, the policy was modified (according to the "Shareholder's Agreement"), so that the SOF are now responsible for the restructuring and privatization of only the large enterprises. The SOF may contract out its activities to consulting firms.

The SOF is supposed to finance its privatization and restructuring activities from its revenue from privatization sales. According to the Privatization Law's unpublished preamble, the budget of the SOF is to be completely separate from that of the state, although the law itself states that any remaining obligations upon liquidation of the SOF[5]

---

[5] The law stipulates that the SOF will be liquidated when the complete (100 per cent) privatization of the Commercial Companies is achieved. If this goal is not attained in seven years, the parliament will determine the future of the SOF and of the administration of the remaining state holdings.

are assumed by the state budget. The SOF is exempt from the profit tax, and in fact forbidden to make any payment to the state or local budgets. Among other uses of revenue, the SOF is allowed to make loans to Romanian natural or legal persons purchasing shares or assets of commercial companies.

The SOF is supervised by a Council of Administration, consisting of seventeen directors, including the State Secretary for Privatization, five directors appointed by the President of Romania and chosen from persons trained and experienced in commercial, industrial, financial, and legal matters, three appointed by the permanent Bureau of Senate and three by the permanent Bureau of the National Assembly, and five chosen from the leading staff of the central public administration and appointed by the Prime Minister. The Council elects a President and Vice-President, neither of whom may be the NAP President, and appoints a General Executive Manager to carry out the Board's and President's decisions.

The Private Ownership Funds (POFs)

The five POFs, created under the Privatization Law, will be organized as joint-stock companies and are supposed to operate on commercial principles. The POFs receive 30 per cent stakes in a set of commercial companies allocated to them by the NAP. Each POF is in turn owned by all adult Romanian citizens through their Certificates of Ownership.

The law stipulates the following objectives for the POFs:

a) to seek to maximize profits accruing to their owners, the holders of Certificates of Ownership (vouchers), and to maximize the value of those certificates through investment and portfolio management;
b) to provide brokerage services for the exchange of certificates for direct shares in commercial companies;
c) to accelerate the privatization of the shares held by the SOF in the commercial companies allocated to them.

This last objective has been clarified through the "Shareholder's Agreement," which divides privatization responsibilities among the POFs, SOF, and NAP and is supposed to be signed by the SOF with each POF. The POFs are given specific responsibility, with regard to the medium-sized companies in their portfolios, for privatizing the SOF holding. It is hoped that this will be accomplished within five years. The statutes of the POFs also require them to announce periodically both the market value and the "nominal" (book) value of their certificates.

The law stipulates that the POFs may distribute their profits as dividends, deposit them in interest-bearing accounts, or use them to finance "other commercial activities within [their] scope of activities" (Article 11). However, the draft statutes require that profits are capitalized and not distributed as dividends during the first three years. The precise scope of activities permitted for the POFs has yet to be determined.

Each POF will be supervised by a seven-member Council of Administration, nominated by the government and approved, separately, by the National Assembly and the Senate. The members of the Councils are supposed to be chosen from persons with commercial, financial, industrial, or legal experience. They elect a POF President and a Vice-President from their number.

Although no shareholders' meetings will be held during the first five years of operation, the certificate holders are nonetheless given certain rights to intervene in the fund management, including procedures to request a financial audit or to replace a member of the Council of Administration. The action must be supported by at least 100 persons holding at least 10,000 certificates in the fund in question. The National Agency for Privatization is the ultimate adjudicator of such actions. After five years of operation, the plan is to convert the POFs into ordinary mutual funds.

4B. Overview of privatization programs

This section contains summaries of the privatization programs for the conclusion of contracts for sale, management, or leasing of assets: programs involving the shares of commercial companies, including early privatization, free distribution and sales; as well as those for land and for housing. More detailed analysis of these programs will appear in future CEU Privatization Project Reports.

Sale of assets, leasing and management contracts

The *sale of assets* is regulated by Government Resolution (G.R.) No. 634/1991 Concerning the Methodology for the Sale of Assets of Commercial Companies with State Capital and by G.R. No. 758/1991 Concerning the Amendment of G.R. No. 634. This program is supposed to provide an opportunity to dispose of assets that are unnecessary for the main activity of the company, do not greatly affect profitability, and might be more efficiently run by a private investor.

The sales may be carried out by the commercial companies themselves, and are generally initiated by the management of the companies concerned. Either a public auction or a sealed bid method must be used, with the starting price set by the company; however, if the starting price is lower than the book value adjusted for inflation and depreciation, the NAP may require a revaluation. In the event that the asset has already been leased or contracted out, the lessee or contractee is preferred, all other conditions being equal; employees are second in priority, and retired employees are third. All three of these groups may also receive various types of special credit arrangements from the company. The company keeps the proceeds of the sale, but is allowed to use them only for investment purposes, for example to update obsolete machinery and equipment, or for the repayment of medium and long term investment credits.

To encourage the sale of assets, the NAP was charged with publishing lists of assets selected by the companies for sale during the twelve-month period following the enactment of the Privatization Law. Several such official lists had been published as of July 1992, containing a total of 5,106 assets. Two-thirds of the assets belong to enterprises subordinated to local authorities, the others to the central government. Table 4B.1 shows the division among sectors of activity: nearly half the total were in trade, and another quarter were in tourism. The annual turnover generated by these assets was about Lei 41.55 bln, and the number of employees was 34,309.

Table 4B.1 Sales of assets in Romania (as of July 1992)

Sector of activity	Number selected	Number sold
Industry	402	49
Agriculture	161	12
Construction	36	2
Transport, communication	43	3
Trade	2,345	317
Tourism	1,544	126
Services	575	42
Total	5,106	550

Source: National Agency for Privatization

As of July 1992, there had been 550 actual asset sales under this program, involving 2,200 employees and annual turnover of Lei 2.75 bln. Total sales revenue amounted to Lei 3.74 bln. As shown in Table 4B.1, over three-quarters of the sales were in trade and tourism. Roughly 80 per cent of the buyers were natural persons, and 20 per cent were legal persons. Although only a small percentage of the total number of selected assets had been sold by August 1992, the process of sales continues.

Leasing and management contracts have been much more common in Romania. They are regulated by Government Resolution No. 1228/1990 Concerning the Methodology for Concessioning, Leasing, and Management Contracts. Arrangements to lease state-owned assets or to contract out are reached as a result of a public auction and are not subject to approval aside from that of the State Representatives Council (see Section 5) of the parent commercial company or the Council of Administration of the *regies autonomes*.

According to incomplete data, from March to December 1991, an estimated 9,160 management contracts with turnover of Lei 36.2 bln and 10,515 leasing agreements with turnover of Lei 8.7 bln were concluded. The average size of the assets in these programs was thus much smaller than the average size of the assets sold, as discussed above. Over three-quarters of the contracts were concluded with enterprises subordinated to local governments; particularly active were the local *regies autonomes*. Regarding the sector of activity, trade dominates even more than in the case of sales, with well over half the total value of assets or turnover.

Early privatization

The Privatization Law made the NAP responsible for selecting commercial companies to be privatized "early," i.e. before the organization of the POFs and the SOF, acting on the proposal of the companies and on the basis of recommendations from branch ministries. According to the law, however, the NAP cannot select more than 0.5 per cent of the total number of commercial companies. The companies receive technical assistance from Romanian or foreign firms.

The selection procedure included the following steps:

a) interested state-owned commercial companies prepare privatization proposals containing technical and economic information;
b) their Councils of Administration (i.e. Supervisory Board; see

Section 5 below on corporatization and governance structures) provide answers to a NAP questionnaire on characteristics of the company and forward the privatization proposals to the respective State Representatives Councils (i.e. the bodies representing the state as shareholder; see Section 5 below). After approval, the proposal is submitted to the relevant branch ministry or local authority (prefecture);

c) the branch ministry or the local authority analyzes the proposal, taking into account average indicators for the economic sector concerned, and makes recommendations on the companies to be privatized;

d) the NAP analyzes the privatization proposals and recommendations, evaluating them in terms of pollution problems, subsidies influencing profitability, price controls on the company's products, degree of horizontal integration, support of the employees for privatization, extent of dependence on the former CMEA market, experience in cooperating with foreign partners, and likeliness of finding a foreign investor.

The NAP made a preliminary selection of sixty commercial companies and included them in a special catalogue sent to foreign firms interested in consulting on the pilot privatizations. The foreign firms were selected by a tender organized by the NAP that evaluated their capabilities; the firms Roland Berger, Ernst & Young, and Samuel Montague were selected. This foreign technical assistance is financed by the PHARE Program (for ten commercial companies), USAID (for ten commercial companies) and the Know How Fund (for five commercial companies).

The consulting firms selected twenty-five companies from the catalog, but, due to various problems, at present eighteen commercial companies are in different stages of sale or preparation for privatization. The first company privatized was a regional brewery in Cluj. Fifty-one per cent of its shares were sold through public auction at the end of the subscription period on July 31, 1992, while the remaining 49 per cent were sold by direct negotiation with a core investor. A garment factory in Vrancea was the second to be privatized. Seventy-one per cent of its shares were purchased by an Italian investor and 29 per cent by the employees. Notably, 20 per cent of the shares purchased by the foreign investor were transferred to the management of the company. The companies that seem most likely to follow include a taxi network and a national publishing company. In addition, another fourteen commercial companies are still under preparation (valuation, search for investors, determination of methods for privatization), out of which four are to be privatized through management and employee buy-outs.

The program is continuing with a further selection of companies. Those selected will not be included in the free distribution program.

The free distribution and subsequent sale of shares program

In theory, the free distribution of 30 per cent of company shares to the Private Ownership Funds (POFs) could be analyzed separately from the subsequent sale of the remaining 70 per cent held by the State Ownership Fund (SOF), because the two processes are conceptually and temporally distinct, although they apply to the same set of assets. But, in fact, both the methods and institutions overlap across the two aspects to such a degree, that it may be both clearer and more convenient to consider them simultaneously, as if they were a single program.

This program applies to the roughly 6,000 state-owned commercial companies (see Section 3A for a description of this legal form, Section 3B for the characteristics of these companies, and Section 5 for the selection and corporatization process). The program fixes the proportion of shares in each company to be transferred at 30 per cent. This 30 per cent share will be administratively allocated to one of the five POFs planned to be established in August 1992 and begin operating in November after two months of staff training, and the remaining 70 per cent will go to the SOF, established in July 1992. The ''Certificates of Ownership'' received by each citizen are actually shares in each of the POFs. These funds are established by the state, and they alone will receive company shares. After five years, the POFs are supposed to become ordinary mutual funds, in the Western sense, and remaining Certificates of Ownership become ordinary mutual fund shares. The entry and functioning of other intermediaries is not yet regulated by law.

The principles for the allocation of companies to funds are basically resolved. The funds are intended to be similar in size, measured by profits, capital, or employment. With regard to 2,500 small enterprises (roughly defined as those with capital of book value less than Lei 50 mln), the funds will be specialized geographically; having head offices in various cities throughout the country is meant to make trading more accessible to the population outside of Bucharest. With regard to medium and large enterprises, special attention is paid to "critical" or "strategic" sectors, which include those in difficult financial circumstances as well as those that are "vitally important and have a great impact on the development of other activities." Enterprises within each of the critical sectors of metallurgy, machinery, chemical and petrochemical, agriculture, banking and finance, commerce, and transportation are supposed to be distributed across funds, while funds specialize in the non-critical, "color" sectors.

Besides taking an active ownership role as the core if not majority investor, the Private Ownership Funds are given the responsibility through the "Shareholders' Agreement" to privatize within five years the remaining 70 per cent share in the State Ownership Fund for approximately 2,000 medium-size companies (the definition is still not precisely determined, but roughly includes companies with book value between Lei 50 and 500 mln and number of employees between 200 and 500). These companies are thought not to require significant restructuring. Small enterprises are intended to be fully privatized (including the POF shares), mainly through management and employee buy-outs; this is supposed to be organized by the branch offices of the NAP together with representatives from all the POFs, which also divide the sales revenue among them. Price is, however, not considered an important criterion for these transactions: the precise role and incentives of the POFs have thus not been fully worked out. The remaining category of large enterprises is to be restructured and privatized by the State Ownership Fund, with no involvement from the POFs. An exception is provided by the Privatization Law in the event that a potential purchaser wishes to acquire 100 per cent of the shares: the SOF is then supposed to delegate to the POF the power to negotiate the sale.

The accomplishment of this division of labor between funds seems to depend on a number of factors that are not yet determined. For instance, the Privatization Law (passed in parliament in August 1991) mandates that the State Fund privatize one-seventh of its holdings annually, so that privatization of these enterprises should be finished in seven years, but granting the initiative to the Private Funds to privatize medium enterprises seems to put this goal beyond the power of the State Fund to enforce. The members of the Council of Administration (functioning like a Supervisory Board) of a Commercial Company, moreover, are appointed at least initially by the State and Private Ownership Funds, 70 per cent from the former and 30 per cent from the latter. Under these circumstances, it may be difficult for the

POF to take the initiative in privatizing the medium-size companies.

Furthermore, it is unclear what incentives the fund managers will be given to accomplish the diverse objectives specified by the Privatization Law. Revenue from sales of state shares would accrue to the State Ownership Fund. The funds, both private and state, will be governed by "Councils of Administration," the members of which are appointed by the government (or organs thereof) for five-year terms, and can be revoked by the same. Compensation of fund directors and staffs will contain both fixed and variable parts, the latter perhaps related to the number of firms privatized, among a number of factors corresponding to the varied tasks faced by the funds, but exactly how remains to be determined.

Turning to the individual participants, the "new owners," all citizens over eighteen on December 31, 1990 – 16.5 mln people – are eligible during the period June to November 27, 1992 to receive Certificates of Ownership (one for each Private Fund). The certificates are issued in bearer form for a fee of Lei 100 ($.38), less than 1 per cent of the average gross monthly wage, meant to cover the distribution cost.

The certificates have uses in both the free distribution and sales side of the privatization program. First, as noted, they are shares in the Private Ownership Funds that will, if retained, become ordinary mutual fund shares in five years. After the first three years, dividends will be paid to certificate holders; until then, all profits will be capitalized. Second, the certificates are tradable on the stock market (due to be established December 31, 1992), or directly with other persons, excluding foreigners.[6] To prevent speculative swings in the price of the certificates, for instance to keep the value from falling precipitously on the opening of the stock market, the POFs are allowed to engage in trading of their own certificates.

Third, the certificates pertaining to a particular fund may be used to purchase company shares from the POF that owns the 30 per cent stake, whereupon the fund annuls those certificates. It is unclear how the price (number of shares per certificate) will be determined or whether the stock market will be functioning adequately to provide some guidance. The law sets no limits on the number of certificates that any individual can use in this way, but the fund's Council of

---

[6] In August 1992 the Romanian Foreign Trade Bank began a brokerage service for the sale and purchase of certificates. Those willing to purchase place an order stating how many vouchers they would like and the price they are willing to pay, and those interested in selling stipulate the quantity and price. It is interesting that transactions are concluded only when buy and sell orders have identical prices.

Administration may set such a limit. Small companies are not intended to be sold in this way. The fourth use of certificates, however, is that employees of those small companies may use them to buy shares from the Private Ownership Fund in the case of an employee buy-out. In this event, the employee may use his or her certificates from all the funds. This is an interesting example where voucher privatization will have been merely a step on the road to another method: insider privatization.

Fifth, the certificates pertaining to a particular Private Ownership Fund may be presented to the State Ownership Fund, when the latter is engaged in the sale of shares in a company belonging 30 per cent to that POF, in order to receive a 10 per cent discount on the public offering price. The reason offered as to why only certificates pertaining to that particular Private Ownership Fund may be used is that this will stimulate trading among certificates for different funds. Restrictions on this use include the provisions that one person may use no more than ten certificates for purchasing shares in a particular company, that each certificate may be used only once for the shares in that company, and that the total value of the discount can be no more than the "market value" of the certificates.

Finally, although certificate holders are the putative owners of the POFs, no shareholders' meetings will be held due to the excessive costs of bringing together up to 16.5 mln people or organizing their representatives. The certificate holders are nonetheless given certain limited rights to intervene in the fund management, as discussed in Section 4A above.

The sale of shares may take any of the following methods: public offering, open auction or an auction limited to preselected bidders, sale of shares through direct negotiations, or any combination of the above.

The Privatization Law sets forth specific provisions for employee preferences. In any public share offer, the employees/management are supposed to receive the right, during a limited time period prior to the commencement of the public offering, to purchase up to 10 per cent of all the shares at a discount of 10 per cent off the public offering price. In an auction, their bid should win if they offer no less than 10 per cent less than the highest bid, and agree to all other conditions of the offer. In connection with a negotiated sale, all terms being equal, the sale is supposed to be awarded to an employee or management offer. Employees or management wishing to purchase shares may also receive financing assistance from the SOF, the POFs and commercial companies, in the form of credits, deferred payment arrangements, or payment by installments.

Agriculture

One of the main features of Romanian agriculture before 1989 was the dominant presence of large Agricultural Production Cooperatives (APCs) and state-owned farms known as State Agricultural Enterprises (SAEs). In 1990, out of the total of 14.8 mln hectares of agricultural land, about 9.4 mln hectares were arable land, out of which the APCs owned 51.3 per cent and the SAEs 20.4 per cent, while the remaining 28.3 per cent, which were mostly hill and mountain areas, belonged to individual farmers.

Law No. 18/1991 (the Land Law) regulates ownership rights on land in Romania, including the restitution of land to former owners. The program in agriculture, completely separate from the restructuring of commercial companies, breaks up the large Agricultural Production Cooperatives. These cooperatives were formed after the Second World War by forcing the farmers to contribute their land. Although legally the farmers were considered the owners of the land in the APC, they actually were not able to exercise their ownership rights: they were not permitted to sell their land, to withdraw it from the cooperative, nor to decide on the use of its fruits.

According to the law, the following persons are eligible for redemption or establishment of ownership rights on land: APC members who have contributed their land to the cooperative, or their inheritors; APC members who have not contributed land, but have worked for at least three years in the cooperative; Romanian citizens whose land has been abusively expropriated, or their inheritors; and, to the extent that land is available, any other Romanian citizen who is willing to move to the countryside and work on the land, as well as civil servants who work in the countryside.

The procedure for land redistribution is as follows. A commission appointed by the prefect's office and headed by the mayor is charged with settling ownership rights on land in every village, town, city and district. Persons eligible to receive land must apply to this commission, justifying their claims. Land is returned first to the former owners who contributed it to the APCs, to persons who were deported and expropriated after 1944, and to Romanian citizens of German nationality who were expropriated, and to cooperative members who have been working for the last three years in the APCs, in this order of priority. The first three groups must provide evidence from the APC registers, from their former titles of ownership, or by deposition of witnesses.

If total claims are greater than the area of the APCs, all claims are reduced by the same proportion so that each category receives some land. If total claims are less than the cooperative land available, then civil servants working and living in the countryside or persons willing to move to the countryside may be allocated land. The former, however, are restricted to receiving only up to 5,000 square meters of land, and only for the period of time that they actually live in the village. If land still remains, it may be distributed to persons from other villages, towns, cities, or districts that applied in their own area but received no land there. In the event that land is still unallocated, the remaining areas are transferred to the state, which can rent or sell them or conclude concession contracts. An Agency for Rural Development is created, under this law, to administer the remaining land. Until the Agency starts functioning, the land will be administered by the local authorities.

Based on the decision of the commission, a nominal Title of Ownership is issued, for an area not less than 0.5 hectares per person and not larger than 10 hectares per family.[7] Persons who were not the former owners and have received land according to the commission's decision are not permitted to sell the land for a period of ten years.

The applicants can appeal the decision to the district commission, and, if it is not resolved, they can further appeal to the district court, which makes the final decision.

The law also provides for the establishment of a liquidation commission (recommended by the mayor and appointed by the prefect's office), which is charged with determining the assets and liabilities of the dissolved APCs. Within nine months from the enactment of the Land Law, these commissions were required to submit a liquidation balance sheet to the financial body of the prefecture. The assets of the former cooperatives are either transferred to a new association created by the former members (see below), or divided among the members, in cash or in kind, proportional to their contribution of land and their work in the APC. A report on the cooperatives' debts to the state and other legal persons is endorsed by the Ministry of Finance which

---

[7] According to the Land Law, a family includes spouses and their single children dependent on parents.

submits it to the parliament, along with proposals for paying off the debts, for final decision.

The State Agricultural Enterprises (SAE) were owned by the state but operated similarly to the cooperatives. Cooperatives were transformed into commercial companies according to Law No. 15/1990, and are included in privatization according to Law No. 58/1991. In the event that former owners claim the land of an enterprise, Law No. 18/1991 stipulates that such land will not be returned, but the former owners can receive, upon request, shares in the commercial company.

Associations of APCs, as well as associations between APCs and SAEs, were operating before 1989. According to the Land Law, these associations may transform themselves into commercial companies, with the former members of the APCs and employees of the associations becoming shareholders. However, these companies are not subject to privatization under Law No. 58/1991. Persons who do not wish to own shares in the newly created company may receive titles of ownership to land that was not contributed by the cooperatives to the association.

As the implementation of the provisions of the Land Law involves the restoration of ownership rights, the process is very complicated and time consuming. Although, as of June 30, 1992, ownership rights had been established (i.e., the commission had determined the ownership rights of individuals or families over the land) for 9.22 mln hectares of arable land, only 79.6 per cent of this land was actually measured, demarcated and distributed. The process of land distribution does not coincide, moreover, with that of issuance of titles of ownership. Therefore, persons who were allocated land do not necessarily have titles of ownership on it, and vice versa. As of the same date, ownership rights had been re-established for 5.1 mln former owners or their inheritors, but only 71.4 per cent were actually in possession of their land. Also, 1.46 mln people had been given ownership rights on land without being former owners. The only information about the distribution of titles of ownership, according to the Ministry of Agriculture, is that, as of May 30, 1992, 97.5 thousand persons had received such documents.

The application of the Land Law resulted in excessive fragmentation of land, incompatible with agricultural equipment designed for large surfaces. This, together with the delay in the establishment of ownership rights,[8] caused a huge decline in agricultural output, resulting in

---

[8] The delay in establishing ownership rights and distributing the titles of ownership is caused not only by the lack of clarity in the ownership rights themselves, with endless trials over property, but also by the nontransparency of the process, mainly controlled by insiders, which leads to possibilities for fraud.

the necessity to import grain. The parliament therefore passed Law No. 36/1991, Concerning the Establishment of Commercial Companies and Farming Associations in Agriculture, encouraging the creation of larger units that would be more suitable to the types of farming equipment available. As of June 30, 1992, 3,854 private commercial companies and 11,376 family associations operating in agriculture had been set up, owning 1 mln hectares of land and 1.7 mln hectares, respectively.

Housing

Before 1989, housing was under both private and state ownership. Private ownership was achieved by purchasing an apartment or house either from a natural person, or from the state, but was restricted to only one housing unit. State-owned housing, mainly in large apartment buildings, was administered by specialized enterprises, and rented to tenants for generally very low monthly rents. The exact proportion of housing that was state and privately owned was not obtained, but some indication of their relative importance can be inferred from recent construction. Between 1951 and 1970, most new housing was built from private funds, but thereafter the proportion declined, so that for the 1951–1990 period privately-built housing accounted for 45.7 per cent of total construction.

Decree-Law No. 61/1990 Concerning the Sale of State-Owned Housing allows for the purchase of state-owned apartments or houses by their tenants. The provisions of this Decree were completed by Government Resolution (G.R.) No. 88/1991 Concerning Measures for the Sale of State-Owned Housing, and G.R. No. 562/1991 Concerning Downpayments and Installment Payments for the Sale of State-Owned Housing, which determine the clauses of the sale contract concluded between the tenant and the specialized state-owned real estate company that administers state housing. Only housing that clearly belonged to the state (i.e. there were no potential reprivatization problems) is covered by these resolutions. Sales prices were based upon the rent and the degree of depreciation of the building. According to these resolutions, the purchaser can pay either the full price when the contract is concluded, or just a minimum down payment of 10 per cent of the price, with the remaining amount to be paid within twenty-five years by monthly installments. The buyer can receive a credit for the downpayment from the Savings Bank with 4 per cent nominal interest, as well as a loan for installment payments extended by the real estate company. The proceeds of the sales are equally divided among the central and the local budgets.

The state set low relative prices, especially for those apartments with extensive depreciation. This, together with the possibility of paying by installments at a negative real interest rate (given the high rate of inflation), created a large demand, and, as of May 31, 1992, 2 mln apartments had been bought by their tenants. The state still owned 2.3 mln apartments, for which the current tenants had filed 600,000 applications for purchase.

Aside from selling to tenants, the state is also selling housing in new, unoccupied buildings, but this process is extremely slow. Many recent migrants from urban areas need housing, for which there is a large shortage, partly due to the halt in construction of many apartment buildings that were in a preliminary stage. The prices for these apartments have been set very high; it is very difficult for the population to purchase them, even though the Savings Bank extends loans with an average nominal interest rate of 4.55 per cent.

An issue of great controversy is returning housing to the former owners (reprivatization), still on the government's agenda. Re-establishing ownership rights for housing that was nationalized after 1945, with or without compensation, is a very complicated process and implies a trade-off between compensation of the former owners, who were abusively expropriated, and the interests of the current tenants, who are not responsible for the decisions of the previous regime. The government is currently working on a second draft law regulating this problem, after the parliament rejected the first draft this summer.

5. CORPORATIZATION

Corporatization, in Romania also sometimes called "reorganization," is the conversion of the former state-owned enterprises into either state-owned commercial companies or "*regies autonomes*" (sometimes referred to as "autonomous units" or "self sufficient administrations"). The state-owned commercial companies are set up as joint-stock or limited-liability companies, designed to have a share-based ownership structure, so that the privatization process can then address the question of divesting the state's sole ownership.

An early measure towards de-monopolization of the Romanian economy was the elimination, in early 1990, of the so-called "*centrale*," the massive state conglomerates which represented an intermediate level between the state enterprises and the ministries, controlling the activity of subordinated units within a field of activity. The *"centrale,"* had an important role in making centralized decisions concerning the allocation of raw materials among enterprises, production, prices, distribution of output, etc. "Holding companies," however, have emerged that group together a number of state-owned commercial companies in a particular sector, as described in the following section.

The law under which the transformation of state-owned enterprises was carried out is Law No. 15/1990 "Concerning the Reorganization of State-Owned Enterprises into Commercial Companies or *Regies autonomes"* (see Section 3A above). The law is applicable to all state-owned enterprises, and its stated purpose is to break up large enterprises and to create new business entities to encourage competition.

Procedures for deciding on the transformation of state enterprises

The division of enterprises between *regies autonomes* and commercial companies was made by the branch ministries and local government, for the enterprises subordinated to the branch ministries and local governments, respectively. According to Chapter II of Law No. 15/1990, which regulates the relationship of the *regies autonomes* with the state bodies and budget, the *regies autonomes* are supposed to remain indefinitely under state ownership, although some of their subunits are being sold through the "sale of assets" program (see Section 4B above).

Although, according to this law, the initiative for corporatizing and splitting up an enterprise formally lies with the government (central or local), there are in practice many cases in which the management and/or the employees of particular units asked for their unit to be separated from the parent company or *regie autonome* and to be set up as a new and independent commercial company. The motivation for such an initiative probably comes from their belief that the new spin company would be able to operate more efficiently and adjust more rapidly than would the parent company. Whenever such a request was considered legitimate by the relevant authority (ministry, department, local government), the proposed split-up was approved.

In state-owned commercial companies, control over important decisions lies with the State Representatives Council (SRC), whose decisions, according to Law No. 31/1990 (Company Law), are supposed to replace those of the shareholders' meeting until the Private Ownership Funds and the State Ownership Fund (see Section 4A above) were established. The SRC was supposed to meet regularly twice a year, and also in extraordinary session when a vital decision had to be made, for example on the sale of assets or the sale of shares under the early privatization program. The SRC members are supposed to be paid a sum equalling 10 per cent of the salary of the general manager.

The law, however, defined clearly neither the mechanisms by which the SRC is supposed to act, nor the incentives for its members to monitor the company's behaviour effectively. There has been some discussion within the government, and in parliament, of the need for further legislation to amend the status of the SRC. As a result, the Law for the Amendment of Article 212 of Law No. 31/1990 was recently passed (July 28, 1992), stipulating that the SRCs will be replaced by "two representatives mandated by the Ministry of Economy and Finance (MEF) and one representative mandated by the branch ministry, or the local authority, respectively." These representatives cannot be members of the Council of Administration (see below) and cannot be directors of the company. However, there are no additions or clarifications to the specific functions of the state representatives at the company level.

The Council of Administration is supposed to have a supervisory role in the company. According to the Reorganization Law, it has seven to fifteen members and its chairman is the General Manager of the company. The members of the Council of Administration are appointed by the SRC or, more recently, the representatives of the MEF and of the branch ministry, and include mostly the directors of different divisions within the company.

Subsequent to corporatization, new "holding companies" were created – voluntary associations of commercial companies in a particular sector, especially in the oil industry, metallurgy, heavy industry, and agriculture. They were established by branch ministries under Articles 33 and 36 of Law No. 15/1990, which allowed for the formation of associations only if the association did not hinder free competition. They are approved by government resolution and registered in the Commercial Register as commercial companies.

Holding companies are based on a cross-ownership structure as follows. Every commercial company willing to enter the holding company transfers 35 per cent of its shares to the company, another 35 per cent is equally divided among all the other companies in the holding, while the remaining 30 per cent goes to the POF.

The role of the holding companies is controversial. Officially, they are not a mere continuation of the former *"centrale"* (intermediary organizations that tightened the control of the center over enterprise activity). The stated motivation for creating holding companies is to help the companies in the sectors most affected by transition, especially with the supply of raw materials (which came mostly from the former CMEA countries, and were centrally distributed) and with selling their products (which were also directed towards the East European markets). The holding companies have no explicit powers of central decision-making, and the companies have complete freedom in deciding whether to join.

The first company of this type was set up in June 1991 in metallurgy. The statute of the "SIDEROM S.A." holding company, used as a model for the companies subsequently established, stipulates that the main tasks of the entities, with respect to the commercial companies grouped together, are as follows: to provide consulting services in marketing, finance and accounting, research and development, insurance, labor conflicts, and environmental protection; to assist in concluding barter arrangements for the supply of scarce raw materials and energy; to coordinate the financial resources allocated by the government for special projects in their field of activity, such as restructuring programs; to supervise the companies' cooperation and to ensure unhindered competition; to assist in advertising and promotion of the companies' products.

The holding companies are nonetheless criticized as a continuation in fact, if not in name, of the former central bodies, thus perpetuating the control of the state. It is also argued that they could hinder the privatization process. Both the ownership structure of the companies in the holding enterprise and how the holdings will be treated in the privatization process remain unclear. All the companies in the holding company, including the company itself, are among commercial companies to be privatized, but they may belong to different POFs. The managers of the holding company have proposed that they be mandated by the State Ownership Fund to take over and privatize the latter's stake (although it is not exactly clear what this should be: the 35 per cent stake that the holding owns plus the 35 per cent of the other companies or 70 per cent of the shares held by each owner) in their companies. Depending on the managers' performance and incentives, this could either impede or facilitate privatization.

The extent of corporatization to date

About 2,000 large state-owned enterprises were subject to corporatization under Law No. 15/1990. They were simultaneously split into smaller units, so that by the end of 1991, about 5,800 commercial companies with state capital were registered. But the process of splitting up and reorganizing has continued so that 7,783 state-owned commercial companies (accounting for about 4.5 per cent of the total number of registered companies) were on the Commercial Register as of June 1992. This number includes about 1,300 branches or subsidiaries of companies which are listed as separate commercial companies, but do not submit a distinct balance sheet to the Ministry of Finance, as well as about 140 cooperative associations that are not subject to the provisions of the Commercial Companies Privatization Law (see Section 4B above, Agriculture). The figure also includes twenty-two holding companies (see subsection on procedures for deciding on the transformation of state enterprises above). By subtracting these numbers we obtain 6,321 commercial companies, which is about the number of companies in the NAP database, undergoing privatization through the free distribution program.

The process of splitting up enterprises can be observed for *regies autonomes* as well, as 390 *regies autonomes* were operating at the end of 1991, while 758 were operating as of June 1992.

At the end of 1991, there were twenty-two holding companies, while five more were in the process of being set up. This total includes eleven holding companies in the agriculture and food sectors grouping together 119 commercial companies (including the eleven holding companies themselves), and eleven holding companies in the industrial sector, with 255 commercial companies. Of these, there are four holding companies in metallurgy, with ninety-seven commercial companies; two in machine building, with twenty-one commercial companies; two in oil processing and distribution, with seventy-two commercial companies; one in material recovering, with forty-four commercial companies; and two in research and development in aeronautics, with twenty-one commercial companies.

Evidence of changes in the organizational structure and behavior of corporatized firms

The corporatization process in Romania was conceived as a prerequisite of the privatization process and was not, in itself, expected to induce major changes in behaviour. The management of the companies has in many cases remained effectively the same. The state has remained the sole owner, and there are few incentives to encourage members of the SRC to take an active role. The economy remains dominated by producer monopolies, and the generalized shortage of material resources means that central distribution is still necessary for some basic inputs and energy.

Commercialization has nevertheless increased the independence of both the commercial companies and *regies autonomes* in allowing them to change their products, choose sources of supply and channels of distribution, and decide on the use of assets and profits, among other things. These are important changes from the hypercentralized economy of the past where few important decisions were made at the enterprise level. However, both groups of former enterprises still receive significant subsidies: in 1991, 37 bln Lei, or about 7 per cent of expenditures in the state budget, were used to cover losses, and an additional 63 bln Lei, or almost 12 per cent of the budget, were spent to subsidize prices.